I Have the Right To

I Have the Right To

A High School Survivor's Story of Sexual Assault, Justice, and Hope

Chessy Prout

with Jenn Abelson

MARGARET K. McELDERRY BOOKS

New York London Toronto Sydney New Delhi

To my sisters, Lucy and Christianna, and
my sisters and brothers in survivorship
—C. P.

To brave girls and women everywhere
—J. A.

MARGARET K. McELDERRY BOOKS
An imprint of Simon & Schuster Children's Publishing Division
1230 Avenue of the Americas, New York, New York 10020
Certain names have been changed.
Text copyright © 2018 by Francesca Prout and Jennifer Abelson
Cover photograph copyright © 2018 by Ylva Erevall
MARGARET K. McELDERRY BOOKS is a trademark of Simon & Schuster, Inc.
For information about special discounts for bulk purchases, please contact Simon &
Schuster Special Sales at 1-866-506-1949 or business@simonandschuster.com.
The Simon & Schuster Speakers Bureau can bring authors to your live event. For
more information or to book an event, contact the Simon & Schuster Speakers
Bureau at 1-866-248-3049 or visit our website at www.simonspeakers.com.
Book design by Sonia Chaghatzbanian and Irene Metaxatos
The text for this book was set in Adobe Caslon Pro.
Manufactured in the United States of America
First Margaret K. McElderry Books paperback edition March 2019
10 9 8 7 6 5 4 3 2 1
The Library of Congress has cataloged the hardcover edition as follows:
Names: Prout, Chessy, author. | Abelson, Jenn, author.
Title: I have the right to : a high school survivor's story of sexual assault, justice,
and hope / Chessy Prout, with Jenn Abelson.
Description: First edition. | New York : Margaret K. McElderry Books, [2018]
Identifiers: LCCN 2017043982 (print) | ISBN 9781534414457 (eBook) |
ISBN 9781534414433 (hardcover) | ISBN 9781534414440 (trade pbk.) | ISBN
9781534425712 (trade pbk. export)
Subjects: LCSH: Prout, Chessy. | St. Paul's School (Concord, N.H.) | Rape
victims—United States—Biography. | Sexual abuse victims—United States—
Biography. | High school students—Sexual behavior—United States. | Sex
crimes—United States.
Classification: LCC HV6561 (ebook) | LCC HV6561.P76 2018 (print) | DDC
362.88/3092 [B] —dc23
LC record available at https://lccn.loc.gov/2017043982

INTRODUCTION

*You can't go back and change the beginning, but you can
start where you are and change the ending.*

—C. S. LEWIS

There is no one narrative for a survivor of sexual assault. We all have our own journey; you'll read about Chessy Prout's in the pages to come. Mine began nearly four decades ago on a winter evening, at a prestigious college campus on the East Coast. I was an eighteen-year-old student, going to a dance at a fraternity house with friends. We danced, we listened to music, we enjoyed the party. Until one young man assaulted me in a crude and insulting way, and I ran, alone, into the cold dark night.

I have never forgotten that night. I was filled with shame, regret, and humiliation, while he was egged on and encouraged by his friends.

Several years later, while working as a legislative aide on Capitol Hill, I was assaulted again, this time by a distinguished guest of the US Congress. I was twenty-three years old, and I didn't say a word to anyone. And then one night walking home from a diner just a few blocks from the Capitol, I was mugged and grabbed. When I broke free, I ran again, alone, into the cold dark night.

I never told anyone. My family didn't know—not my husband, my children, my friends. The truth is that my experiences are not remarkable or unique. Sadly, they are all too common.

I lived in silence for most of my life. But in June 2016, Emily Doe, the survivor of the brutal assault by Brock Turner at Stanford University, bravely shared her story. Her powerful words and the severe failure of the justice system to hold her assailant accountable inspired me to publicly tell my stories. Since that time, I've been heartened to see more courageous young women come forward to shed light on the all-too-persistent culture of sexual violence in our nation.

I was blown away when I saw Chessy Prout's interview on the *Today* show in August 2016. Her poise, strength, and courage reflected a young woman wise beyond her years. I saw in Chessy someone who wasn't satisfied with the status quo and who was ready to take matters into her own hands.

I also had the realization that forty years of my generation's silence had helped create the system that Chessy and her contemporaries are fighting to tear down. A system that blames the victim. A system in which justice is too easily escaped by those who prey upon their fellow students, service members, and citizens.

It is time to push back.

As Chessy was going public with her story and taking back her own identity, I was inspired by her and other survivors to begin working on Capitol Hill to establish a group dedicated to ending sexual violence. Sexual violence is not a Republican or Democratic issue: it's a challenge that faces all our communities, our military, and our institutions of learning.

I was encouraged to find members of the US Congress, men and women, Republican and Democrat, who were willing to take on this effort. The Bipartisan Task Force to End Sexual Violence is still growing in numbers but is already beginning to serve as a catalyst for change. We continue to educate our fellow lawmakers and push for reforms that will help empower survivors and prevent these crimes from occurring.

We can change the laws, but what really needs to change is the culture of sexual violence. That begins with conversations and the strength to speak truth to power as Chessy is so bravely doing.

I first met Chessy and her family in a coffee shop on Capitol Hill. We told our stories and realized that we shared a mission of education, advocacy, and empowerment in our quest to end sexual violence.

I invited her to join our panel for a film screening and discussion on Capitol Hill focused on the challenges the digital age is presenting to survivors of sexual violence. With her confidence and quiet resolve, Chessy made quite an impression on the members of Congress she met that evening. Chessy is helping to lead a generation of young people who are shaking up the system and saying, "Enough is enough."

Since that time, I've had the opportunity to work and meet with Chessy on several occasions and I continue to be impressed by her courage and resolve. So much of what she eloquently writes about has been a mystery to me for the past forty years of my life. I recognize the tears, the nightmares, the anger, and the loneliness, even when our family and friends surround us with love. But luckily, and most importantly, I recognize the inspiration, the resolve, and the hope for a better world that motivates us to become advocates.

Chessy embodies the inspiration and the courage to rise up and take back what is rightfully ours—our voice, our autonomy, our hopes and dreams, our future. It's an honor to stand with incredible survivors like Chessy to create a kinder, better, and safer world for everyone to thrive and succeed.

I was in the third class of women at Dartmouth College and I have lived in the shadow of St. Paul's School for sixty years. Chessy's description of the hierarchy of influence and privilege on campus and the fear of challenging the status quo is all too familiar to me. For the past forty years, I was silenced by shame and self-blame. But now, through Chessy's courage to stand her ground, I have found my voice.

Chessy did not know that, two years after her trial and one year after she went public on the *Today* show, revelations about Harvey Weinstein's behavior would have millions tweeting Tarana Burke's #MeToo, showing solidarity with those who have experienced sexual harassment and sexual assault.

Chessy's case is one of many that led us to the present, where we're challenging institutions, Congress included, on the power imbalances that lead to sexual oppression and a system that's set up to keep people silent.

In short, we have arrived at a cultural tipping point. What are we going to do about it?

Together, we can lead a movement for change in our schools and in our society, so that every person can thrive in a world of respect and autonomy.

When I was a young lawyer, raising two sons with my husband, Brad, and managing a demanding workload, I spoke up about fairness and equality for women, promoting equal pay, flexible work schedules, and paid family leave. I remember a male colleague admonishing me—"You're rocking the boat, Annie. Don't rock the boat."

Chessy, I am a certified boat rocker and I can't think of a better first mate than you. I believe in you. I am proud of you. And I am honored to change the world with you.

Ann McLane Kuster
US Congress
Concord, New Hampshire

Representative Kuster
claiming her rights.

PROLOGUE

I t's May 31, 2014, the night before my older sister, Lucy, graduates from St. Paul's, the boarding school we both attend in New Hampshire. My extended family is here in Concord for the weekend festivities, and Dad, a St. Paul's alum, is bursting with pride.

I'm a freshman and I'm hanging out with Lucy and our cousin Katie, watching an awards ceremony honoring student athletes. We arrive too late to get seats in the wooden bleachers, so we end up standing near the road overlooking a pond. Everyone is clapping and cheering.

But I can't put my hands together. I should be mesmerized by the midnight-blue water reflecting everything beautiful around it, the clementine sun sinking in the sky, the redbrick academic buildings, the ethereal pine trees. But my knees are wobbly and my legs feel like Jell-O.

A sticky breeze ripples across the flag. It's warm outside and the guys are sweating in their royal blue and crimson blazers and straw hats. Lucy and her friends are wearing strappy sundresses. I have on a loose-fitting blue shirt and white jeans so I can cover my body, cover everything that he touched last night.

I look over again at the pond. I used to be obsessed with that view. I took a photo of it almost every week this spring as I walked from the dining hall to my dorm. How could a place that's so beautiful, so filled with endless promise, cause so much ugly pain?

Suddenly I notice Malcolm Salovaara staring at me and whispering to him, to Owen Labrie, a popular senior and captain of the soccer team.

Four days ago I received an invite from Owen to climb hidden steps and bask together in the nicest view on campus. I knew what it was—a Senior Salute invitation. It's a tradition at St. Paul's in which seniors try to hook up with younger girls before graduation.

As much as I love an artsy Instagram photo, I didn't want to be just another sexual conquest. Besides, Lucy had briefly dated him and told me to stay away. But after I sent Owen a sassy rejection, a friend who lives in Owen's dorm confronted me.

"Owen's not going to pressure you or do anything to hurt you," my friend promised. "He's a nice guy. He just wants to spend time with you."

My friend kept insisting I go. Owen had a secret key with access to a cool view. Didn't I want to see that? I'm only fifteen years old, but I've lived overseas in Japan and I've been on my own at boarding school for a year. I could handle a rooftop excursion with an eighteen-year-old senior.

If I'm honest with myself, I didn't mind kissing him. Owen's cute and a golden boy, beloved by teachers and bound for Harvard University in the fall.

I glance over at Lucy and I'm afraid to tell her what happened last night. I don't want to ruin graduation weekend. It's the first happy milestone for our family since the 2011 earthquake in Japan uprooted our lives. But I feel shattered like I did back then, my world unraveling beyond my control.

St. Paul's was supposed to be a rock of stability after a difficult few years. It felt safe and familiar, the natural place to be after Dad and Lucy attended. But in one horrible night, I ended up with Owen in a dark, locked room. My fierce independence, my youthful innocence, stolen.

I look up and see Malcolm playing connect-the-dots with his eyes, staring at Lucy, then at me, and then at Owen. His smirk sends shrapnel through my body.

I blink back tears. I need to get away from here, from him, from what he did to me. I don't know who to tell or what to do. As I walk with Lucy and Katie uphill past the pond and the squash courts, a stillness comes over my body. I have to tell Lucy. I know she might be angry that I didn't listen to her, but she would understand that I didn't want this to happen. She knows me better than anyone. She'll know what to say, what to do.

"He had sex with me," I say, tears slipping out of the corners of my eyes, "but I didn't want it."

Lucy wraps her arms around me. Then she utters four of the most important words I need to hear: "It's not your fault."

Before I can say anything more, fury flashes across Lucy's face.

"I'm going to kill him," she says.

A few hours later, Lucy hunts down Owen on the chapel lawn, her silky brown hair swaying violently across her back.

"This is for taking my sister's virginity," Lucy yells.

Then she punches him in the face.

I make it through graduation on Sunday without breaking down, and Lucy has left campus along with the rest of my family. Now I'm studying for math and science finals. But I'm overwhelmed. Word has spread, and students in my dorm confide that Owen has violated other girls too. I need to focus on something else.

I decide to check email, and then I change my Facebook cover photo to one of me and Lucy from yesterday's graduation. Lucy has me in a semi-headlock and is holding a celebratory cigar in her right hand. Classic silly sisters picture.

A few minutes later a classmate writes Owen Labrie's name in a comment under the photo, as if we were notches on his bedpost. My head begins to spin, and I hear my phone ringing. It's Lucy. She's shouting.

I'm upset that Lucy is upset, but I'm not mad at her. I'm mad at me like she's mad at me. But I'm also mad at Owen Labrie. I race through my dorm crying, trying to figure out what to do. I still don't understand what happened to me. Should I tell an adult? Do I go to the hospital?

Later that night, the friend who pressured me to go out with Owen texts a sickening manifesto:

> Chessy, I know what happened with you and Owen, and I just wanted to say I'm really sorry . . . I know him really well and if he thought he was doing anything to hurt you physically or emotionally he would've stopped . . . So before you tell anyone names, I just want you to consider the circumstances. Owen is starting a new life in a new place, and next year will be a fresh start for you too . . . I just love you both and I know what he did hurt you, and maybe you didn't necessarily hate what he was doing at the time. I don't want to see either of you get hurt.

Maybe I didn't hate what he was doing? Is this some kind of threat? My body convulses and I shriek uncontrollably.

Dr. G., a dorm adviser who lives next to me, hears me and brings me into her apartment. I start to tell her what happened, using hypotheticals, because that's what we were advised to do at orientation in the beginning of the year when talking about serious stuff with adults.

"What should I do?" I wail.

"Call your mother," Dr. G. says. "How you handle this will inform the rest of your life."

ONE

March 11, 2011

I had only one question on my mind as I walked toward my sixth-grade math class: Which bedsheet would make me look like a *real* Grecian goddess?

Later that night was the annual Bingo fund-raiser at our all-girls school in Tokyo, and this year it was a Greek-themed event. You'd never seen Bingo like this: the entire gymnasium and cafeteria filled up with students, parents, and teachers who pounded their fists on the tables in frenzied excitement.

Some of my friends were already wrapped in exquisite togas. I was twelve and loved any excuse to dress up, but was holding out until I found the perfect sheet. In the meantime, I wore my regular school uniform: navy knee-high socks and a white button-down shirt tucked into a thick polyester blue-and-green-plaid skirt.

I hoped Mom would let me borrow one of the nicer sheets that shimmered in the light. She was chair of the silent auction and had been working on the Bingo fund-raiser for months. Maybe I'd even thread leaves into my blond hair like the wreaths worn at the ancient Olympic Games.

As I made my way into Mr. Martindale's room on Friday afternoon, I noticed some girls giggling as they climbed under their desks, pretending there was an earthquake only they could feel. Nothing was moving.

In Japan, earthquakes were pretty routine. Sometimes we had one every week, and we had just felt one on Wednesday. I'd lived in Tokyo since I was six months old, so I barely noticed the small quakes anymore. But new kids at my school, the International School of the Sacred Heart, usually freaked out at the tiniest tremor.

Just before the bell rang, I was knocked to my knees. Windows rattled back and forth and books tumbled off the shelves. This was no pretend earthquake anymore: it was the biggest one I'd ever felt.

I squeezed under a cluster of metal-legged desks for safety with five of my classmates. My head banged against the hard bottom of the desk as I was tossed around like a rag doll. Mr. Martindale stood by the sliding doors and grasped the frame to steady himself. White geometric cubes rained down from the windowsill as the tree branches shook angrily outside.

I locked eyes with my best friend, Annie. I thought we were going to die. My eyelids shut like I was trying to avoid the scary part of a movie. I didn't want to see how this ended.

When the tremors paused, the loudspeakers blared: "This is an emergency."

"Get up," Mr. Martindale shouted. "We're evacuating."

The clock at the front of the room read 2:54 p.m. Thumbtacks fell from the bulletin board, sending a poster of Albert Einstein to the floor. We hurried past blue lockers in the hallway and filed out the side emergency stairs. Students streamed out of every door of the building, turning the hilly driveway into a sea of shivering white togas.

We always gathered outside for earthquake drills in case buildings collapsed. But it didn't feel any safer there. Electrical wires swung like vines in the jungle. A gray building towering over Sacred Heart moved across the blue sky as if it were a cloud.

I stood on my toes while my class descended the giant hill leading down to the parking lot. I searched frantically for my older sister, Lucy, a freshman at the high school, and my four-year-old sister, Christianna, who attended the pre-K program. It was close to pickup time for the younger kids, which meant Mom was probably close by. I spotted her across the parking lot with Christianna, and I waved wildly. Relief washed over me. Thank God they were safe.

"Mom, I'm okay!" I shouted over the commotion, and threw my fist in the air with my thumb pointing to the heavens. Hot tears filled my blue eyes as I wove my way through a knot of cars, parents, kids, and teachers. I flung my arms around Mom. I wiped away the wetness before anyone saw. You didn't show signs of weakness in Japan. Being stoic and humble were the most admired qualities.

But sometimes I couldn't help myself. Lucy was a teenager— fifteen—and better at keeping things buttoned up. She had dark hair and hazel eyes and looked more like Dad, who is half-Japanese. I had the all-American looks from Mom's family.

We found Lucy with the rest of her class farther up the hill. She was sitting on the ground in a daze, hugging her knees.

"This is so cool," she mumbled.

Aftershocks forced us to crouch defensively on the hill. My sisters and I huddled together and listened to the crescendo of rattling windows to our right, looking fearfully at the large poles with dangling electrical wires to our left. Mom worried that cars parked along the steep driveway would start rolling sideways if there was another jolt.

I just wanted to go home. The principal eventually allowed students to leave if their parents were with them, so we began our climb up the hills through the University of the Sacred Heart, which is next to our school.

We made it to the top of the second hill, grabbed our bikes from the rack, and walked them up the third hill. I thought about taking my handlebars and running, but Christianna wouldn't stop crying while we wound our way through the ancient university gardens.

As we trudged through the eerily abandoned streets, shards of glass from broken streetlamps littered the cracked sidewalks. We arrived home less than an hour after the earthquake.

The color returned to Mom's face when Dad finally called. He had had trouble finding a cell signal in central Tokyo, where he worked as CEO of Invesco Japan, a division of the American company Invesco.

"I'm okay, I'm safe," he said. "But turn on CNN."

In stunned silence, we watched thirty-foot tsunami waves wash over entire coastline towns ninety minutes east of us. People, real people, were drowning before my eyes. I couldn't blink. News anchors reported that the quake had a 9.0 magnitude, the largest ever recorded in Japan. I grabbed Christianna's hand, trying to soothe her as much as me.

Dad called again a few hours later. "I'm going to stay to make sure everything is fine with the business. Is it okay for some employees to sleep at the house tonight if they can't get home?"

"Of course, whatever you need," Mom said.

Mom grabbed everything she could find in the cupboards and cooked like she was feeding an army. A somber haze enveloped our apartment as news anchors switched between the tsunami waves and dire concerns about radiation leaking from the damaged Fukushima nuclear power plant. I staggered around the apartment, unable to form words.

It was amazing how much could change in twenty-four hours. The night before, our home had felt like a party after Lucy received her acceptance to St. Paul's School in Concord, New Hampshire.

Lucy was three grades ahead of me and president of her class. She had that angsty I'm-too-cool teenager thing going. But when the St. Paul's acceptance email flashed on the computer screen, Lucy cried and pleaded, "Can I go? Can I go? Can I hit accept?" She was so excited she literally ran out the front door and sprinted around the neighborhood at nine p.m.

Dad had attended the prestigious New England prep school as a scholarship student back in the 1980s, and he secretly hoped that we would follow his path. A huge smile spread across Dad's face whenever he talked about his days playing baseball and basketball at St. Paul's. He made lifelong friends there and still kept in touch with his basketball mentor, who taught him the importance of integrity and compassion. Dad was especially proud that the boarding school had started a Japanese language program at his request.

I wanted to be happy for Lucy, but I was devastated at this news. Lucy was my best friend, and the thought of her leaving me ripped a hole in my chest. I couldn't believe that she would go so far away to boarding school. We had our typical sister fights: she tried to get rid of me during sleepovers with her friends, and I loved "borrowing" her clothes. But at the end of the day, our bond of sisterhood ran deep.

When we were younger, we'd wake up and spend hours together with our Barbies. We still loved playing hide-and-seek with the other kids in our three-story yellow-brick apartment building. Lucy had a secret hiding spot that she wouldn't tell me about. All I knew was that I could hear her voice from inside the beige hallway walls.

Our life in Tokyo revolved around a few square blocks that Lucy and I could navigate with our eyes closed. Our neighborhood in Hiroo was filled with both Japanese and gaijin (foreigners) like us. Each morning we greeted the stoic guards at our school, who had watched my sisters and me graduate from strollers to bikes. I knew some Japanese, but we mostly spoke with them in broken English with hand motions and head nods. After school, Lucy and I rode our bikes to the local sushi shop, where the old lady knew my daily order: a toro and scallion roll, ikura nigiri, and inarizushi, marinated tofu skin wrapped around rice.

Almost every weekend, our family brought in dinner—usually udon noodles or hamburgers and shakes—and we played karaoke on Wii Nintendo in the living room. Mom had a beautiful voice and always belted out a song from her favorite band, Earth, Wind & Fire. I loved all music, from Taylor Swift to Run-DMC. Christianna, Lucy, and I had spontaneous dance parties that spilled from room to room, growing in energy and tempo. We liked to jump on Dad's black lacquer coffee table, which he'd bought when he was a bachelor. It was low to the ground, and we used it for everything, from stage to dinner table to game station to dance floor.

"Come on, Christianna, let me twirl you," I'd say, spinning her tiny body around on the table. "Now follow me."

"Okay, Chessy," Christianna squeaked, copying my dance moves.

Dad would cheer us on from the couch. Even though he worked long hours at his job, family came first on weekends. And Dad was a staple at our sports games and other school events at Sacred Heart, always clapping the loudest.

On Sundays our family walked together to church in Omotesandō, and I devoured curry doughnuts at Andersen's bakery on the way home. I loved those fluffy dough balls so much I dreamed about them in anticipation: they were soft and crunchy at the same time and filled with curried minced meat, potatoes, and carrots.

16

Our life in Tokyo was perfect. This was our home, where we—all five of us—belonged.

And Lucy was leaving all this behind, leaving me behind to attend St. Paul's.

On the day of the earthquake, nobody was leaving. The subway and train systems shut down in Tokyo, and hotels were mobbed with businessmen and stranded tourists. Dad waited until nearly all his employees had found a place to stay and then began the long trek home with several others past the Hotel Okura and through the streets of Roppongi.

I emailed my best friend Annie to see how she was doing:

> Are you guys ok??? Are you home?? Im sooo
> worried!! :(I hope you all got home safely . . . Lots of
> aftershocks . . . we r watching cnn and all the tsunamis
> and lots of fires. ohmygosh. Sooooo scary . . . all covered
> in black debris. Email me back when you are home or
> safe!! I hope you all are ok and prepared for the other
> shocks. :(

Annie wrote back a little while later:

> Omg I'm not okay!! :(everyone is so frantic here!! My
> house is so BAD I'm Serious!!! Everything fell!! I'm so
> sad n scared. please help! I'm not even sleeping in my
> house!!! :((((

I wished I could bring Annie and my other friends home so we could protect each other; safety in numbers. My friends at Sacred Heart were my second family. But now we were separated, and I couldn't comfort them. I watched the devastation and loss of life on

TV. All these people were dying, and there was nothing we could do to save them. I felt terrified and helpless. But mostly I was numb.

Lucy moved into my pink butterfly canopy bed so Dad's employees could sleep in her room. We curled up together and listened to the wooden shoji screens shake with every tremor. I tried to lie perfectly still, as if that would stop the aftershocks, and prayed, "Please don't get bigger, please don't get bigger."

Mom was supposed to host a baby shower for my piano teacher on Sunday. She loved throwing parties and knitting together new friendships. I always looked forward to our massive Halloween bashes, when Mom and Dad would lead dozens of kids on candy hunts through the neighborhood. I learned from Mom the importance of building community, and I tried to welcome new girls to Sacred Heart and invite them to my birthday parties and sleepovers.

I was excited about the baby shower, but in the hours after the earthquake, no one could think about celebrating life to come when there was so much death and destruction in the country we called home.

Sacred Heart closed school indefinitely. Dad heard from friends in the US military and Japanese government that the nuclear crisis was far worse than it was being portrayed. Mom and Dad huddled together and came up with a plan. Instead of our family heading to Okinawa for spring break at the end of the month, Dad enlisted the help of a friend to get Mom and us girls on a flight out of Japan. Dad needed to stay behind to take care of the business.

We tearfully said good-bye to Dad in the driveway. I flung my arms around his waist and refused to let go. Yeah, he was the head of a company, but he was our dad first. He should have been coming with us. The earthquake had already done so much damage; why did it need to tear apart our family, too?

Mom promised we'd return to Japan in a few weeks when things got back to normal. We were just taking a short trip to our vacation home in Florida. We'd spent every summer and winter break in the United States, hopscotching between family and friends in New England, New York, and Florida. Lucy dubbed us "vagabums" because we lived out of suitcases. I tried to convince myself that this was another journey to America. But the feelings of doom would not recede.

I passed out on the long flight, exhausted from the fear that had been marathoning through my body for the past three days.

Suddenly I was jarred awake. I looked over at Mom, who was trying to buckle in a wily Christianna before we began the descent into Chicago for our connecting flight. We walked into the terminal and camera flashes blinded us. Journalists pushed microphones into our faces. Somebody mentioned that we were the first flight from Japan to land in Chicago since the earthquake.

Before I said anything, Lucy told me my teeth—newly without braces—were now stained yellow from the curry udon I ate on the plane. I kept my mouth shut.

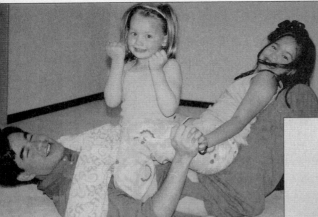

I loved playing in our apartment in Hiroo with Lucy, Christianna, Mom, and Dad. I'd dance around in my school uniform before heading to International School of the Sacred Heart.

My family enjoyed taking trips around Japan, including visiting Aunt Fueko (below). We wore matching robes during a visit to a ryokan, a traditional Japanese inn (left).

TWO

Naples, Florida

I prayed every night for Dad to stay safe and for everyone who had been killed in the earthquake to have a place in heaven. Days stretched into weeks, and before I understood what was happening, our temporary evacuation had turned into an indefinite stay in Florida.

In early April, after many arguments around our kitchen table, Mom enrolled me and my sisters at a private school near our house in Naples. I missed Dad, my friends at Sacred Heart, and life as we knew it.

On the first day of school—April Fool's Day, of course—my nerves were eating away at my stomach as I worried about the culture shock and whether I'd fit in. I had left my self-confidence back in Japan with the rest of my stuff.

I wanted to blend in so much that I'd disappear, so I picked out the most boring outfit possible—a khaki skirt and a white polo shirt. When Mom dropped me off in the middle school parking lot, I looked around and noticed all the girls were dressed in different shades of pink. So much for blending in.

I was assigned a buddy, Kate, to help me adjust. It was like someone had switched the characters in the movie of my life. I had always been the one who welcomed new kids to Sacred Heart.

Everyone in Naples was tan, a perfect Florida bronze. It was so different from Japan, where pale skin was prized and women shaded themselves from the sun with dainty umbrellas.

I quickly discovered that I couldn't hide here. Everyone had been together since kindergarten at the Community School of Naples (CSN), and they'd all heard about the Japanese kids who'd escaped the earthquake. They seemed utterly confused that I was a blond-haired, blue-eyed girl with an American accent.

The kids stabbed me with questions: "You're the Asian girl? You're the one from Japan? Do you speak Chinese? Do you eat dog?"

I was surprised by some of their ignorance but didn't want to embarrass them. I took a deep breath before answering and forced the corners of my mouth to turn up.

"No, I don't speak Chinese," I said. "But I do know some Japanese."

The bell rang and I hurried into homeroom. At first I wondered if I was in the right place. There were boys sitting in the classroom, and I couldn't stop staring. They threw stuff at each other. They talked back to teachers. I tried to stifle the nervous laughter that kept rising in my chest. I was in total disbelief that this was now my life.

At the end of the day, I stomped out of school, a fist clenched around my heart. I missed Annie and Hana and the other girls at Sacred Heart. I desperately wanted to go back to Japan.

I marched over to Mom's car and quickly locked the door after I slid inside. I made sure no one was looking before I shuddered with horror. "I can't believe how rude the boys are! This would never fly at Sacred Heart!"

I refused to give up hope that we would return to Japan, even though there were frightening reports about shops running out of food and meltdowns at the Fukushima power plant. Our black duffel bags sat by the front door, ready to go back to Tokyo. We FaceTimed with Dad every day, and he told me to stay strong.

"We're going to figure this out, Chess," Dad promised. "You focus on school and be good to Mom."

It was my third day at CSN and I tried to do a better job at fitting in: I put on pink pants from Lucy's closet and a white polo shirt. Maybe if I looked good, I would feel better on the inside. I woke up every morning with a tornado in my stomach.

Today, it was swirling at epic speeds. I went to the school bathroom and saw a bloodstain in my underwear.

"Think fast, Chessy," I muttered under my breath. I'd never had my period before, so I was completely unprepared. And I didn't have any friends yet, so I couldn't ask them for help.

I worried that people would think I was pooping if I spent too much time in the bathroom. I grabbed a fistful of toilet paper and wrapped it around my underwear. Things couldn't get worse.

Then lunch happened, and the school cafeteria was its own kind of hell. I sat at a long lunch table of about fifteen girls, all gabbing about who said what and who liked who. I took my first spoonful of minestrone soup as I sat back and listened to the day's gossip. Suddenly I lost my grip on the cup, unleashing a second crimson tide on my sister's pink pants. My white shirt was a battlefield of carrots, celery, beans, and onions.

Kids looked at me and grimaced and then offered napkins. I ignored them and ran to the bathroom, where I broke down in a stall. A classmate, Macy, knocked on the door. I'd met Macy at a theater program for kids during a summer vacation a while back, but I still didn't know her very well.

"Chessy, I have an extra pair of gym shorts. Do you want me to go get them for you?"

"Yes, please," I said, pretending that I wasn't crying. "Thank you so much."

Macy sprinted to the gym lockers three buildings away and brought back her shorts. She also gave me a yellow T-shirt from the school store. I was the new kid who soiled herself with soup and had to wear clunky gym shorts and a yellow shirt that happened to be the color of urine. It was mortifying.

Mom cried when I told her about my day. It didn't take much for either of us to turn on the faucet of tears. She tried to make things better by bringing home a chocolate cake to congratulate me on "becoming a woman."

Christianna looked puzzled but didn't bother asking questions. She just wanted cake.

"This is too much to handle," I whined as I shoved forkfuls of frosting into my mouth. "Why does this have to happen now?"

As much as I missed the fierce sisterhood at Sacred Heart, I began to find the boys at CSN fascinating. Zach and Scott were always making funny faces and playing practical jokes on each other. I had trouble suppressing my laughter during class.

It was hard getting to know the boys. At lunch, they ran around on the fields while the girls sat and gossiped. I thought about how I used to play volleyball at Sacred Heart during lunch and climbed the yellow slide from bottom to top during snack break with Annie. We got sweaty and didn't care what we looked like.

At CSN, some of the girls were in a constant state of primping: touching up mascara and reapplying eye shadow. It seemed like so much effort for sixth grade. They were obsessed with boys, and it was hard keeping up with their crushes. They changed them so frequently, as if they were pairs of shoes.

"Chessy, who do you like? Who's your crush?" Bella asked me from across the picnic table at lunch.

"I don't have a crush on anyone," I stuttered. "I'm still getting to know everyone."

"Well, you should think of one soon," Bella advised.

Zach and Scott seemed pretty cool, but I didn't know what a crush was supposed to feel like. Maybe there was something wrong with me.

Then one day, Zach asked me out on a date, and I said yes. But I'd never been on one before—what were you supposed to do on a date? Did I have to talk to him? I was so out of my element.

Thankfully, Lucy stepped up to help.

"Just be normal," she said. "Zach's such a nice kid and so is his sister."

Lucy was friends with Zach's sister, so the four of us made plans to go to the beach for Zach's birthday. Lucy reviewed my many outfit changes and let me borrow her blue ruffle bikini bottoms and a pair of red sunglasses.

Zach showed up with his new birthday present: a black-and-white paddleboard. First he paddled me around while I lay on my stomach and let the warm gulf water rush between my fingers. Eventually, I gained enough confidence to stand and paddle on my own. I felt so powerful gliding on the water.

After a few hours, we dragged the board back to shore. I tried balancing while the board was resting on the sand.

"No, no, Chester," Lucy warned, using the nickname she'd given me. I was her Chester, she was my Lester. "Don't do that."

"You could break it," Zach's sister chimed in. "There's a fin on the bottom."

"I'm just practicing," I insisted. "I've got this!"

Nope. I broke the fin. Lucy shot me the *I told you so* stare. I hated that look, but I was also thankful that she was there with me. I was afraid of being alone with people, especially when I pulled moves like this. Lucy was my best protector. She understood me better than anyone.

"It's okay," Lucy reassured me. "It's just a board."

What was I going to do when she left for St. Paul's? It was really happening. Wouldn't she miss me? Didn't she need me, too?

Mom and Christianna arrived to pick us up soon after the paddle-board fiasco. Rather than wait in the car, they joined us on the beach. Christianna ran over to me and began inspecting the broken board. Mom chatted with Zach's mom, and they hit it off immediately, as if they'd known each other for years.

All I wanted to do was get out of there. Somehow, my first date had turned into a family affair.

As the summer wore on, Lucy retreated further and further away from me. At sleepaway camp in Maine, she wouldn't even sign up for activities with me. All she wanted to do was hang out with her friends.

When we got back to Florida with just a few weeks left together, Lucy and I kept getting in fights. She had one foot out the door and I wanted to glue her body next to mine. She babbled on about her new boarding school, how awesome her new roommate at St. Paul's seemed.

"Lauren's going to be on the volleyball team with me. Her older sister is already there and captain of the team, and she's going to look out for us," Lucy prattled on.

"Whatever," I said, kicking my toes into the ground.

Lucy was so strong. She didn't need anyone's help. Who was going to look out for me, for Christianna, for Mom?

I'd start in with Lucy over stupid things, just to rile her up, so I could feel her presence, absorb every part of her before she vanished.

"Honestly, I just want to get away from here and from every-thing," Lucy groaned.

"Fine, leave!" I snapped. "I don't care."

But I did care. And Lucy left.

Dad swore he was searching for someone to lead the company so he could move to the United States. I understood that he wanted to put the business in good hands, but really, how long was this going to take? It had been six months already and it was just three of us in Florida now that Lucy was away at St. Paul's.

I should have been thankful that I escaped a natural disaster, but I was twelve and focused on my little universe. My family had fallen apart and I was floundering.

I worried about Dad's safety and missed our time together: inhaling the scent of purple wildflowers on our morning walks to Sacred Heart, licking the empty salt packets during our yakisoba cooking sessions, and embarrassing Lucy at her sports games by starting a two-person wave.

I tried to make things less stressful for Mom, since she was basically a single parent now. I cleaned up after my little sister and attempted to keep my behavior in line, but I was constantly filled with rage. I blamed Mom for bringing us to the United States and keeping me from my perfect world in Japan.

"You took my life away from me. Why is it that we always have to do what you want?" I yelled. "When are we going back home?"

"Chessy, I'm not in control of the world right now," Mom sighed with exasperation. "You have to understand that I'm not trying to do this to you. I didn't want the earthquake to happen. I don't like being separated from Dad either. But this is what life is right now."

"I know the earthquake wasn't your fault, but that doesn't make me any less angry," I hollered back, with poison darts shooting from my eyes.

I was also scared that Mom and Dad might separate. I couldn't believe that life was going on without Dad. Maybe Mom would realize she didn't need him. Whenever he came home for short visits, they seemed to fight about his job.

I was bitter that I never got a chance to say good-bye to my friends at Sacred Heart. It was so hard to start over in middle school, especially when all the kids had known each other since they were five.

To make matters worse, Lucy was totally MIA. She wouldn't respond to my messages for days at a time, and I was pretty sure she blocked me from seeing her photos on Facebook. She was missing my thirteenth birthday, my first teenage year. We'd never celebrated a birthday without each other. I guess this was the new normal.

I was in a fight with everyone, including God. Why would he let an earthquake kill thousands of people who didn't deserve it? Why would he allow the earth to be destroyed, all these people's lives to be destroyed, my precious world to be destroyed? What was the purpose of all this if everyone was going to die?

I was spiraling into darkness and feeling tired and sad all the time. Mom took me to a few doctors, who diagnosed me with a severe vitamin B12 deficiency, multiple food allergies, and a high gluten intolerance. Go figure, my favorite meal was pasta.

I started seeing a therapist, Dr. Sloane. At first I pretended nothing was wrong. I kept up the perfect facade I had been trained to have in Japan. It was really awkward because Dr. Sloane would sit and wait for me to say something.

I realized it was going to be a waste of her time if I kept acting like everything was fine. Anyway, she was an expert, so she could probably see right through me. After one session and a week of contemplation, I started talking. And talking. I was relieved to have an outlet where I could say anything and not be judged.

I told her I was exhausted from trying to infiltrate the tight-knit groups at middle school. I wanted people to like me and respect me even though I was new. I was worried that the students thought I was damaged because of the earthquake. Dr. Sloane introduced names into my vocabulary for the torpedoes in my stomach and the black blanket wrapped around my brain: anxiety and depression.

I let my new best friend, Arielle, in on a few secrets, like how I was feeling tired of life and of being a burden to Mom. Arielle came with me every day to get my vitamin B12 shots at the school nurse's office. Arielle was also new at CSN and had strawberry-blond hair and a laugh that was, incredibly, louder than mine.

We spent every moment together, except when Dad descended on Naples. Then the world came to a standstill. I wouldn't let him out of my sight. We rode bikes, played volleyball and catch, and cooked our favorite meal of fried spaghetti. We stayed up late watching YouTube videos of funny pranks or episodes of *NCIS: Los Angeles*.

When we were throwing footballs around, I realized I was sick of sitting at the picnic tables with the other girls. I had a good arm and I could take on these boys. So during lunch at school, I marched onto the field with Arielle by my side. I saw Scott and Zach (we hadn't lasted beyond that first date when I broke his paddleboard). We told the boys we wanted in.

"Wow, you're good," Scott said as I hurled a football. "You can play with us anytime."

I was excited to tell Lucy about my new friends when she came home for winter break. We'd seen each other a few times, but I didn't really understand her life. Mom was mad because Lucy never called. She claimed she had bad cell reception in her dorm room and was too embarrassed to talk on the landline in front of other people.

It was a pure lovefest when we finally got Dad and Lucy together with the Naples gang of three. I stole glances at Lucy out of the corner of my eye. She was wearing more makeup and had that carelessly tousled prep-school hair.

I was desperate to get her alone. I wanted to know everything. Was St. Paul's like *Gossip Girl*? Or more Hogwarts? Dad had his stories, of course, but they were ancient history. Lucy wasn't sharing much when everyone was around. After Christianna went to bed one night, I finally cornered Lucy on our brown couches outside.

"So, seriously, what's it like?" I asked.

"It's kind of crazy." Lucy smiled slyly. "You're totally free to do whatever you want after class is done. There's no one to check in on you. No one is looking over your shoulder."

"Wow, that's pretty amazing," I said. Sometimes Mom made me write up lists that broke down what I was doing minute by minute so I could keep "on task." I craved the freedom that Lucy described.

Lucy talked about how great the volleyball team was, how her teammates got breakfast and dinner together.

"I'm thinking of doing club volleyball here in Naples," I chimed in.

"That's awesome!" Lucy said enthusiastically. "It will totally put you at an advantage if you come here to St. Paul's."

I got goose bumps hearing that Lucy wanted me there with her. I missed her so much. I pictured us strolling through campus together and sharing sister dinners. Then Lucy began to word vomit.

"I have to tell you the boy stuff is crazy. There were all these guys who wanted to score me."

"Score you?"

"Yeah, that's the word everyone uses for hooking up," Lucy explained. "You can't have too many of them, but you need to do some or else people will get mad."

My eyes were saucers about to fly out of my head.

"That's weird," I said.

"Everyone does it."

I couldn't get words out of my mouth. I looked away. I was afraid of saying something to upset Lucy. She usually stopped talking to me when she got mad, and that was the last thing I wanted.

"Okay, if you say so," I said.

I hoped that Lucy knew what she was doing, but she was only fifteen. I thought she was way out of her league. I couldn't stop worrying about her, so I eventually told Mom. To be honest, I always told Mom everything.

A little later, Lucy stormed into my room, whirling with anger.

"I'm never going to share anything with you," she screamed. "Never mind. I'm never going to speak to you ever again."

"I'm sorry. I'm really sorry. I didn't know Mom would get upset," I said. "But you can't tell me things and assume I'm not going to say anything."

"I thought you were my friend," Lucy snarled. "But I guess we're just sisters and not friends."

She scorched me with her eyes. My heart crumpled. Then Lucy slammed the door. What had St. Paul's done with my sister?

The following June, Lucy and I traveled to Japan for the first time since the earthquake. Things were good again between us, and I wanted to keep them that way for our big journey abroad to visit Dad. Mom was staying home with Christianna, and I felt so grown-up traveling on my own. Mom and Dad could be protective, but they always encouraged me and Lucy to explore and be independent.

I could barely sit still for the twelve-hour flight. My toes tingled each time I thought about walking the streets of Hiroo, visiting Sacred Heart, devouring tonkatsu (fried pork cutlets) and endless rolls of sushi. I was so close to getting my world back, even if it was just for a short farewell tour.

But once we landed, I quickly realized that nothing was the same. Dad had moved out of our beloved apartment and was staying at a hotel in another neighborhood. Many of my Sacred Heart friends had left Tokyo. The rest of the students were on summer break, and everything there seemed to be under construction.

Dad worked during the day, so Lucy and I slept late, swam at a nearby pool, and then watched a marathon of *NCIS: Los Angeles* episodes. We could have been anywhere.

One afternoon Lucy and I finally got motivated to return to our old neighborhood, then walked up and down the main street, Nisseki Dori. Only a year had passed, but some of our favorite shops had closed. Our kind sushi lady was still in business, and we placed our usual order.

We took our food to a nearby playground and sat down on some rocks. I devoured my toro and scallion roll, ikura nigiri, and inari-zushi. But nothing could fill the emptiness that gnawed at me.

"So much has changed in just one year," I said to Lucy between bites. "I thought I'd be at home here, but I'm not. I feel like I don't fit in anywhere."

"You'll come with me to St. Paul's in a year," Lucy said. "You'll find your place there and we can be together again."

I smiled. I wanted my Lester back. And I wanted a community, a place where I truly belonged.

Lucy and I leaned on each other when we relocated to Florida after the earthquake. It took me a while to adjust to my coed school, and I went on my very first date (below).

THREE

October 2012

My stomach was doing flips as I walked up the steps to a gray stone building, Sheldon Library. It housed St. Paul's admissions office and featured a sweeping view of Library Pond and the redbrick chapel across campus.

I followed Mom and Dad into a rotunda decorated with portraits of the rectors who had run the school since 1856. I turned around to look at them and saw a bunch of old white men staring down at me. I shifted my weight from side to side, trying to shake off my nerves, and pressed my sweaty palms against my new skirt.

"Just be yourself," Dad said as I stared stoically ahead.

A soft-spoken woman named Ms. Carega introduced herself and brought me upstairs to a room lined with books. I sat across from her on a couch and shared my background growing up in Tokyo and then moving to America. I had memorized all the points I wanted to make about my dreams of studying Japanese and piano, two things I'd lost after the earthquake. I mentioned that I hoped to play volleyball with my sister and was excited about the international community at St. Paul's.

My chest puffed up a little as I hit everything on my list. Then Ms. Carega asked, "Do you have any questions about the school?"

I wasn't prepared for that. I sat dumbfounded for a few seconds.

"Um, well, my sister goes here and my dad went here, so I got a lot of information from them," I said, my body deflating.

I walked downstairs, irritated that I hadn't come up with a single question. I stood in the rotunda and prayed that I could follow in Lucy's footsteps, in Dad's footsteps.

Dad's position was likely getting transferred to the Hong Kong office, and I loathed the idea of starting over again in a new country. I had just gotten used to life in the United States, but I was ready to leave Florida.

Naples was beginning to feel suffocating, especially with the 2012 election. I was surrounded by white, wealthy conservatives who had never really accepted that we had an African American president. I yearned to be in a place that was progressive and diverse. St. Paul's seemed to promise that as I thumbed through yearbooks and glossy brochures that featured students of different races and ethnicities and information about financial aid.

I looked out the wall of windows into the pond reflecting October leaves streaked with crimson and tangerine.

The school's two thousand acres of rolling green hills felt indulgent after spending twelve years in densely packed Tokyo. I still missed having chocolate cake fights with my friends on the roof of our apartment building and scootering in the alleys around our neighborhood in Tokyo. But my favorite memories of Japan were the weekend trips we took to Mount Fuji, where I ran with Lucy through plains of susuki grass taller than me. St. Paul's had that same expansive feeling.

Mom and Dad went upstairs to meet with Ms. Carega and talked about their potential move to Hong Kong. They explained how they saw St. Paul's as a place to rebuild a community for me and Lucy, something that had crumbled after the earthquake.

St. Paul's stitched together the people and places that were important to Mom and Dad. Mom was a New England girl who grew up in Connecticut and attended College of the Holy Cross in Massachusetts. She had family and friends who lived nearby. St. Paul's was home to all of Dad's fondest memories, and some of his old classmates and teachers were still there and could look after me. My parents thought St. Paul's would provide a world-class education and a safe, gentle transition to college.

After we finished the interview, Lucy stopped by Sheldon with a Nikon camera hanging around her neck. She wanted to take some black-and-white pictures of me and develop them for her photography class.

I grasped the wrought-iron railing with one hand and stood at the top of the stairs to the admissions building. I smiled confidently, my eyes captivated by the opportunity all around me. When I looked at that same photo years later, I saw a girl who knew nothing about St. Paul's, a girl who was too young and naive to go to a place like that.

I was walking with Mom and Dad to Lucy's volleyball scrimmage when Lucy called and said the team might need an extra player.

"Grab some clothes from my dorm. This could be awesome."

Holy crap. I was going to play with the St. Paul's varsity team? I raced past Library Pond to Kehaya, the nicest dorm on campus. It looked like an old English manor house, with a brick exterior, a stone courtyard, and a sprawling manicured lawn. Lucy had one of the biggest rooms, with a floor-to-ceiling window and a spacious loft. At St. Paul's, it was the lap of luxury—so much so that the girls living there were called the Kehaya princesses.

I ransacked Lucy's room, grabbing spandex shorts, a gray tank top, athletic socks, and sneakers. I couldn't find any extra ankle guards or knee pads. I was just going to have to tough it out. I took deep breaths.

"Don't get your hopes up, Chess," I muttered to myself. "Enough girls may show up."

But what if they didn't? This could be like an unofficial tryout for the team! I walked slowly into the athletic center, which had recently had a $24 million makeover. I marveled at the vastness of the place— an Olympic-size swimming pool, an indoor track, a wrestling arena, and two basketball courts. I climbed the V-shaped staircase to the volleyball court and stood awkwardly behind the glass. The coach, Doc Reynolds, waved me onto the court.

"All right, Chessy, we're just going to rotate around positions," Doc said, towering over me with his toothy grin. "Relax and give it your best."

I started in the back row and lasered my eyes on the ball. I could hear Dad cheering in the stands, like he used to when we played sports at Sacred Heart. I tuned him out when I saw Lauren Rusher—Lucy's roommate from last year—go for the ball on the opposite side of the court.

Lauren was one of the biggest and fiercest girls on the team. She hit the ball so hard she'd supposedly given several girls concussions, earning her the nickname Rusher the Crusher. Lauren had a wild look in her eyes as she lifted her arm up and smashed the white sphere, knocking the moon out of the sky.

It was heading straight for my face in what was sure to end with a broken nose. I took a step backward and stuck my arms out. The ball hit my skin so hard I felt like I'd been stung by a thousand hornets. I wanted to collapse, but if I moved, the ball would shoot sideways. I clenched my jaw and returned the missile to Lauren's side of the court. Not an ideal bump, but at least it didn't land on the floor next to me. Doc looked impressed.

Moments later, when I rotated to the front row, I was face-to-face with Lucy. We jousted at the top of the net and I blocked her spike. Lucy beamed with pride. Sweat was pouring down my head by the time the scrimmage was over.

Dad rushed off the bleachers onto the squeaky parquet floor as if I'd won an Olympic medal. He put one arm around me as Doc ambled over.

"Chessy's got a spot on the team next year if she wants it," Doc said to Dad. "I'll make sure to put in a good word with admissions."

"Oh my gosh, thank you so much," I said. "It was such an honor to play with the team."

"That's our newb," one of the varsity players called out to me.

I was elated. The volleyball team was like Lucy's second family. The girls ate dinners together, walked to classes, and hung out on weekends. I was beginning to see this as my community, my new home.

A few weeks later Dad and I visited Lucy to see her compete in a New England semifinal match. I imagined myself on the court playing next to Lucy and Rusher the Crusher. Some boys on the bleachers were shirtless and covered in red body paint. I couldn't help but gawk at one guy who had written PROUT MAKE ME SHOUT across his back.

Unfortunately, St. Paul's lost, but Lucy was still in a good mood when we headed out to dinner with her boyfriend, Brooks, and their friends Duncan and Jackson. Dad had been a year ahead of Brooks's father at St. Paul's, but the two hadn't known each other well because Dad mostly hung out with the minority scholarship students.

Lucy's friends piled into our rental car, and I ended up squished in the back between Duncan and Jackson. They started teasing that they'd "watch out for me" when I got to St. Paul's and walk me to class.

"We'll take you out," Jackson said. I turned cranberry red with embarrassment and giggled nervously. Lucy rolled her eyes at their blatant attempts to unnerve her.

I leaped out of the car when we arrived at our destination, the Common Man. It was a two-story restaurant that looked like a charming New England home, with dark wooden beams and rooms with upholstered couches and floral curtains. There were quotes from politicians and athletes painted on the bathroom walls, like John F. Kennedy's "Forgive your enemies but never forget their names" and Vince Lombardi's "Winning isn't everything. It's the only thing."

At the dinner table, I was sandwiched again between Duncan and Jackson. We played hangman after we ordered food, and Duncan tried unsuccessfully to get the phone number of our waitress. What was up with these boys?

I looked over at Jackson, who was wearing a burnt-orange Texas Longhorns baseball hat backward on his head. He started in with Lucy again and suggested that he'd date me next year, and then she could go out with one of his younger brothers when they enrolled next fall.

Lucy burst out laughing. "She's in middle school. Don't even think about it."

On the drive back to St. Paul's, Duncan put his arm around me and Jackson stuck his thumb up in front of my face as Lucy snapped a photo. I pressed my lips together and smiled. I was flattered by the attention but didn't exactly feel comfortable. I was only thirteen and in eighth grade, after all. And they would be seniors by the time I got there next fall. If I got there next fall.

"The boys were acting really weird," I said to Lucy at the end of the night.

"Yeah, don't worry about it," Lucy said. "They're just being dumb."

Boys will be boys, I guessed.

I didn't think twice about Jackson or Duncan once I was back in Naples. I'd been dreaming about Dean, a boy in my grade with chocolate-brown eyes. We loved playing basketball and watching

TV with Zach and Scott. Dean understood my sarcasm—somewhat of a rarity—and we binge-watched episodes of *Impractical Jokers* together. By Thanksgiving, a fuzzy more-than-friend feeling enveloped me whenever Dean was around.

I mostly ignored it until we ended up at a bonfire party after Christmas. I stuffed my face with marshmallows and chocolate from the s'mores supplies and swung wildly from a rope hanging off the trees. When I finally sat down, Dean gently took my wrist and slipped his hand into mine.

At school the next week, Dean picked me up after class and kissed me in front of our lockers. We were officially boyfriend and girlfriend. Our science teacher scolded us for kissing in the hallway.

Dean had an infectious laugh, and when I was with him, the hamster wheel of anxiety in my brain slowed down. I was still seeing Dr. Sloane and had started taking medication to treat my depression and anxiety. I told Dean a little bit about what I'd been going through, but I tried to keep things light and fun.

I wasn't ready for anything super serious, so I liked having Zach and Scott around as buffers. My friend Jackie was close with Dean, and she constantly wanted relationship updates.

"Chessy, do you love him?" Jackie asked.

"I dunno," I said. "He's not family."

"Chessy, he really loves you."

Yikes. Was I in love? What did love feel like?

I was too embarrassed to ask Mom. I knew Mom had had serious boyfriends in high school and college, but she didn't talk much about them. She grew up in a very Catholic household—sex before marriage was forbidden—and her own mother wouldn't even acknowledge some of Mom's relationships. There was no real sex talk yet, and that was fine by me. That felt like light-years away.

But with Valentine's Day fast approaching, I felt pressure to tell Dean how much I enjoyed being around him. While I was sitting in

French class, I wrote Dean a note on a stray index card, and it was kind of mushy. I cringed when I took it out later that night and read it again. I worried about putting myself out there too much and getting hurt. So I tucked the note into my diary and wrote him a new, toned-down card.

Dean showed up on Valentine's Day with roses, a box of chocolates, and a picture frame with a photo of us in it. I kept the roses for weeks, until they were wilted and blackened around the edges. I worried that our relationship would soon look like that, because it was seeming more likely that I'd be heading off to boarding school.

Decision Day—when St. Paul's emailed its acceptance letters—was in early March, and it was marked on the kitchen calendar with four exclamation points!!!! I'd be in Colorado for a national volleyball tournament, possibly my last one with my team. I was excited because one of my old friends from Sacred Heart was supposed to be there playing with her new school.

Dad was meeting me in Colorado—his job was now based in Atlanta, so he commuted to Naples on weekends. I didn't feel well when I boarded the plane in Florida. I started sweating and shaking. Everything I touched sent pain shooting through my veins. It had to be the flu or some wicked virus. When we got to the hotel in Denver, I collapsed in bed. My teammates tracked down some medicine, and I fell into a NyQuil-induced haze.

I woke up in a pool of sweat, my eyes crusted shut. I rubbed away the sleep, but my vision was still blurred. It took a while before I could make out Dad smiling at me from across the room, with an iPad in his lap. It was March 9, he reminded me. Decision Day.

"Check your email! Check your email!" Dad yelped as he handed me his iPad.

A video popped up featuring admissions officers, students, faculty, administrators, and the school mascot, the Pelican, dancing in various picture-perfect settings on campus and waving red-and-white signs imploring me to SAY YES TO SPS!

I looked over at Dad, and he had tears in his eyes.

"This is so wonderful. We'll be on the same reunion-year cycle, sweetie," Dad said. "This is going to be a lifelong bond for us."

Dad had left his home in New York City in the fall of 1979 and arrived at St. Paul's as a sophomore, a lanky scholarship kid excited about the school's strong athletics program. He was the fourth of five children from an Irish-American father and a Japanese mother whose own parents were pioneers, attending college in the United States—Mount Holyoke and Harvard. Dad was really tall and towered over his siblings. He liked to joke that he got his height from all the milk he drank as a kid. Dad guzzled the stuff because he was collecting as many cartons as possible to exchange for free tickets to Yankee Stadium, his favorite place on earth.

At St. Paul's, Dad was not part of the prep-school legacy crowd—the many students who had generations of Paulies in their blood. But he found a core group of friends through sports.

Mom hadn't heard of St. Paul's until she met Dad. She was the daughter of public school teachers from a small working-class town in Connecticut. She got her first glimpse of the campus when Dad brought her to his ten-year reunion. They were newly engaged—after meeting on a flight from Tokyo to New York—and Dad linked arms with her as they walked in the alumni parade along a path that cut through the emerald landscape.

"Do you think we could send our kids here?" Dad asked.

They weren't even married yet, and he was already asking to give up their future children? She thought boarding school was where kids were sent away as punishment. Mom crossed her fingers behind her back before answering.

"Maybe," she said.

Dad's job in finance led us to Japan, and Mom set aside her career in marketing to take care of us girls. But Mom always wanted us to have an American education before we attended college. Months before the earthquake, Dad lobbied Mom to open the door to the family nest and let Lucy apply to St. Paul's.

Her acceptance a day before the earthquake seemed like a sign— here was a stable and safe place that could care for Lucy the way Sacred Heart had. Two years later, as Dad prepared for another transfer abroad, Mom felt confident entrusting me to the St. Paul's community.

"This is so great, Chessy," Dad said as he replayed the St. Paul's video acceptance over and over.

All I knew was that my head needed to meet the pillow or else the world would end. I started to close my eyes when Dad shook me: "Call Mom! Call Lucy!"

It barely rang once before Mom and Lucy picked up the phone together and squealed with excitement. Lucy was home for spring break, and Mom promised a proper celebration when I returned to Naples.

I was laying in the hotel bed and scrolling through Instagram when I stumbled across a cryptic posting from my boyfriend:

> Through God all things are possible
> Please pray for my family.

I tried calling Dean, but he didn't pick up.

I texted Jackie to find out what was going on, and she responded that Dean's brother was hospitalized in the intensive care unit after trying to hurt himself. It didn't make sense. Was this a NyQuil hallucination? The room was spinning, so I pulled the covers over my head and fell back asleep. I never made it onto the volleyball court.

When I returned to Naples, Mom, Lucy, and Christianna presented me with a gluten-free cake they'd baked themselves, canvases with CONGRATULATIONS and SPS YEA! CHESSY '17 DAD '82 AND LUCY '14 painted in red, and crimson-and-white balloons to match the St. Paul's school colors.

My family was ecstatic, but I was having trouble matching their excitement. I was worried about Dean's brother and anxious that my friends at CSN would ditch me when they found out I'd be leaving. Arielle usually did not get emotional, but she teared up after I broke the news.

I refused to let Arielle out of my sight when we took a school trip to Washington, DC, a few days later. I even made her sit between me and Dean on a two-person bench during a bus ride back to the hotel. Dean wasn't talking much about his brother. He was acting distant, and I couldn't tell whether he was upset about his family stuff or my acceptance to St. Paul's. I wasn't sure how to navigate this.

It didn't help matters when I left with Mom for New Hampshire in early April 2013 for St. Paul's Revisit Weekend. The trip gave prospective students one last look at the school before deciding whether to go.

When we arrived on campus, I picked up registration materials at the Lindsay Center for Mathematics and Science. It was a massive brick structure named after an alumnus and had a greenhouse, a solar observatory, and a Foucault pendulum that hung down a stairwell. Mom quickly made friends with a family who had an older daughter, Allie, starting in the fall. I hoped I could make friends that easily.

I opened a glossy crimson folder embossed with the St. Paul's crest: a pelican ripping meat from its own breast to feed its young. Yikes, what a horrific image. I wasn't sure why they would choose that.

I met my student host in the common room of Coit, one of the dorms attached to the main dining hall known as the Upper. My host was friendly and gave me a tour of her dorm, including the laundry room. Most kids paid to have their clothes cleaned and delivered in neatly folded piles—a negligible expense when you considered the annual $50,000-plus price tag to attend St. Paul's.

I met other girls who told me how fun the school dances were and that they never got in trouble for violating the dress code. Apparently, female students at nearby Phillips Exeter Academy were always complaining about how faculty forced them to change clothes because they were wearing something too revealing or "distracting."

The girls here seemed so sophisticated. I thumbed through one of the brochures in my folder etched with the St. Paul's motto: "Freedom with responsibility." That sounded right up my alley. I could choose when I woke up, what I ate, and when I did my homework.

I was in awe of famous alumni like then secretary of state John Kerry and cartoonist Garry Trudeau. Who wouldn't want to be a part of this exclusive club?

Later that night the students put on a variety show, where all the different a cappella and dance troupes performed. I could already imagine myself singing on that stage. After the show, Lucy found me along with Jackson and Brooks. Jackson introduced me to one of his younger brothers, who would be in my grade.

"Hi," I said shyly.

"Hi," he said without looking at me. Neither of us could get out any more words. Awkward.

I started scrolling through Instagram to check in on my friends back home. I saw pictures of Dean with his arm around a girl from my school. My stomach dropped to my feet. I showed Lucy the photos and asked her what she thought I should do.

"Forget about him," she said. "That's not a real relationship anyway. When you come to school, you'll realize what a real relationship is."

"Yes, it *is* real," I insisted.

Lucy annoyed me when she played that older sibling card—the one where she knew better because she was *soooo* much more mature than me.

"Lucy, we're only a few years apart," I said.

"You're going to break up soon because you're leaving," Lucy said. "All these boys here are interested in you. I'll get a picture of you with them to make Dean jealous."

When I got back to Naples, I learned that Dean had cheated on me with the girl in the photo. I unleashed my fury at home. I thought about setting fire to the picture frame he'd given me for Valentine's Day, but that seemed like more effort than Dean was worth. Instead I ripped up our picture.

A wave of calm washed over me when I saw him at school. Dean walked over and tried to give me a bullshit explanation. I cut him off midsentence.

"You know what? I don't want to hear it. I'm leaving," I said.

His mouth twisted with sadness, and then I softened my tone.

"I want the best for you. I want to make sure you're okay," I said. "But we're done."

I walked away before he could get another word in. I was done with Dean, done with CSN. As much as I had tried to make Naples my home, I had never truly fit in. It was small and homogenous and closed off—the opposite of my world in Tokyo. I had so much hope for St. Paul's to provide a place of love and stability and community that I sorely needed.

While Mom and Dad packed for Hong Kong, I spent the summer getting quality sister time with Christianna and Lucy. We biked together to the beach and splashed in the water. Lucy had recently gotten her license, so she drove us around Naples blasting country music at top volume on Gator Country 101.9.

Mom helped me pick out a pretty blue-and-white comforter for my bed at St. Paul's and shop for posters for my dorm room. She also got me a few prep-school essentials: black Hunter boots, a navy Longchamp bag, and a forest-green Barbour jacket.

I filled out a roommate questionnaire for St. Paul's that asked me about my living style: was I clean or messy, was I quiet or loud, did I go to bed early or late? Lucy really wanted me to room with Ivy, the little sister of her roommate, Georgina, and so I put down the request.

One night Lucy sat down next to me on the glider couch on our patio as the warm gulf breeze swept over us.

"Chester, I'm so excited for you to come to St. Paul's," she said, and squeezed my hand. "We're going to play volleyball together and have sister brunches on Sundays."

"It's going to be so fun, Lulu," I said, using one of my various nicknames for Lucy.

"I know we'll probably still get in fights, but you can't be rude at school. You really can't talk back to seniors."

"Okay," I said.

"And I just want you to know that what you do in the first couple of weeks is how you'll be known. Everybody remembers everything," Lucy explained. "So don't dress too slutty or revealing at Nash Bash. Don't kiss any boys during the first month. You don't want to be known in that way. Boys will try to talk to you all the time. You can ignore them."

Lucy had good intentions and I trusted my older sister. But I was offended that she felt the need to even tell me these things. I knew how to protect myself. This was my life.

"I'm going to figure it out on my own," I said.

"You don't understand: the school is a whole different world than down here."

"I have to make my own mistakes," I told Lucy. "You made your mistakes. I'm going to make mine."

"Fine," Lucy sighed. "You'll figure it out."

I had fun visiting Lucy's dorm at St. Paul's (left) and playing in a scrimmage with her volleyball team (bottom left). Lucy took this photo of me after my interview with admissions in fall 2012 (below). I was so excited to join her at boarding school.

My family celebrated after I got accepted to St. Paul's. During Revisit Weekend in April 2013, I reunited with Lucy and took photos of my favorite view of Library Pond.

FOUR

St. Paul's, September 2013

'd finally made it. Mom and I were waiting in the Rectory, a stately gray house in the middle of campus, so that we could meet the head of school and sign my name in a big leather-bound book.

I recognized Rector Michael Hirschfeld from visiting Lucy over the last couple of years. I'd already met his son, Dylan, the year before, when he and his older sister had dinner at our home. Mr. Hirschfeld had a frozen grin on his face and robotically stuck out his hand when Mom and I made it to the front of the line.

"Hi, Chessy. We're so glad to have you here," he said. "Dylan is really looking forward to seeing you."

I eagerly picked up the pen and signed my full name, Francesca Prout, in black ink. It was my first official act of independence—*I* enrolled myself in the school. The next four years of my life started now.

Mom and I linked arms and walked along the path the way she

and Dad had years ago at his reunion. My dorm, Conover Twenty, or Con20, was a redbrick building with a pitched green roof. It faced the chapel and was conveniently located next to the Schoolhouse, where most classes were held.

I knew my room was not going to be as posh as Lucy's at the Kehaya castle. Still, I was stunned at how tiny the space was: it had originally been used as a single, and there was just a body's length between the twin beds. I could deal. I was used to cramped spaces in Tokyo.

I noticed a pale girl with jet-black hair sitting on a bed and a bunch of DJ equipment stuffed in the corner. She had a rocker look, with lips stained red and black combat boots. I went in for a hug.

"Hi, I'm Chessy. It looks like we're going to be living together. Yay!" I said, immediately regretting how dorky I sounded.

"Hey, I'm Tabitha," she said coolly, barely looking up. "Some people call me Tabby for short. But I don't really care what you do."

I quickly learned three things about Tabitha: she was from the West Coast, she was obsessed with all good music, and she gave zero shits what other people thought of her. I liked her bluntness; it reminded me of Arielle. But I worried that Tabitha assumed I was some lame Florida chick who only listened to pop music.

Mom was busy chatting with my head of house, Colin Callahan, and of course they made connections. Mr. Callahan's dad had taught Mom in college at Holy Cross. I lived next door to another dorm adviser, Dr. Theresa Gerardo-Gettens, who everyone called Dr. G.

I left the adults so I could grab more boxes from the car when I ran into Ivy—the younger sister of Lucy's roommate. We hugged each other as if we were best friends, even though we'd never actually met in person. Ivy was tall with long blond hair, perfectly straight white teeth, and a beauty mark under her right nostril. She lived on the Upper East Side in New York City and could have stepped off the set of *Gossip Girl*.

"Chessy! I can't believe they didn't match us as roommates, but it's soooo good that you're just down the hall," Ivy squealed. "We're going to have so much fun."

Her peppiness was contagious.

"Definitely," I said, my voice sliding an octave higher. "I can't wait!"

We swapped cell phone numbers and made plans to walk to dinner. I was relieved to find a friend right away, especially someone who seemed so confident and upbeat. I pictured us becoming best friends and doing sister outings together.

Later that evening there was an opening-night dinner for third formers—what they called freshmen at St. Paul's. It took place at the Upper, the main dining hall, which was tucked inside a hulking Gothic building. Ivy and I stuck close together as we entered a narrow hallway lined with dark wood panels engraved with the names of St. Paul's graduates.

The dining hall itself was straight out of Hogwarts, with tall arched ceilings and long rows of wooden tables. During dinner, a stuffed snowy owl that looked like Harry Potter's pet, Hedwig, flew across the cavernous room on a wire. I couldn't decide whether this was magical or creepy. Maybe magically creepy.

After the meal, we traipsed across campus to the smaller old chapel for First Night Service. After a short ceremony, where Mr. Hirschfeld welcomed us, we spilled out into the dark night. Seniors, dorm leaders, and faculty surrounded the chapel and cheered the new kids, known as newbs. I saw Lucy on the lawn and ran to hug her.

"We're finally here. Together," I said, my eyes glistening.

"Yes, we are, Chess," Lucy said, and squeezed my hand.

I spotted Mr. Hirschfeld's son, Dylan, out of the corner of my eye and waved at him to come over.

"I need something good to wear for Nash Bash," Dylan announced, referring to the dance the following night, when everyone dressed up in neon colors and crazy outfits.

"Totally. Lucy has a box of costumes we can search," I said.

Dylan texted me so that we had each other's numbers, and we agreed to meet the next day to raid Lucy's stuff and find him some spandex biker shorts. I was eager to be as helpful as possible. The pressure to find friends and make this community my own weighed on me. People seemed to orbit around those with knowledge, and I was not afraid to use mine.

As I straightened up my room before bed, I got a text from Ivy.

Ivy: Hey so 7:45 walk to breakfast?

I grinned as I texted back.

Me: Yess! The first of our long walks to the upper . . . 🙈
Ivy: Ahhhh! Let the adventure begin 😌

I tried to pay attention during the rest of orientation, but I felt like this stuff was beneath me. I'd lived overseas and knew how to take care of myself. Still, I made a few mental notes: if I wanted to discuss a serious issue with an adult, I should talk in hypotheticals to avoid mandatory reporting to outside authorities.

And if I got drunk, or knew a friend who was wasted, we should "sanctuary" ourselves. We wouldn't get in trouble if we turned ourselves in to the health center and said we were concerned about our safety. Of course, the school didn't phrase it precisely this way—but that was the message.

At a dorm meeting about Nash Bash, the adults were more blunt with their advice: "People will be inappropriate. Boys will try to touch you. Try to ignore it and don't participate."

That advice felt wrong somehow. The senior girls (sixth formers) then suggested that we come up with hand signals to get out of any sticky situation. Ivy and I were skeptical but ultimately devised a plan: thumbs-up if a boy was cute. Thumbs-down if things looked sketchy.

Ivy and I raced to the Athletic Fitness Center blasting music on her iPhone—a "Summertime Sadness" remix by Lana Del Rey and "No Interruption" by Hoodie Allen. We sauntered into the dance, as if we owned the place. I was wearing a yellow crop top, black Converse sneakers, and high-waisted purple-and-black shorts with a galaxy-like print that I borrowed from Ivy's roommate, Faith. Ivy had on a tight white T-shirt showing off her tennis abs, blue-and-pink shorts, and a pink headband with a bow on top. She looked like a cotton-candy swirl.

We made our way to the dance floor and created circles with groups of girls. I didn't notice when a freshman hockey player snuck up behind me and slipped his hand under my shorts. I was so flustered that I grabbed Ivy's hand and pleaded, "Say we have to go to the bathroom!"

I didn't want to cause a scene and show my disgust at the first social event of the year. In the bathroom, other girls told me that same boy had groped them, too.

"Can you believe this?" I said to Ivy after the escape.

"It's gross. But just forget about it," she said, leading me back to the dance floor. "I'll protect you."

I would quickly learn that boys at this school felt entitled to stake a claim to things that were not their own, including girls' bodies. I struggled to make sense of it all at the time, because the behavior was so normalized, woven into the fabric of St. Paul's. Whenever I wanted to get a meal at the dining hall, I first needed to walk through a common area that Lucy had warned me about: the senior couches. Here, seniors—and *only* seniors—were allowed to sit on the maroon leather couches and walk on the senior rugs.

The couches usually faced outward so the boys could stare and call at girls who passed by on their way to the dining hall. All I could think was, *Oh my God, somebody is looking at my butt right now.* We were all on display.

As a fourteen-year-old, I reveled in my newfound freedom at boarding school. No one told me when to go to bed, do my homework, or clean my room. St. Paul's, or Millville as the nickname went, was every teenager's dream. I picked the electives I wanted and took naps during my free blocks in the afternoon.

I loved that classes, sports, and clubs were all right there for me—the way it was at Sacred Heart. Making varsity volleyball as a third former was kind of a big deal. Even better, I scored jersey number thirteen—my lucky number, same as Taylor Swift.

Rusher the Crusher still intimidated me, but I appreciated having friends outside the newbs. The older girls were encouraging and invited me to dinners and lunches at the Upper. Sometimes we went to Coach Doc's house for ice cream and waffles or deep-dish pizza. It felt like a family.

Ivy also made varsity volleyball, and the two of us seemed unstoppable. We had sister brunches in the Upper with Lucy and Georgina and often retreated to their oasis in Kehaya. Lucy and Georgina and their third roommate, Zoe, had pushed their beds together to create an amazing megabed. Ivy and I loved flopping on the bed and sharing memories.

Georgina, shorter and more petite than Ivy, had dark hair and a mean streak. And she was always talking about how much she hated their mom.

"She didn't raise us. We were raised by our nanny," Georgina complained. "And I had to help raise Ivy. She, like, owes me everything."

"I wuv yoouuu," Ivy said.

"Oh my God, remember that time when I thought you looked cuter than me with your blond hair so I tried to dye it black?" Georgina recounted.

"I knooooow, that was so funny," Ivy said, dissolving into a fit of giggles.

I sensed that Georgina was envious, but this sounded diabolical. I pretended to laugh and looked sideways at Lucy. She met my eyes with a knowing look.

Later Georgina asked Lucy whether she ever got jealous that Ivy and I were adjusting so well to St. Paul's.

"Oh my God, I never want to be a newb again," Lucy said. "I want her to have a better go at this than me."

I soon realized that Ivy could be just as competitive as Georgina. When I told her I had an audition for an a cappella group, she decided to try out and somehow ended up singing one of the songs I had practiced. When I confided that I thought Jackson's younger brother—the boy I had met during Revisit weekend—was cute, Ivy said she had a crush on him too. I wasn't going to let boys get in the middle of my most promising friendship, so I immediately backed off and rooted for her. That's what you were supposed to do, right?

In just a few weeks, Dylan and I had collected a big group of friends from our dorms and classes. Ivy knew several kids from the New York City private-school world, including Catie, who lived in our dorm, and Harry, a scrawny guy who loved his blazers.

We moved across campus in the safety of herds, from the Upper to classes to Tuck Shop, the student center, where kids hung out at night to see and be seen. It reminded me of the picnic tables at CSN—girls gossiped about boy crushes, complained about classes, and admired/judged each other's outfits. I liked Tuck for the snacks and usually devoured mozzarella sticks or raw cookie dough, or both.

The newbs were still getting to know each other and finding common ground: Did you summer in the Hamptons or Martha's Vineyard? Ski in Vail or the French Alps? They name-dropped rich and famous people they'd met and shared selfies of themselves in front of black diamond runs. Some of the lingo my classmates used was nuts, like substituting the word "gucci" for good. As in, "Sounds gucci!"

I knew I lived a comfortable life, but my parents never talked about money, and as a kid, I didn't really think about wealth or class or where my family fit in. I didn't understand what a rarefied world I was entering when I got to St. Paul's. Girls wore couture to formal seated meals. The level of affluence and one-upmanship was astounding.

And I wasn't immune. When people asked where I was from, I always made sure to mention that I grew up in Japan and was part Japanese. It was all true, obviously, but I knew it made me sound more interesting and worldly. I was kind of ashamed of saying I lived in Florida, and I wanted them to know that I wasn't just some blond ditz.

It took me a while to get used to the selfie situation at St. Paul's. The girls constantly took pictures of themselves, always posing to accentuate their "good side"—something I thought only happened in cheesy movies about mean girls. Ivy taught me how to create a "thigh gap" by placing my feet together and bowing my legs out. I tried it once, but I felt like I dislocated my knees.

Photos were uploaded to Snapchat, Instagram, and Facebook, and everyone kept track of how many likes or comments they received. The pictures were carefully curated as if they were displayed in an art gallery. Some social events were simply an excuse to show off our phenomenal prep-school lives—Fall Ball, Nash Bash, Dorm Day, and sports games included. Older guys were just as photo obsessed, especially when it came to taking pictures with the newbs.

At Ecofest, a pseudo Earth Day gathering in the fall, kids dressed in plaid flannels and drew names on each other's foreheads, something that resembled a branding ritual. I had to borrow a shirt from Lucy because I'd lent out all five of my flannels to girls in the dorm.

"Chessy, you have to stop giving away your clothes," Lucy scolded me. "People are not going to give them back."

"I just want other people to like me," I said. "I feel bad saying no."

We headed over to an orchard behind Lucy's dorm and took photos in front of trees bursting with magenta and canary yellow.

Lucy's friends chatted with me about life as a newb. Then Owen Labrie sidled up to me. Lucy had broken up with Owen sophomore year because he moved too fast. Now he was captain of the soccer team and had on a red shirt and multicolored headband that held back his long brown hair. He was attractive and assertive.

"Oh, can I take a photo with you?" he asked as he squeezed his arm around my shoulder.

"Okay," I said, already under his grasp.

Then he walked away without saying anything more. Kind of a rude weirdo. I didn't understand why someone would want to take a picture with me and not actually have a conversation. But the photo of the two of us went up on Facebook, making it look like we were the best of friends.

I started to find the scene at Tuck tiresome, especially as the nights got colder. I preferred hanging with Tabitha, listening to cool music she had discovered, or chilling with a bunch of girls in Ivy's room.

Ivy and her roommate, Faith, had one of the larger spaces in the dorm, which could easily fit fifteen people sprawled out on their blue and pink rugs, beanbag chairs, and raised beds.

We'd do homework together in there, which really meant Ivy studying and me goofing off with Faith and Catie, who lived down the hall.

We liked to procrastinate by shopping online or giving each other makeovers. One night the three of us sat on the floor, one in front of the other, curling each other's hair. I was in the front and had my laptop open while Faith wound my locks tightly around the hot iron.

"How does it look?" I asked Catie in the back.

"Oh my God, you're like Shirley Temple!" Catie burst out laughing.

"It's so cute, Chessy!" Faith said, defending her work.

"Everyone needs to be quiet!" Ivy huffed from her bed, not looking up from the MacBook resting on her legs.

We giggled and would stay quiet for five minutes, max. I liked Faith a lot. She was sweet, with thick auburn hair and a throaty laugh. But it was clear she was out of her league when it came to Ivy. Faith lacked Ivy's sophistication and confidence and sometimes followed Ivy around like a lost puppy.

Early on, Ivy had spread rumors that Catie was crazy, but I thought she was hilarious and down-to-earth. I saw Catie every morning when we waited at the Clark House health center, where nurses dispensed meds in two lines: one for students with names A–L and the other for M–Z. Catie wasn't embarrassed to be seen picking up her morning Rxs. Nothing actually seemed to bother her.

She didn't balk at "dirty dinnering," which meant showing up at the Upper without taking a shower first. It was a big no-no among third-form girls, but Catie didn't buy into most of the social norms at St. Paul's.

"Who gives a shit what I look like at the Upper?" Catie said. "I'm there to eat."

"Amen," I agreed.

Catie and I bonded over our shared ability to finish an entire pizza by ourselves. That girl had an appetite like me. She'd text late-night snack orders for Tuck:

Catie: mozzarella sticks ice cream and a lemonade
ooh and a burger
Me: Got u burger but i want 2 mozzarella sticks

We were more interested in eating food and having fun than pursuing boys. I found her lack of social ambition refreshing. If we ever took photos, we were usually giving each other silly, weird looks. Catie was adorable, with bright, mischievous eyes, wavy brown hair, and an upper lip that disappeared whenever she smiled. Which was often.

Catie was constantly buying fun stuff online or at the Target in town. I was pumped when she showed up one night with two scooters.

"Oh my God, these are fantastic. I used to have a Razor scooter that I'd ride to school in Tokyo," I said wistfully. "I'd race home through all these alleyways."

"Let's race then," Catie said as she took off down the hallway of the dorm.

I loved this girl.

When we were up late at night, too hyper to sleep and way past check-in time, we'd have high-speed chases inside. Mr. Callahan, the head of house, would roll his eyes at us as we whizzed by.

One night Catie confided that her shopping binges were funded by guilt money from her dad, a Wall Street financial executive, over serious problems in her parents' marriage. Catie was one of the few people who let on that her life was not perfect. She was open about how hard it was to live in the shadow of an older sibling at St. Paul's.

Lilly, a girl down the hall, shared her struggles with me when I spent hours in her room and we divulged our life stories. When we were alone, Dylan sometimes admitted that St. Paul's wasn't living up to the fairy tale he'd imagined as a child growing up there.

There were rampant rumors of kids with substance abuse problems and their miserable parents who cared more about their reputations and vacations than their own children. I was surprised to learn that boarding school was filled with so many teenagers from dysfunctional homes.

But most students at St. Paul's would never fess up to real problems. I'd been seeing Buzz Whalen, a counselor at the health center, since I started at St. Paul's. She was my new Dr. Sloane to help me with the transition to boarding school.

Buzz wore her whitish-blond hair in a ponytail and talked in a soothing voice that rolled out of her mouth like ocean waves. Buzz, like most of the adults at St. Paul's, juggled multiple responsibilities: coaching the varsity girls' field hockey team, serving as a dorm adviser, and working as a counselor at Clark House.

I confessed to Buzz that I still struggled with low moods and felt like I couldn't escape my past trauma. I knew I was lucky to be at St. Paul's, but I also expressed frustration that no one showed any vulnerability on campus. I certainly didn't think I could; if I did, people would believe I was weak.

It was exhausting trying to be perfect all the time, and I felt that pressure when I was with Ivy. Sometimes, I could let my guard down with Catie and Dylan and be my goofy, weirdo self. They were my partners in crime and loved exploring the campus at night.

For my fifteenth birthday near the end of October, we decided to go stargazing. We walked over to the soccer fields and spread out near the center line. It was chilly, so I covered myself in a blanket I'd brought from the dorm.

I lay down on the grass and sipped in the crisp fall air. I saw my first shooting star that night diving across the oily black sky. I watched in awe when fourteen more soared above, as if the sky was putting on a show just for me. I turned my head to each side to smile at Dylan and Catie. Somehow, this night felt perfect.

It was mid-November and I was overwhelmed by upcoming exams and a volleyball tournament. I was having a tough time sleeping and adjusting to my medications for anxiety and depression. I had recently rehashed the earthquake with a school-referred psychiatrist, and it left me in a funk.

Mom, Dad, and Christianna felt so far away in Hong Kong, and I really worried about my little sister. It was the longest I'd gone without smushing her in a koala hug. She was the best remedy for bad moods.

Catie came up with a great distraction: she ordered food from my favorite Thai place, Siam Orchid. I shoveled pork gyoza and hot and crazy noodles while my friends daintily picked at their meals. They were all talking about their Saturday night plans, and I had none.

I could have gone out with them, but I felt the black blanket wrapping around my brain again. Lucy was busy with her friends, so I checked in early for the night.

Tabitha was gone. I closed the door and turned off the lights. The tears I'd been holding back fell like sheets of rain.

I curled up in bed and closed my eyes. Painful memories were painted on the back of my eyelids: huddling under the desk during the earthquake in Tokyo; my family getting ripped apart; overwhelming thoughts of being a burden to my family; Dean's brother hurting himself; my first love cheating on me with a classmate.

People thought I was this popular, confident girl, but at times I felt so isolated from everybody at St. Paul's. No one knew what I'd been through. It was my fault. I wanted a clean slate here and I hated troubling anyone with my problems.

My chest was pounding, my hands sweating. I had so much pain in my heart and my head. I wanted to move the hurt somewhere else. I stood up and let the feelings of hopelessness and exhaustion wash over me.

Without thinking, I grabbed a bottle of nail polish remover from the bottom drawer of my desk. I took a sip and it felt like someone had lit a match inside my esophagus. Oh my God. What had I done? Were my insides going to burn? I didn't want to die.

I called Lucy and whispered into the phone, "I don't know what to do. I just . . . drank a little nail polish remover."

"Holy shit, Chessy," Lucy said, panic rising in her voice. "What happened?"

"I'm okay, you don't have to worry about me. I'm fine."

"I'm coming over and we're going to Clark House," Lucy said.

"No, I'm fine, I'm really fine."

Shit. They were going to think I was crazy and send me home. I couldn't have that happen. Where was home anyway?

I had soaked up the tears on my sleeve by the time Lucy sprinted into my room. I became agitated when she said an adviser would meet me at Clark House.

"Why would you do that?" I whined, immediately regretting my attempt at self-harm. "This is not a big deal. I'm fine. I'll get over it."

"You need Mom and Dad," Lucy said, and led me to Clark House with her roommate Zoe.

I wanted to go back to my room to sleep, but the health center insisted I stay overnight. The next day lots of friends stopped by, but I didn't want anyone to see me weak like this, so they left notes instead. Ivy wrote a nice message but somehow tried to make my sadness revolve around her.

> Dear Chessy,
> You are my best friend and sister. . . . I'm beyond sorry
> if I did something I never want to hurt you. You can
> talk to me tom. if you want I'm always here.
> Love you more than life,
> Ivy

Catie texted repeatedly, but I didn't answer at first. Eventually, she sent an offer I couldn't refuse.

> Catie: I have no sports and I was wondering if you need a
>   buddy I can bring the kardashians and gummy bears
> Me: Aww wanna watch tv with mee??
> Catie: yeah I'll come

Catie snuggled with me in the health center bed as we watched television together. Later that day I had a meeting with Buzz. By now, I was used to the therapy thing, so I didn't hold back in telling Buzz what was going on in my head.

"I honestly wasn't trying to kill myself," I explained. "I just wanted to feel the pain somewhere else."

She nodded her head sympathetically. "It's a lot of pressure here being away from home," Buzz said gently. "Everybody needs a break sometimes and I think you could use a break. Don't worry about your schoolwork. We can get that all figured out."

I resisted at first but ultimately agreed to go on a health leave. A lot of kids took them at St. Paul's, so I knew it wasn't that big of a deal. We'd been planning to celebrate Thanksgiving together in Florida, so Dad booked an earlier flight from Hong Kong so he could pick me up at St. Paul's and take me to Naples.

Before I left, Ivy stopped by and gave me a gold signet ring with her family crest on it. She and her sister both had one, and they wore them all the time.

"Keep this over the break. It will help protect you," she said. "I love you, Chessy."

"Thank you, thank you," I gushed. "I'm so lucky to have you as a best friend."

Lucy was relieved I was going home. I thought it was the right thing too. I knew my big sister couldn't be the only one to take care of me.

"I'm sorry I got mad at you for bringing me to the health center," I said. "I know you were scared and just trying to help."

"Chess, I love you so, so, so much," Lucy said, holding me tight. "You mean the entire world to me. It physically hurts me to think that something bad could happen to you."

I reveled in my new life at boarding school: decorating my dorm room (top), signing my name into the school ledger (above left), playing volleyball with Lucy (bottom left), and bonding at Ecofest in our flannel shirts (above right).

FIVE

Traditions Begin

I returned to St. Paul's after Thanksgiving break, and the girls in Con20 smothered me with love. There were constant hugs, kisses on the forehead, and invites for heart-to-hearts. Even some of the boys in my grade swung by to welcome me back. We didn't talk about what led to my health leave, but I could tell they were being more thoughtful. It was all very sweet, though I hated having the attention on me. I wanted to go back to normal.

I assured Mom and Dad that I was feeling better, but they were worried. I was afraid they would go into protective mode and try to bring me to Hong Kong. Lucy never gave them any inkling about how tough things could be at St. Paul's, and I certainly didn't want to make them concerned.

We had spent Thanksgiving huddled as a family in Florida. I devoured Dad's turkey and gravy and Mom's pumpkin chiffon pie.

Mom literally latched herself onto me at the airport. They spoke with Buzz, who promised we'd meet regularly. My doctor also adjusted my medication again. I was still processing the tumult from the last several years, and I knew I'd have to take things one day at a time.

I tried to pray every night like Mom had taught us growing up. Praying helped me focus on the things I was grateful for in my life. I'd cuddle up in the dorm bed with Bearsie, my pink stuffed Build-A-Bear, which I'd had since I was six, and clasp my hands at my chest. I faced the wall as I silently recited the same prayer: "Dear God, please bless Mom, Dad, my sisters, and me. Please bless Uncle Tom with good health. Keep Grandpa safe in heaven. Thank you for blessing me with a wonderful home, family, life, and thank you for making me healthy."

These little moments helped ground me. And so did Lucy. She was hanging around a lot, keeping a watchful eye on me. I'm not sure if Mom and Dad suggested this, but to be honest, I didn't mind. Lucy was a safety blanket I wanted to wrap myself in. We ate sandwiches for lunch on my bed between classes, took long walks to the docks, and studied together at the Works, a cozy sandwich shop in downtown Concord.

Lucy confided that she'd been having a hard time too. Since she'd ended things with Brooks over the summer, her guy friends at St. Paul's had ditched her in obnoxious ways. Recently, she'd been catching up with Andrew Thomson near the senior couches outside the Upper. But when Andrew spotted some guys approaching, he abruptly cut Lucy off.

"Oh, never mind," Andrew said. "I forgot I'm not supposed to talk to you."

Lucy's jaw dropped. She'd been friends with Andrew before she started dating Brooks. Part of the reason Lucy broke up with Brooks was because he was too demanding. Now his possessive tentacles were trying to strip Lucy of any meaningful relationships. It was a disgusting display of social power.

To make matters worse, the senior boys were flirting relentlessly with me as a way to piss off Lucy. Before my health leave, Andrew and Duncan emailed me and Ivy an invitation for a "secret snuggle." I wasn't sure what a secret snuggle entailed, but Ivy and I agreed it was creepy and weird.

By this point, I knew how much power the senior boys had, and I didn't want to do anything to come off as a bitch or provoke them into targeting me more. So I tried to banter over email without committing to anything or rejecting them.

> Duncan: secret snuggle?
> Me: is it even a question?
> Andrew: yeah im more than down
> Duncan: secret snuggle. time and place?
> Me: Your call boys
> Andrew: My lap tonight at 9pm

Gross. Conversation over. I wasn't interested in casual relationships, and all these guys wanted was to score. Kiss. Touch. Go all the way. Scoring covered any and all of that. I'd later learn that if you scored a lot, you were known as a slayer. This was all so foreign and scary, because I'd only kissed before I got to St. Paul's. I didn't want to have sex. It wasn't even on my radar as a fifteen-year-old.

A few weeks earlier, Ivy's sister had dragged me out to Tuck and insisted I get together with her friend Jason. I didn't buy into the scoring culture, but I wasn't confident enough yet to renounce it outright.

And I was flattered that Jason liked me and I felt as though I should give him a chance. I was curious, as any teenage girl might be. Jason was nice enough, but I called it off after we kissed twice over the span of two weeks. I didn't know this guy. I didn't like that he kissed me in the middle of a sentence.

For weeks I'd been trying to keep at bay two hockey boys who kept messaging me and Ivy, commenting on our photos, asking when we could hang out. Hockey players were at the top of the social ladder at St. Paul's, and "no" wasn't a word they were used to hearing. I wanted something special. I wanted a guy who knew me, liked me for who I really was, and most of all, respected me.

But that seemed impossible at a place like St. Paul's, where everything was about status, tradition, and hierarchy—and guys ruled all three. They ran most of the clubs, dominated class discussions, and determined girls' worth by whether or not they wanted to score them.

St. Paul's first began accepting girls in the 1970s, but it might as well have been yesterday. When Lucy earned the same grade as a guy in her modern China class, he remarked that she must have flirted her way to the A. It wasn't just the students who reinforced this male hierarchy. When we gathered at the oval wooden table for my humanities class, the teacher listened intently to the boys and fluffed their egos while dismissing girls' opinions as "wrong." The teacher was so rude a girl once fled the class in tears.

One day after humanities, I accidentally bumped into a male classmate as we slogged through the slippery snow. I apologized and joked, "Oh, well, I'm lucky you can't push a girl." Suddenly my friend grabbed my shoulders and shoved me into a snowbank and kept on going.

I was shaking when I pulled myself up and looked around. I tried to laugh it off as I made my way, soaking wet, to the dining hall, where someone would undoubtedly leer at my butt as I passed the senior couches. It was clear the school could not shake its century-plus history as a boys-only institution.

There was only one time a year when the gender dynamics at the Upper were inverted, or perverted, depending on your view. This was at the annual Boar's Head Dinner, where students voted for the senior boys they wanted to see shirtless, carrying a ham around the dining hall. It was completely absurd.

I couldn't believe the school sanctioned this. At the same time, I was amused by the idea of boys being objectified the way we were whenever we walked into that dining hall. This year administrators tried to tone down the Boar's Head Dinner by requiring the guys to wear tank tops. Still, it didn't change anything. I refused to vote.

I noticed Logan the first time he walked by Con20. He was wearing a purple-and-blue tie-dyed sweatshirt and was leading a pack of guys. He was the cutest boy I'd ever seen, and lucky for me, he was in my Japanese class. Logan was a year older, a fourth former, with a thick mess of blond hair and a huge grin.

He was sweet and normal—if that was possible at St. Paul's—and always asked about life in Japan. My stomach fluttered whenever I saw him in the hallway or he asked for help with assignments.

Logan seemed genuinely interested in getting to know me, not just getting in my pants. So I happily accepted his invite to attend the Christmas party at Nash, one of the boys' dorms.

It was a tradition for guys to escort their dates, so Logan and his roommate picked up me and Faith for the Christmas party. I preferred hanging out with Faith when Ivy wasn't around. Faith was more relaxed, more herself, if she wasn't trying to please her roommate, the queen bee.

"You don't have to agree with everything Ivy says or does," I told Faith. "It's good to have your own opinions. We love to hear what you have to say."

"I know," Faith said. "I try."

Everyone was dressed in festive outfits at the Nash Christmas party. I was wearing a red dress with three-quarter-length sleeves that I borrowed from Lucy. I let Logan take my hand as we danced to Michael

Bublé's Christmas hits, and I was surprised at how smooth and self-assured he was, swinging me around the room. I was having fun.

All of a sudden, Brooks swooped in between us and grabbed me and started dancing. I saw the flash of a camera, and just like that he was gone. It was super rude, but I didn't want to confront Lucy's ex.

I couldn't find Logan and was searching for any friendly face when Owen Labrie approached and asked to take a picture with me. I'd smiled at him a few times on the school paths since Ecofest but had never had a real conversation. He was wearing mustard-yellow pants and a blue-and-red sweater. It was too much color at once. I clenched my jaw and smiled as Owen put his arm around my right shoulder in that same tight grasp as at Ecofest.

I was about to turn around to find my friends, but Owen asked if I could take a photo of him and Andrew Thomson and a short girl named Gwen. They thought the height difference between Gwen and Andrew would be funny.

"Sure," I sighed as Andrew handed me a camera.

Later that night, I was in my room looking at Facebook photos from the party. Another senior posted the picture of me and Owen. Malcolm Salovaara was one of the first to like it. Malcolm had graduated from St. Paul's the year before, and he had a reputation for scoring lots of girls.

A few other kids liked the photo, so I gave it the thumbs-up too. As conflicted as I felt about St. Paul's, I was still trying to find ways to embrace this community, to have this community embrace me, to go along to get along. That's what you were supposed to do at St. Paul's. You liked the things that happened even if you didn't enjoy them at the time. Everything was perfect.

I was browsing through the rest of the photos when I noticed the one of me and Brooks together. Some jerk commented that Brooks was moving on to the next sibling. It was so disgusting. They thought Brooks was going to leap from Lucy to me? I felt like a piece of raw meat in the lion's den. Before I even talked to Lucy, she attempted to take back control of the conversation with her own comment.

Lucy: We try to keep them in the fam.

I wanted to hurl my laptop at these idiotic boys and knock them out cold. Instead I called up Mom in Hong Kong, crying. She told Dad, and he exploded when he saw the photo. A few minutes later, Lucy was howling at me through the phone.

"Why did you take that picture with Brooks?" Lucy yelled. "You know how upset I am at the way he's treating me and telling all my guy friends to stay away. Dad just screamed at me, as if this is my fault."

"Lucy, I didn't ask for this. I didn't want to take a picture," I said. "I was literally grabbed and pulled away! I just want that photo down. These boys are so stupid!"

"I don't know what I can do," Lucy said in a huff, and hung up.

My ears burned with anger as I threw myself on the bed. It wasn't fair for Lucy to be mad at me. She was hot and cold with Brooks, and I never knew where they stood. Did she really expect me, a little freshman, to push away her ex-boyfriend? She understood that wasn't how things worked here. I hadn't asked to take the photo with him and I wasn't the one who posted it. Lucy should have been pissed at Brooks and his friends, not me. But the boys were never at fault at St. Paul's.

I was trying to keep my distance from the seniors, but Andrew Thomson, who roomed with Owen, couldn't help himself and sent me a single rose for Valentine's Day. The card was blank except for a heart. I tried to give Andrew the benefit of the doubt because I liked his younger sister, Haley, who was on the varsity volleyball team and in my music class.

Besides, I had other things on my mind—mainly the winter formal. I was going with Blake, who was a year older, and Ivy had said yes to his friend Raymond. The boys had called us outside in the middle of a snowstorm to invite us.

The winter formal was one of many important social events at St. Paul's. Guys sometimes asked out dates months in advance. Having a boyfriend didn't make things any easier. In fact, it was the opposite. Girls rarely got asked to go to dances by their boyfriends. No one could explain why. It was just another warped tradition at St. Paul's that everyone here accepted as normal.

I didn't know Blake that well, but he seemed sweet whenever we crossed paths on campus. He was a legacy kid and a total jock, tall with blond hair. I was excited that a boy might genuinely, platonically like me. I was tired of the games the older boys played.

In the weeks leading up to the dance, Ivy fretted that our dates didn't match her social-climbing ambitions. Her sister said she could set us up with two seniors instead.

"Are Blake and Raymond really cool enough? Are they popular enough?" Ivy wrinkled her nose.

My eyes nearly rolled into the back of my head. At first I felt sorry for Ivy, because her sister seemed to thrive on making her younger sibling insecure. But then I got annoyed by how shallow Ivy could be sometimes. She was my fun friend, but she needed to stop obsessing over social expectations.

I talked Ivy off the ledge and assured her we'd have a good time no matter what. We both bought dresses online for the dance and got ready together in her room. I wore a backless turquoise-blue velvet dress. Ivy had a sparkly champagne-colored dress with the sides cut out.

We went out to dinner with two other couples to O Steaks & Seafood in downtown Concord. I was nervous about one of the other girls, Sally. She was a status seeker like Ivy and loved being the center of attention. In group pictures, Sally was usually in the middle with her tongue sticking out.

After dinner, we waited near the entrance of the restaurant for our cabs. Sally blocked me out of the group with her body, making it impossible to join the conversation. I didn't like having to insert myself, so I just checked my phone. My date, Blake, saw the slight and gave me a warm smile, which helped to ease the anxiety creeping up my throat.

The winter formal had a gambling theme, so it looked like a WASPy Las Vegas. Green felt poker tables were scattered around the wood-paneled ballroom. The boys were dressed in sport coats and ties, and the girls had donned glitzy cocktail dresses.

I ran into Harry, a third former from Manhattan who was close with Ivy and Catie. Harry was short and kind of dorky but already influential in the larger prep school world. He knew how to secure coveted invites to the annual Gold & Silver Ball, a super-selective dance around Christmas in New York City for private school students. I hadn't been able to attend this past December because I was home in Florida, but Harry promised I'd stay on the list.

We grew closer over the winter because we both did recreational skiing and were chairlift buddies. He even helped coax a terrified Christianna down the slopes when she visited—bribing her with a cookie. Harry wasn't an alpha male like a lot of the St. Paul's boys, but he still did their dirty work and twice asked me if I wanted to score older guys. I felt bad rejecting them outright so I told Harry I didn't know.

The small talk at school social events bored me, so I ditched Harry and headed with Ivy to the dance floor and got so sweaty that the sticky boob cups I was wearing to keep everything in place slipped off.

I asked Ivy to come and help me, but she preferred to hold court on the dance floor. I ran to the bathroom to wipe myself down and adjust the cups. These were the perils of fancy dresses with no backs. I was embarrassed walking to the bathroom by myself, let alone having to hold my dress to my chest. Luckily, I ran into an older volleyball teammate who kept me company.

Later that night, while I was looking at pictures from the dance, I noticed Sally and Ivy had photobombed me and Blake, jumping up behind his shoulder with their tongues sticking out.

I wasn't sure if Blake actually had a good time until I got a text from him after one in the morning:

> Blake: Assuming you'd like to hang out more
> Me: We'd like that haha
> Blake: Hahaha I'm glad
>   As long as you come I'll be excited

We hung out a couple of days later in his room with a mutual friend, and then Blake walked me back to Con20. He was easy to talk to and look at. But I was not going to make the first move.

He finally kissed me one night in my math classroom in Lindsay. I felt like I could relax around Blake when it was just the two of us. But I got nervous whenever I saw him on campus with other people. Lucy told me that I needed to say hi when I ran into him at the Upper or on the paths.

One night I texted Lucy from the couch of his friend's room while I was mingling with other boys. I wanted to know if it was a good or bad thing.

> Me: Does that mean hes trying to get me in with his
>   friends??
> Lucy: Hahaha it just means it's fun idk
>   Probably to show you off

Blake and I became exclusive, but I wouldn't call him my boyfriend. I felt like I was walking this tightrope between the norms

St. Paul's foisted on me and what I really wanted.

We agreed to stay together over spring break in March while Lucy and I visited Mom, Dad, and Christianna in Hong Kong. Blake and I would decide whether to keep hooking up when we got back to campus. While sitting on my bed, I gave Tabitha the latest update on my nonrelationship relationship.

"Seriously?" Tabitha asked.

She had an uncanny ability to make you question everything in life with a single word.

"You don't *really* like him, do you? He's like the quintessential white boy."

"But he's really sweet," I explained. "It's nice just having somebody nice. It's enough for right now."

Tabitha ended our conversation with her trademark eye roll.

I appreciated that she was honest and blunt like Arielle back home. I'd felt more comfortable confiding in Tabitha since my health leave. Late at night, we'd turn off the lights and talk for hours. I shared my darkest moments: my attempt to hurt myself and the earthquake trauma.

Tabitha told me about her own struggles with self-harm and anxiety. She confided that she'd been sexually assaulted when she was younger, and her parents had downplayed what happened. I'd never known anyone who'd gone through something like that. It made me feel sick.

Tabitha said she refused to be used by anyone ever again. She tried to make sure I wasn't either by calling me out on my bullshit, usually when I went running down the hall to help Ivy with her latest boy drama.

I was attempting to steer clear of that land mine. At night I'd walk with Ivy and my friends on their way to Tuck, but then I'd ditch them halfway and head into the music building so I could practice piano. I was taking music theory and piano instruction and needed all the extra playing I could get.

Sometimes I'd close the shades so that no one could see me from the outside. I had saved some sheet music from Tokyo and rehearsed songs that I'd been learning before the earthquake. It was my personal oasis, where I could be alone and lose myself in classical music, my fingers dancing on the keys. Once in a while, Dylan, Lilly, and Catie stopped by to hear me play. I didn't mind sharing my secret hideaway with them. Sometimes we all needed a refuge from St. Paul's.

When we came back from spring break in early April, Blake and a bunch of guys in his dorm were supposedly busted for weed. His punishment was early check-in, which meant we stopped hanging out.

> Me: We need to talk tonight. I can't drag this out, I need to know where we stand.
> Blake: I'm in tuck quickly if you wanna come over but I have to leave soon.

I walked briskly over to Tuck with Catie around seven fifteen p.m. and found Blake outside.

"It's not fair to you to keep this going now that I have to check in at seven thirty every night," he said.

"Okay, is that what you really want?" I asked.

"It's just not fair to you," he responded.

It sounded like a cop-out, but I wasn't going to argue with him. I met Catie downstairs in Tuck after Blake left so we could eat our feelings. We loaded up on pints of ice cream, pizza bites, chocolate icing, Ritz cheese crackers, mini Reese's peanut butter cups, and Airheads candy.

"Put it on my credit card," Catie said, flashing a smile.

"You're the best," I said. "You always know how to make me feel better."

My fling with Blake was fun while it lasted, and I was thankful that he never tried to go beyond my comfort zone of kissing. I got so grossed out when Ivy told me that a friend had recently given a guy a blow job in a classroom in Lindsay. I was instantly nauseous whenever I thought about a boy's private parts. I didn't want to see that. I worried how I'd ever have children, because the idea of sex repulsed me. Sometimes I pretended with my friends that I was cool discussing this stuff, but in reality, it made me shudder.

Lucy had been accepted to Georgetown—Dad's alma mater—so you'd think she'd be coasting through the rest of her senior year. But no, she had a full load of classes, an independent study project, and events to plan for the Japanese Society. She kept breaking dates with me and shooing me away as if I was an annoying fly. She acted like a pretentious senior imposing the St. Paul's hierarchy.

I vented to Mom that Lucy was being a jerk. Mom said Lucy was stressed about her schedule and friends. She suggested that I give Lucy some space to enjoy her last few weeks of school. I was going to be on my own in the fall, Mom said, and needed to find my way. A few minutes after we hung up, a new message arrived.

> Mom: I love you Chess - and want to see you navigate all that's tricky about SPS/boarding school life. If you lash out at Luce re what I shared with you I will be very unhappy. This is her time to feel good about her work thru HS. Please recognize that. She's also trying to be there for you the best way she knows how - never will be perfect, but I know she sincerely tries.

Mom was right. She was always right. I had to rely less on Lucy. She wouldn't be here for much longer. So I needed to figure things out on my own. I decided not to bother her when a senior, Tucker

Marchese, sent me a corny email asking me out. Tucker was a quiet guy who'd lost a bunch of weight this past year. I'd never talked with him or had any interaction, but I heard he had scored Ivy's sister.

> chessy,
> as the days grow longer, so mine here grow shorter. in
> an effort to enjoy every last one, i'd be delighted to have
> your presence one of these warmer summer evenings.
> given the nature of the proximity of our school, my
> lips are shut if it so pleases you. i promise i'll show you
> something cool at the very least. mull it over.
> tucker

It was a classic Senior Salute invitation. The Senior Salute was a well-known ritual at St. Paul's, where sixth formers tried to make out with as many younger girls as possible before graduation. It usually started around May, when they invited girls to a secret spot with the hopes of hooking up. Once in a while, senior girls went after younger boys. Everyone knew about it. The Senior Salute was even mentioned in a scoring dictionary that appeared in the student paper, the *Pelican*.

Two advisers told us that they were working hard to stop the tradition and not to feel obligated to respond if we got an invite. Before the Senior Salutes started rolling in, Buzz told me to be careful and that she was trying to educate the rest of the school about why this was bad.

I wanted no part of it. I thought it was weird and creepy that older guys were pursuing freshmen so impersonally over the Internet, where they could easily hide. I was pretty sure Tucker had sent the same email to Ivy. It seemed so generic.

We'd heard he was in a competition with Andrew Thomson and Owen Labrie to score the most girls before graduation. Still, I tried to be polite when I sent my rejection. I didn't want him to think I was rude or bitchy. I wasn't raised to ignore people, especially those who were older than me. And I knew Tucker and the other senior boys had all the power at the school and they could spread rumors and destroy my reputation in an instant. I wasn't ready to risk that.

> tucker,
> although your invitation is tempting, i must decline. I hope you enjoy the last of these evenings, and i will see you around. . . .
> Chessy Prout

I was still rolling my eyes over this when I was hanging out a few days later with Catie and Dylan before a school dance. Dylan was my go-to guy at parties. We'd gravitate toward the corner of a room and check in on each other to make sure we were okay. I felt comfortable around him, like he was the brother I never had. Dylan was the opposite of some of the other third formers in our friend group like Owen MacIntyre, who was always flirting with girls and mansplaining.

Dylan had stolen vodka from his dad's liquor cabinet and asked me to bring empty water bottles. We walked past the soccer fields to the edge of the woods and started taking swigs. I should have known better—alcohol didn't mix well with my meds and getting caught would have landed me in front of the disciplinary committee. But I rationalized that I couldn't get in that much trouble if I was drinking the rector's alcohol that his own son had smuggled out of the house.

The vodka hit me hard. I felt a fire in my throat as I sucked in the chilly May air. So much for those warm evenings Tucker forecasted. I ran, skipped, and hopped to the dance but didn't stay long. Dylan and I were both kind of a mess. I ushered Dylan away from the chapel lawn and walked with some friends halfway to the docks. I barely remembered how I ended up in Catie's room. It wasn't a fun night. I realized how stupid it was when I started getting texts from Lucy.

Lucy: Not cool at all chess. I am so disappointed.

Me: I know what you're talking about, and you have every right to be disappointed. It was only a little, and I am completely fine.

Lucy: I am so disappointed chessy. Hope u think about this. Night.

Ugh. I hated upsetting Lucy. Catie's room was spinning. I rolled over and went to bed.

Scoring Dictionary

Score -noun- a hook up; the action involved in scoring

Score -verb- to hook up with someone

Scoring -adj - a label used to describe people who are in a casual relationship

hangout -verb- to chill; to relax with references of scoring
   e.g: Jordan: Sally, maybe we can hangout sometime. Sally: sure, I'd like that

Walk back -noun/verb- The act of escorting a fellow student back to their dorm with intentions to scone

Senior Salute -noun/verb- (often during the spring term) when a senior requests to score someone in a form below them; usually it only occurs once

Secret Score -noun/verb- to score/ the act of scoring someone under the radar; usually to avoid unnecessary complications

Noob Score: noun - the act of scoring between two new students

Dating -adj - having surpassed the label of scoring; thus implying a more serious relationship

desperate -adj - having a strong desire to score someone; often looked down upon
   e.g: Gosh, he is so desperate he'd score a pillow.

goggles -noun -(In reference to living at a fully residential boarding school) theoretical/ imaginary goggle that skew your perspective / judgement of someone's appearance

RG '15

The hook-up culture was so pervasive at St. Paul's that the student newspaper printed this scoring dictionary (above).

I took a selfie with the rose that Andrew Thompson sent me on Valentine's Day (right).

SIX

Another Senior Salute

I t was Wednesday, May 28, and I was in the Upper eating lunch with Ivy. I couldn't believe it was almost the end of the year and my days as a newb were numbered. She was freaking out about how to fit in studying for finals when the weekend was chock-full of graduation activities. I zoned out and checked my phone. An email from Owen Labrie popped up.

> francesca,
> while the thought of my name in your inbox makes me
> blush perhaps more than it should, there's something i
> want to share with you and my evenings left to do it are
> growing fewer by the evening. there's a door here that's
> been locked since before we were born, but in a moment
> of divine intervention the night before last, its hinges swung

open in my hands. if you want a definition of the word
bittersweet, think of me spending three years trying to
open it, yet now only having three nights to remember
the view. i want to invite you to come with me, to climb
these hidden steps, and to bask in the nicest view millville
has ever had to offer. i hope you're all right with heights.
if you're not otherwise engaged, mull it over. i ask only
that you let me know soon--these days they're not
making time quite like they used to.

yours,

owen

I burst out laughing. I could feel the pretension dripping off my phone.

"Oh my God, Ivy, look at this," I said. "Owen sent me a Senior Salute."

"That's sooo funny," Ivy said.

"Lucy *has* to see this," I said.

We agreed that this called for a meeting of the sisters. I read the email again and concluded that the "nicest view" Owen referenced must be the chapel bell tower. It was undoubtedly one of the coolest places on campus, and only the bell ringers were supposed to have a key.

I was conflicted. I wanted to see the top of the chapel and take awesome pictures. I loved having Instagram cred. But I hated the idea of the Senior Salute. I'd never had a real conversation with Owen. Everyone knew that he was smart, an intellectual type. Owen was not outwardly macho like the hockey boys, which probably made him more attractive to the ladies.

I had heard rumors recently that he'd scored Mallory and Whitney, both girls in my grade, and that he could be pushy. I didn't want to be just another notch in his belt. Of course, there was Lucy. Owen and

Lucy had dated briefly when they first got to St. Paul's, and they'd hung out again earlier this year. I definitely needed Lucy's help.

Later that afternoon, Ivy and I walked over to Kehaya. I plopped down on the megabed and passed my phone around so everyone could read the message.

"Look how stupid this is," I said.

"Ivy, did you get one from Owen?" Georgina asked.

"No," Ivy said.

"Are you sure?" Georgina asked, raising her sculpted eyebrows. "Check your phone again."

"I didn't," Ivy insisted.

"Can you believe this?" I snickered.

"You don't have to reply," Georgina said. "You can just ignore it."

"Yeah, don't answer," Ivy echoed.

"Maybe I could get a good Instagram picture and that will be it. *I* could be the one using *him*," I suggested. "It doesn't have to be anything else."

Lucy shook her head. "Just don't engage," she advised.

"No, I have to reply to this," I said as my voice rose with indignation. "This is the second Senior Salute I've received. These boys just think it's okay to do this stuff and it's not. I don't want some other girl to get the same copy of this message. I have to make sure he knows that it's stupid."

I crafted a response on my iPhone with Lucy's help and read aloud some choice lines.

But I refused to show Lucy the final version, because I feared she would try to talk me out of it. I knew the stakes were high to rebel like this. I had bitten my tongue all year because I was insecure and afraid of what would happen if I called out the almighty boys. But the school year was ending and I was tired of holding back.

At 9:09 p.m., in the safety of my room, I emailed Owen a big fat rejection:

owen,
while the thought of your name in my inbox gives me
a sense of dejavu, (Lucy and I are very close sisters,) and
although I would like to climb those hidden steps with
you, I have to decline.
I would like to climb that, not the list of third formers that
have spent quality time with you.
Chessy

One minute later, Lucy texted and asked me to show her the final cut. I chuckled but didn't send her the note.

Me: I sent it as is . . . 😬 I have to stick up for myself!!
Lucy: Chess you made my evening

I woke up the next morning to another email from Owen in my inbox:

probably one of the sassier emails i've ever received, my
sweet lord. and minus chavez and macintyre, i'm afraid
that list is slimmer than you might think. pretty much
nonexistent this term, even, but do as you please, mon
chere, i'd have taken you either way.

He ended the note with a line in French. All I could understand was that it was something about a queen.

Oy. I felt bad. Maybe I'd been too harsh. Either way, I needed to focus on more important things.

Days earlier, Mom had arrived so she could spend time with Lucy and plan graduation festivities before all the relatives descended. Mom's mom (aka Grandma Prusaczyk) was coming, along with Uncle Bernie, Aunt Blair, Aunt Frannie, and cousins Cameron and

Katie. Dad's cousin Ken—a chef in Boston—was preparing a sushi feast for all of Lucy's friends on Saturday night. It was the first big celebration for our family since the earthquake three years ago.

Before I plunged into graduation mode, I needed to help Catie finish a poster for her physics class. I was getting dressed to go to the lab at the Lindsay building when I saw an email from Duncan with a cryptic-sounding Senior Salute.

> Duncan: . . . running out of sunsets

Ugh. Duncan was a nice enough guy, and I still felt a little bad about what I'd written to Owen, so I refrained from sending any more feisty emails. Instead I kept it simple.

> Me: . . . Too true

It was chilly out, so I put on a long-sleeved black-and-white-striped shirt. I found Catie in her room, grabbing a pink sweater. I looked around the room—about double the size of mine—and yammered about how fantastic life would be in the fall when we were roomies. Catie and I were planning to get a couch, shelves, and maybe a hammock. It would feel like a real home instead of a prison cell with DJ equipment.

Catie and I wandered over to Lindsay and found her physics lab on the first floor. The rooms all looked the same, with rectangular wooden islands with shiny black countertops. The teachers were gone for the night, and it was just me and Catie at first. She plugged her phone into the classroom speakers and blasted music. After she turned off the lights, I used my phone as a strobe light and swirled it around. I was climbing from table to table, ecstatic that our study hour had morphed into a procrastination party.

Other kids arrived, and so it was time to settle down. Owen

MacIntyre and two other boys in my grade came over to where I was sitting. I'd been friends with Owen—or O. Mac, as people called him—since the fall, and sometimes we'd studied together in the library. But he'd gotten more annoying in recent months. O. Mac was a wannabe hockey bro and acted cocky like the guys on his team. We tried to keep him grounded by poking fun at his highlighter-yellow polo shirts and flat-brimmed baseball hats. Tonight he had on a blue-and-white T-shirt with his hat turned backward.

"So I heard you got an email from Owen Labrie," he said.

I stared at him without saying anything. I knew they lived in the same dorm, but why was this anyone's business?

"Yeah," I finally said. "I'm not going to go."

"Oh, he's a nice guy," O. Mac said. "And he has the keys to a building. Wouldn't it be cool to see the place?"

"Yeah, but he's been with all these other third formers like Whitney and Mallory. I don't want to be another girl on his list."

"The Whitney thing is not true at all. She has braces," he said. "And the Mallory thing happened earlier in the year. Don't be a bitch."

Ouch.

"I just want to see the view," I said.

"Owen's not going to pressure you or do anything to hurt you. He's a nice guy," he said. "He just wants to spend time with you."

I sighed. Maybe I'd judged Owen Labrie too harshly. I felt bad for being rude when I rejected his invite. He was a golden boy, a dorm leader. All the teachers loved him, and he was going to Harvard in the fall.

Truth be told, I was flattered that one of the most popular boys thought I was special. I didn't know Owen, but it felt nice to have him take an interest in me. Ivy didn't even get an invite. More than anything, I was excited to see the chapel spires—something none of my friends had done before.

Looking back, I shudder at the vanity and false confidence that led me to reconsider.

"Okay. Yeah, I'll go," I told O. Mac. "But make sure he knows all I want to do is go up to see the view. I don't want him gloating to his friends or Lucy."

When I got back to my dorm, I emailed Owen in French, apologizing for my first email. Then I said yes to his invitation.

Me: Only if its our petit secret

Later Catie turned to me and asked, "So, how far would you be willing to go with him?"

I laughed nervously, my reflex in uncomfortable situations. I wasn't totally naive.

Catie knew how inexperienced I was sexually. But I didn't want to sound like a baby. Even with Catie, I couldn't fully let my guard down sometimes.

"I'd be willing to make out," I said. "But I won't go as far as second base."

Owen wrote back two hours later and attached a picture of the words BELIEVE IN ANGELS spray-painted in white on a brick wall.

Owen: what a golden change of heart. you've saved it
until the very end--there's not a lot of time, but I'm sure
we can figure something out.
ps your french is amazing. not a soul needs to know

It was Friday, May 30, and Dad and the rest of the family arrived to kick off graduation weekend. I knew it was a dream come true for Dad to see his oldest child receive a diploma from St. Paul's. Most of the time, I felt lucky to be part of the SPS family. I got the chance to learn Japanese, play the piano, and meet smart, talented people from all over the world. I could stroll around the enchanting campus, wildflowers pushing through the soil, believing it was possible to become anything I wanted.

But all I wanted right now was for the chapel bells to stop ringing in my ears. It was the daily alarm clock telling me I had five minutes to get dressed, pick up my meds, and run across the street for morning services. I was feeling extra lazy this morning. I stretched my arms over my head, grabbed my iPhone resting on the desk, and scrolled through my email. I saw a weird one sent in the wee hours from David, Lucy's prom date.

David: we should hang out tomorrow.
P.S. im the sexiest asian at the school.

I immediately told Lucy about David's note, but I didn't mention Owen. I still wasn't sure I'd even go. Around lunchtime, Duncan sent me another message.

Duncan: I might be able to make room for you tonight

Might make room for me? Who did Duncan think he was? I'd never said I wanted to hang out. These guys were so condescending and presumptuous. Besides, I had plans. Owen messaged me on Facebook to make sure we were still on.

Owen: it might be a little crazy for the tower but i can
take you somewhere else that's pretty sweet

It should've been a red flag. I was disappointed, but I knew there were other interesting spots to explore. Just last week, I'd ventured out with Catie, Dylan, and a few others to the chapel late at night and opened a grate on the floor in the back section for latecomers.

We squeezed our bodies through the hole and crawled around the dark underground tunnels.

I wanted to seem easygoing to Owen, so I didn't press him on the plan.

Me: That sounds perfect haha

I saw Ivy in her room and told her that I was meeting up with Owen after dinner. She looked surprised.

"Do you really want to go?" she asked with a hint of judgment.

"Nothing bad is going to happen," I insisted. "O. Mac said Owen was really sweet and just wants to hang out."

I didn't say much to Ivy when we were sitting together at dinner later that night. Lucy and her friends had organized a dinner with all their families at the Centennial, the fanciest hotel in Concord. I smiled as much as I could and listened to the grown-ups and their small talk. But I had this cloud hanging over me—it always appeared when I kept things from my family.

Back at the dorm, I took off my pale blue dress with pink flower petals and searched my closet for something more casual. I picked out dark denim shorts, a magenta T-shirt, and an oversized navy zip-up sweatshirt that I'd stolen from Dad.

Tabitha shook her head. I knew she was about to take out the bullshit detector. I'd miss this next year when she moved to another dorm across campus.

"Chessy, don't do this," she said. "It's stupid. You know he doesn't really like you."

Why weren't people getting it? I could protect myself. I'd lived and traveled all over the world and I'd been on my own at boarding school for a year. No one was going to disrespect me. And *I* had the power. Owen wanted to hang out with me, not the other way around. I was using him to get a cool view and impressive Instagram photos.

"This is my choice. I'm going to be fine," I said. "If I get uncomfortable, I'll leave."

At 9:15 p.m., I slipped out the back door of Con20 and met Owen in front of the Schoolhouse. I was reassured when I saw he was wearing a backpack. Phew. He had somewhere else to go after. This would be a quick trip.

The campus was teeming with parents, students, and alumni, and I was nervous about running into someone we knew. But I was also excited: I'd made this decision by myself and nobody else had told me what to do. This was what life was going to be like next year when Lucy wasn't around.

We headed together toward Lindsay until Owen spotted a security car parked out front and decided we should split up.

"You go in this way and I'll walk in another door. Meet me inside near the pendulum," he said as he bolted to the other side of the building.

I waved to the security guard and opened the door facing the Schoolhouse. I waited under the pendulum for a couple of minutes. Maybe he was going to ditch me. I felt a bit relieved.

Owen eventually arrived and started sprinting up the stairs two at a time. I was having trouble keeping up in my flimsy red leather sandals. They had small wooden heels that kept catching on the stairs.

I was out of breath with wobbly ankles after four flights. Owen took out keys to unlock the door. I felt a pit in my stomach.

"Where did you get the keys?" I asked.

Owen put his finger on his lips and shushed me. Students broke into places all the time. I guessed it couldn't be that bad. He walked deeper into a dark room. All I could see were blinking red and green lights, and I heard loud whooshing noises coming from machines. I wasn't sure what this was—a storage closet, an attic, a mechanical room?

"Can I use your cell phone as a flashlight?" Owen asked.

"Sure," I said, and handed him my phone.

I heard him unlock another door and then followed him up several steps. Finally we were on the roof.

The sky glowed dusky lavender. The wind brushed my face as I dangled my arms over the chest-high ledge. "Oh my gosh, this is really pretty," I said.

Owen was casing the perimeter of the roof. I wasn't sure what he was doing and I really didn't care. I looked down at Moore, the brick building where I took my music theory class, the Schoolhouse, and my favorite willow tree in between the two. The branches bent all the way to the ground, creating a natural fort, and it reminded me of the trees back at Sacred Heart in Tokyo. I kept telling Catie we needed to picnic there.

I inhaled the damp air and fell deep into a nature coma, losing track of everything around me. I felt lucky to be at St. Paul's, so thankful that my parents had allowed me to attend. We'd been through a lot as a family, and this place would never fail to be beautiful.

Owen interrupted my thoughts, barking orders: "Come on, Chessy, let's go inside. It's soggy and gross out here. Let's go back down."

I wasn't sure what he meant. There were puddles and some raindrops, but they didn't interfere with the view. I needed to snap some photos.

"Can't we stay longer? It's so nice," I said, waving my hands in the air. "We've only been here a few minutes."

"Let's go. It's getting cold," Owen said, and walked inside and down the steps.

I followed his white sweatshirt as he meandered through the dark room and then dropped his backpack on the ground. He turned toward me and, without saying a word, wrapped his arms around my waist and pressed me against a wall. He put his lips on mine, sliding his tongue in my mouth. He wasn't a bad kisser. He'd clearly had practice. But I was still shocked. We hadn't even had a conversation.

Then he took off my blue sweatshirt and peeled off my T-shirt. His speed and deftness with this was astounding and confusing. By the time I'd processed my sweatshirt on the floor—and the fact that we were moving to second base—Owen ripped down my bra straps and scratched my shoulders.

Oh my God, I didn't want this. I pulled the straps back up, sending a message. He tried to grab my breasts under the front of my bra but then stopped. *Okay, Chessy, this is fine,* I told myself. I had this handled.

Owen took out a flannel blanket from the backpack and laid it on the floor. He kissed me and fell to the ground, bringing me down with him. Then he got up again and pushed me against a wall. He pinned my hands above my head. I had seen this in movies, couples aggressively kissing against walls, but this was not romantic. He held on to my wrists, nailing me to the wall. Stuck. I was uncomfortable.

My sandals were off and I could feel the cold, hard concrete under my feet. Owen kept one hand on my arms above my head and used the other to take off his belt. I heard the clanging metal buckle. His shorts fell to the floor.

I began to panic. I thought I'd brought us back to first base, and now the belt. What was I going to do? I didn't want to offend him or make him think I was an inexperienced little girl. I needed to get out of there.

I tried to relax when he put his hands on my shoulders and started to massage them. But suddenly Owen pushed me to the ground and grabbed my breasts, my shorts, my zipper. He tore my bra down completely. He was shirtless on top of me and then moved me around so I was on top of him. Then he was back on top of me.

Owen unbuttoned my shorts and told me to lift my waist up. He pulled off my shorts and threw them aside. He tugged my underwear down from the side of my hips, but I instinctively grabbed them and pulled them back up. I was desperate to keep my underwear up.

"No," I mumbled as he kissed me.

It was as if the universe splintered into two. Owen buzzed around like a bee stinging me rapidly and I was trapped in a honey jar, my brain covered in goo. How were things happening so quickly?

I could barely make out Owen's face. I saw shadows and felt his wet mouth all over me. On my neck. Biting my ear. Chewing my breasts. I was scared.

Before I could process more, he pulled the bottom panel of my underwear to the side and stuck his fingers inside me. I don't know how many were in there. I felt them scraping around and around.

It was so painful, but I couldn't move. It was as though I was bolted onto the flannel blanket. What could I say that wouldn't make him angry?

I was always going with the flow with my family, with my friends. But I was scared he could get more aggressive. At this point, he didn't seem like the Owen everyone said he was. At least not the guy who'd emailed me BELIEVE IN ANGELS and promised me a sweet view. I was trying to form thoughts in my head, but the pipeline that delivered words to my mouth was gone.

Owen took his fingers out of my body and licked my stomach down to my vagina. His head was down there when he tried for the second time to pull off my underwear. I forced them back over my hips and dragged Owen's face away from my underwear. I would put a stop to this now.

"No, no, no, let's keep it up here," I said, and let out a stuttering laugh.

Finally, words.

Owen scoffed. "You're such a tease, Francesca."

My face contorted with confusion. What did he mean? I was saying no. Why was he calling me a tease? I obviously didn't want any of this. I'd pulled up my bra straps, my underwear, his head. I felt paralyzed. I couldn't yell. I couldn't kick. I couldn't say a word. I'd never experienced this. I'd been lifting my head off the blanket as if that would help me stay in control of the situation.

His mouth was down there again. My head banged against the floor in defeat. Owen stretched my underwear to the side, and then bit the outside of my vagina. Why wasn't he listening to me? I'd said no several times. What else could I have said to make it stop?

I looked up at the rectangular metal pipes on the ceiling and then felt myself float above my body. I couldn't believe this was happening to me. This person, who was not listening to me, was violating me in the most intimate place, and I was lifeless.

I couldn't feel my body anymore, so I shut my eyes and focused on the deafening sound of the machines.

The whooshing air. Chessy, listen to the whooshing air. This will be over soon.

When I opened my eyes again, I felt something pushing inside me. I suddenly realized that Owen's hands were planted next to my shoulders. That meant what I felt was not a hand. I was in shock.

"You're such a tease," Owen said again, this time sounding frustrated. "Would it help if I yelled?"

What the fuck was that supposed to mean? I sank deeper into deadness.

He thrusted again. My whole body jerked backward. He was having trouble getting inside me and I could tell that he was angry. He paused and moved his mouth past my stomach and spit on my vagina. I could hear spitting into my body.

I was freezing, a dead fish on the cold floor. I saw Owen's hand move over my face to reach for something in his shorts pocket. He was back inside me. He moaned.

I was lying there unresponsive when Owen stood up and quickly got dressed. I put my hands on the floor and tried to push up my limp legs. I was so dizzy as I gathered my scattered clothes. I felt drugged. Could that be possible? I held on to the wall as I put on one of my sandals. The room was spinning. My legs were pudding. I lost my balance as I hunted for my second shoe. I braced myself with two hands on the concrete floor.

Then I found my phone. It was 10:18 p.m. How could that much time have gone by? I was completely disoriented.

Owen was in a rush to get to an a cappella concert. He walked over, grabbed my face, and kissed me on the lips. My mouth was numb. I couldn't form words. Owen gestured that we needed to hurry up.

"How are we going to do this?" he asked.

"Don't worry," I mumbled. "You go first."

"Well, that was fun." He smirked.

Owen ran down the stairs and didn't look back. I was trembling. The feeling started to return to my body: my breasts were sore and there was a horrible pain between my legs. What the hell had just happened?

SEVEN

The Immediate Aftermath

I walked slowly down the stairs and squinted under the harsh fluorescent lights. I secretly hoped that the security guard was still around and could see me through the glass windows in the stairwell. Maybe he would ask me what was wrong, or help me piece together the last hour. Because I had no clue how to explain it.

At the bottom of the stairs, I opened the door to the hallway and saw Dylan and two other friends who'd gone tunnel hunting under the chapel with me last week. They were racing around on black wheelie chairs. Dylan and I stood face-to-face in the hallway as I let the door close behind me.

"Hey, Chessy, why are you here so late?" Dylan asked.

I started spilling words: "I think . . . I just had sex with Owen Labrie. I don't know if that's a good thing or an awful thing. I don't know whether to be proud or happy or . . ."

"Did you want this?" Dylan asked.

I touched the back of my head. My hair was a rat's nest. I was so confused. How could it get that messy? Dylan looked shocked and frightened as I untangled the knots in my hair and stared off into space.

"No, I don't know," I muttered eventually. "I don't know how to feel."

"You don't look okay. Do you want to talk?" Dylan asked. "Let me walk you back to your dorm. You can't go by yourself."

I noticed his eyebrows furrow, and I immediately snapped out of it. I had to pretend that everything was normal.

"No, no, no, no, no. I'm fine, I'm fine," I said. "Don't worry about me."

Dylan and the other boys walked me out of the building, but I cut across the lawn to get away from them. I needed to be alone. I clawed the tears off my face as I trudged back to my dorm. I gazed at the night sky and prayed it would swallow me whole. I saw alumni up ahead celebrating on the chapel lawn after the a cappella concert that Owen had been racing to see.

How could they be happy when I was so messed up? I felt filthy and contaminated. I convinced myself that I was being too sensitive, too much of a baby. Dylan started pelting me with texts as I walked into my dorm.

> Dylan: I am worrying I don't like him.
> Me: I stood my place and pushed, don't worry.
> Dylan: So he forced you?
> Me: Kinda, but he's notoriously aggressive.
> Dylan: Ugh I am so sorry
> Me: I made a decision, I have to deal with the consequences.
> Dylan: ugh I'm still mad
> Me: I know.

I had to get it together and fast. I needed Catie but she wasn't in her room. I drifted down the stairs to the basement and ran into Ivy and Faith on their way to make cookies in the kitchen downstairs.

"So," Ivy asked, "how was it?"

I ushered them down the steps and into a quiet part of the basement.

"Guys," I said, my hands shaking, "I think I just had sex with Owen Labrie."

Ivy's jaw dropped. "Whaaaat? That didn't happen."

"Yes."

"Oh my God, Chessy, are you okay?" Ivy and Faith gasped.

I promised that I'd talk about it when Catie got back. I tried to pretend that everything was fine and joined the circle of girls on the floor and couches. I avoided direct eye contact with Lilly, who was sitting across from me.

I wanted to collapse on my own bed, but I was afraid of seeing Tabitha. Not after she'd cautioned against this. Not after what she'd been through. So I retreated to Catie's room on the other side of the dorm, hoping no one would follow me. I needed to figure this out for myself.

I grabbed a carton of Goldfish crackers off Catie's shelf and sat on the floor next to a blue beanbag chair. I put some crackers into my hand and accidentally dropped a few stragglers on the floor. They would have to live there. Possibly forever. Maybe I would join them, getting crushed by footsteps until I was pulverized into nothing. I was already dead inside.

Ivy and Faith walked in over my Goldfish graveyard. Moments later Catie burst through the door, looking as if she'd seen a ghost.

"Guys, check this out," she said as she pulled down her sweatpants and revealed bloodstained underwear. Her boyfriend, Carter, had fingered her for the first time, leaving a gruesome scene for us to witness. This night was a total train wreck.

My first instinct was to ignore what had just happened to me and take care of my friend. But Ivy and Faith didn't forget, and eventually they turned their attention to me. If I refused to talk about what happened, I thought it would raise more red flags.

At first I was nervous and giggly, recounting the rooftop, the kissing. My words crashed into each other, I was speaking so fast.

"He took off my shirt and shorts he kept trying to take off my underwear but I wouldn't let him he fingered me and tried to eat me out I lifted his head up and I said let's keep it up here but he kept going down there and I said no and he called me a tease."

My friends looked at me and then at each other, their eyes bouncing like pinballs around the room.

"Oh my God," Ivy whispered.

"That sounds aggressive," Catie said.

I tried to keep it together, like this was no big deal. I checked my phone and saw Owen's name in my inbox. I thought I might vomit.

> francesca you're an angel.
> much love
> owen

Stay calm, Chessy, I told myself. *Figure out what the hell happened before saying anything more. Stick to the script he gave you.*

> Me: you're quite an angel yourself but would you mind
>   keeping the sequence of events to yourself for now?
> Owen: comme tu veux belle fille.

I plugged the sentence into Google Translate to figure out what he was saying in French: "as you want beautiful girl."

I looked up at my friends. The words tumbled out again.

"He bit my breasts and then he pinned my arms above my head and I couldn't get them down," I said, trying to steady my trembling hands.

"What do you mean?" Faith asked.

"Yeah," Catie said. "Show us. Do what he did on Ivy."

"Fine, I'll show you," I sighed.

I got up from the floor and positioned Ivy so she was standing with her back against the closed door. She was wearing a white T-shirt and baggy red sweatpants with ST. PAUL'S emblazoned in white.

I lifted up her arms and kept her elbows slightly bent, making a diamond shape around her head. I clasped both of my hands on her wrists and pressed them against the door. She couldn't move. Like I couldn't move. Catie took a picture. Ivy was searching my eyes. I could tell she was worried.

"He fingered me and then I was confused because both of his hands were near my head and I still felt something inside me. It was really confusing. I was just lying there."

"Shit, did Owen wear a condom?" Catie asked.

"I dunno," I sighed. "He reached for something in his pocket but I couldn't see what it was."

"You could get pregnant, Chessy," Ivy gasped. "You need to ask him if he was wearing a condom. You have to find out."

I felt like an ax had crushed my skull. I could be pregnant?

"I can't ask him. What would I even say?"

"You need to," Ivy insisted. "Get your phone." My fingers were slipping as Ivy dictated an email. But I was too embarassed to use the word "condom." I sent it at 11:09 p.m.

By any chance, were you using anything tonight?

Owen responded in Spanish on Facebook messenger instead of his St. Paul's email.

¿que?

Could this guy just fucking speak English?

"Now what am I supposed to say?" I groaned.

"Just spell it out for him," Catie said.

I was freaking out inside. My friends demanded that I get answers, but I was worried about setting off any alarms or offending him. I didn't want him to lash out or retaliate against me. I wrote back, drawing out my words with extra vowels to make it sound more casual. The girls read and approved every message.

> Me: Liiike a condom? Just incasee . . .
> Owen: yeah
> Me: Haha okaay thanks
> Owen: are you on the pill?
> Me: Nope
> Owen: praise jesus i put it on like halfway through

Why was he praising Jesus? What did he mean halfway through?

"This is serious, Chessy," Catie said, stitching her eyebrows together. "You need to stop being polite and figure this out."

> Me: Are you sure?
> Owen: yee i think you're fine

Wow. Think I'm fine? Were we like fifty-fifty here? Because I was 100 percent certain that I didn't want to be pregnant.

> Me: Hopefully, do you know for sure?

Owen didn't respond for nearly two minutes. The girls insisted that I get explicit about ejaculation. I was mortified.

> Me: Like before or after you came

Owen: hahaha i put it on long before i knew i would
  i would say you're good to go
  but i guess it's your call?
Me: haha sorry for all the technical stuff
Owen: you're a gem let me know if there is anything else
  i can do
Me: you're not too bad yourself

I fidgeted with my bracelets and tried to keep my shit together. I didn't want to let on how upset I was. I didn't want to be weak. I didn't want Ivy and Faith to think I was a withering little girl.

I was in control. I felt that maybe this was my fault. I hadn't been clear enough to him. Maybe I should have done more to stop him.

Faith and Ivy hugged me and then headed downstairs to deal with their cookies. They were probably charred by now.

After they left, Catie looked me straight in the eyes. "Are you really okay?"

"No, Catie, I'm not," I said, gnawing on my lower lip. "I'm scared. Look at this."

I slowly lifted up my shirt and revealed red bite marks near my nipples.

"Holy shit, Chess!" Catie said. "That's not okay."

"I need to take a shower," I said. "I need to get everything off me."

A couple of tears leaked out from the corner of my eyes.

"Can I use your shower and stuff?" I asked Catie. "I don't want to go to my bathroom."

"Yeah, of course, of course. Here, let me get you a towel."

I hid in a bathroom stall and felt a shooting pain inside me as I tried to pee. I was paralyzed again.

Eventually, I stood in scalding-hot water and scrubbed the filth off my body. I wanted it gone. I tried to rub my skin raw, but my body recoiled from my own touch. Tears slid down my cheeks and swirled into the drain. I was empty, like something had been ripped out of me.

Catie, who never allowed anyone to touch her sheets, let me crawl into bed with her and wear her pajamas. She gave me a white T-shirt, white shorts, and white underwear. She cradled me and fed me Goldfish crackers until I fell asleep.

My head was pounding when I woke up. I had to face my parents. My sick grandmother. My little sister. I had to be okay. First I needed clothes. I skulked down the hall to my room, praying that Tabitha wouldn't see me. I tore through my closet. Nothing felt right. I needed to cover my body. I put on a loose-fitting royal blue shirt and long white jeans.

I met my family outside the dorm for the alumni parade. Dad was beaming, so happy. We were about to march from the chapel through campus down Rectory Road, the same path that he and Mom had walked along when they were newly engaged. The oldest alumnus led the line, followed by other classes celebrating their reunions, and the form of 2014 in the way back.

Dad put his arm around my shoulder and squeezed me. "Chessy, remember we're going to be on the same reunion cycle, so you and I can share this for the rest of our lives."

"Yeah, I know," I said, trying not to flinch.

Lucy looked gorgeous as always in a white dress with pink and red flowers. After the parade, we made our way to the hockey rinks for the celebratory luncheon. Christianna held Lucy's hand while they walked with my parents, and I slipped away to catch up with Dylan. He was with Haley—Andrew Thomson's little sister.

"Are you all right from last night?" Dylan asked.

I shook my head no, holding in my breath. Dylan gave me a warm side hug.

Haley looked perplexed and I began to unload. I was still unsure

104

of how to describe it. Haley put her arm around my shoulder and pulled me in, too.

I moved in a fog from the parade to the luncheon to the crew races, my head down, staring at the red bricks beneath my shuffling feet. Mom and Dad took pictures every two seconds, and I was exhausted from fake smiles. All I wanted to do was hold Christianna. I kept putting her on my lap and squeezing her. I needed comfort and home and safety.

The one event I was mildly excited about was a performance by the female a cappella group, the Madhatters. I planned to try out in the fall. It was a short show that night—just fifteen minutes before the Flagpole Ceremony, when students received athletic awards.

We arrived too late to get seats in the bleachers surrounding the makeshift stage in front of the flagpole. I was standing in a crowd next to Lucy and our cousin Katie when I noticed Malcolm Salovaara staring at me. I'm not sure what any girl saw in him.

Malcolm smirked and then whispered something to Owen, who was standing next to him. I saw Malcolm moving his beady eyes from Lucy to me and then to Owen.

I was back in the mechanical room, pulling up my bra straps, yanking up my underwear, and dragging Owen's face away from my vagina. *No, no, no, let's keep it up here.* His hands were by my head. There was something inside me. Tears pushed open my eyes and I saw Malcolm looking at me again. I tried to tamp down the panic rising from my gut.

As Lucy, Katie, and I walked uphill past Library Pond and the squash courts, a stillness came over my body. I had to tell Lucy. I knew she might be angry that I hadn't listened to her advice, but she would understand that I didn't want this to happen. She knew me better than anyone. She'd know what to say, what to do.

I stopped her in front of Sheldon, the gray stone admissions building, where a year and a half earlier, Lucy had taken a photo of me after my interview.

"I went with Owen last night," I said, as tears escaped. "He had sex with me, but I didn't want it."

Lucy pulled me in tight and threw her arms around me. Then she uttered four of the most important words I needed to hear: "It's not your fault."

Before I could say anything else, fury flashed across her face. "I'm going to kill him."

She ran away in her white dress and red flip-flops and headed back to the flagpole. Katie and I raced behind her.

"She can't do this," I pleaded to Katie. "This can't happen."

"Lucy, please don't cause a scene," I begged from behind, trying to catch up. "I'm okay. Don't worry, don't say anything, don't do anything. I don't want to ruin the weekend."

Lucy was already at the flagpole, yelling at Brooks. I hung back with Katie until Lucy returned with news: Brooks already knew, and Owen had snuck away.

"So where exactly did he take you last night?" Lucy asked.

"He had keys to the roof of the Lindsay building, but then he brought me inside this noisy room." I sniffled.

Rage returned to Lucy's eyes. "He took me there too. He's not getting away with this."

We were so late for dinner and total messes when we finally showed up. Mom looked *pissed*. She'd worked so hard to put together the perfect evening, getting special permission to host the celebration in the courtyard of Kehaya. Lucy had a gray hooded sweatshirt covering her dress and folded her arms across her chest as if in protest. Mom thought she was spoiling every picture on purpose.

Lucy blinked back tears and whispered to her best friend, Zoe. I walked over to the tables of food and grabbed a plate of Uncle Ken's salmon rolls, knowing full well I was allergic. I didn't care about the consequences.

I clearly was not doing a decent enough job of holding it together, because Mom came over and scolded me: "If you're going to look so miserable at this dinner, the least you can do is go play with your little sister."

It was the best punishment. I took Christianna by the hand and led her to the trampoline near Lucy's dorm. I felt free for the first time, jumping high in the air, pushing through the pain still searing inside me. Maybe if I jumped high enough, I'd disappear into the sky.

My throat was closing up and my lips were swelling from the salmon. Mom said I needed Benadryl, so I stopped at Clark House with Ivy to pick up medicine. Later that evening I headed across the street to the chapel lawn to wait for the end of the Last Night Service. It's a tradition where the underclassmen line up to celebrate the sixth formers as they walk out of their final chapel service before graduation.

I joined in on the clapping and cheering and searched for Lucy. Finally she walked out. We locked eyes and both began to bawl. She embraced me in a big-sister hug and said, "I'm so sorry, Chessy."

Then she snarled: "I'm going to get Owen."

She had a determined look in her eyes as she hustled toward the throng of students celebrating on the grass. I finished saying goodbye to other senior friends and then escaped to my dorm.

Lucy called later with an update: she had marched over to Owen with her girlfriends by her side.

"This is for taking my sister's virginity," she yelled before punching him between his nose and cheek. He looked stunned, a deer in headlights. For the first time, Lucy said, Owen didn't have a witty comeback. Her knuckles still stung, but she swore it was worth it.

That blew my mind. Lucy hated confrontation as much as I did. I couldn't believe she'd done that. I was still trying to process it all when Briana, a senior in Con20, called me into her room.

Briana was small and feisty—her nostrils flared whenever she was angry or happy. She had a sister the same age as Christianna, and she was very protective of the younger girls in our dorm.

"What happened?" she asked.

"I'm still so confused," I said. "I don't really know what's going on."

I recounted the night: the rooftop, the kissing, the bra straps, the underwear.

"I said no but Owen ignored it," I sighed. "His fingers were inside me and then the next thing I know his hands are above my head and I realize something is still inside of me."

"Oh my God, Chessy, he did the same thing to me during junior year," Briana said.

It was dark, she couldn't see, and he was very aggressive. She told Owen she didn't want to have sex. He had one hand on her thigh and a finger inside her vagina. She was okay with that. But then Briana suddenly felt both of his hands on her thighs and pressure inside her. She sat up and it ended abruptly.

"Chessy, you did nothing wrong," Briana said.

I wanted the words to sink in, but I was wearing my protective armor to get through the weekend. If I hadn't done anything wrong, then someone had done something wrong to me. I'd lost control. I couldn't accept that.

Just after midnight, Owen messaged me on Facebook.

> Owen: chessy, here are my thoughts. i think you're an amazing girl--i'm sure you'll crush it next year. fourth form was the best year of my life by 10,000 miles. anyways, people have been saying all kinds of things to me today (which i don't really care about), but i don't want your sister, who i also think is sweet, to leave with a bitter taste in her mouth. lucy and i were really tight at one point. all i want to say is that, when a boy actually takes

your virginity, i hope it's golden. i hope he loves you to
death and i hope he treats you like a goddess. there's a
difference between making love and messing around. if
only the rest of the world understood--maybe you can help
them. you're an absolute gem. bisous, owen
ps i checked in lindsey for your earring this morning. i
couldn't find it!!

He was backtracking. Did Owen think I was an idiot? But I still
wasn't willing to confront him like Lucy.

Me: Thank you so much for that owen, things have been
difficult and I haven't been making the most pleasing
decisions (to lucy) recently, and that makes me feel
terrible. I hope for what you said as well. On a happier
note, félicitations, diplômé! And thank you for looking.

Done. Or so I thought.

Owen: yeaaahhhh you sister punched me in the face after
    last night service.
Me: I am so sorry . . . Shes very protective . . . . .
Owen: hahahha all of her friends ran after me
    never have i been attacked by so many crying yelling girls
Me: oh my god thats every guy's worst nightmare hahahaa
    And the emotions don't help at allll

I wasn't sorry but maybe an apology would make him go away.
The last thing I wanted to do was cause a scene. I was too weak to
tell him he deserved getting slugged. I just needed this idiot to leave
me alone.

ooooo

Graduation day had finally arrived. I was counting the hours until my family left so I could exhale. It was exhausting pretending to be fine. I was running late and had to save seats for Grandma Prusac-zyk. But Catie insisted that I go get Plan B first.

I was leaving Catie's room, my new home base, when I ran into Veronica, a fifth former in my dorm. Veronica was very mindful of the newbs—she was one of the girls who told us to come up with hand signals for Nash Bash, and she drew up a list of good boys and bad boys at the beginning of the school year.

Veronica pulled me aside in the hallway and whispered, "I know I probably shouldn't be telling you this, but Owen did the same thing to two of my friends."

One of the girls was like me and had no sexual experience.

"She had no idea what was going on," Veronica said.

My eyes bulged and anger bubbled in my stomach. I couldn't believe he'd done this to so many girls. And I was shocked that everyone knew about it too.

"I was so confused," I said. "I don't even know if he used a condom. I have to get Plan B."

"If you don't want to go to Clark House, I can buy it for you downtown," Veronica offered.

I briefly considered it, but decided I needed to clean up my own mess.

"No, it's okay," I said. "I'm going over to get my meds anyways."

I still hadn't fully accepted the whole Plan B thing. I was supposed to get my period any day now. It was the first time in my entire life I was praying for it.

"Well, I'm here for you," Veronica said, and gave me a hug. "Let me know if you need anything at all."

I started weeping the second I stepped foot into Clark House and told the nurse I needed to talk to her about Plan B. She led me into a private examination room and left me alone while she got some paperwork. I sat and reminded myself that I couldn't make this day about me.

The nurse returned with a checklist and began ticking off questions: Had I taken Plan B before? Did I understand what the medication was for? Could I already be pregnant? She saved the hardest question for last. Was it consensual?

I couldn't cause any trouble. Through tears, I said yes. I was already running late. I still thought it might be my fault. And this was Lucy's weekend, not mine. The nurse kindly offered me a tissue and said that the medication would be available in a couple of days.

I rushed out of Clark House and was blinded by sunshine and a sea of white. All the senior girls wore white dresses with red flowers pinned to their chests. I couldn't help but think of my friends in white togas at Sacred Heart on the day of the earthquake. The day everything changed. I felt like I had back then: shocked and scared. What had I done to deserve so many bad things in my life?

I didn't have time for a pity party. I needed to get in line to reserve enough seats for our family. I was glad Grandma Prusaczyk was there, even though it was hard seeing her sick and in a wheelchair. I knew how much she loved us, and how happy she was that Lucy and I had returned to the United States. She and Mom have had a tough relationship over the years. I don't think she ever got over Mom and Dad moving to Japan for so long.

My eyes were glued downward during the graduation ceremony, as if I was having a staring contest with the grass. Mrs. Hebra, the school's vice rector and an adviser in my dorm, announced the names of the graduates. I took deep breaths when she called out Owen Arthur Labrie. I didn't clap for him. That was my big act of defiance. I forced my head up when I heard Lucy's name.

Dean of Students Chad Green then took over the microphone to announce student awards. Rusher the Crusher received the Benjamin Rush Toland Prize for her intellectual achievement, athletic ability, and gallant spirit. Then came the Rector's Awards for students whose "selfless devotion to school activities have enhanced our lives and improved the community shared by all at St. Paul's School."

I was stunned when I heard Owen Labrie's name. All the breath got sucked out of my chest as he sauntered across the stage in his royal-blue crew blazer. Why did all the adults think he was this perfect gentleman? Someone had to know he was a sick guy who took advantage of girls. Owen smiled and mouthed, "Thank you" to Mr. Hirschfeld as he shook his hand and took the award.

I could tell the end was finally near when someone started handing out cigars to the graduates. This turned into another picture-fest. I gritted my teeth.

After Mom and Dad said their farewells, I returned to my room to get changed. Tabitha was there and I tried flashing her my best fake smile. But when I unzipped my strappy blue dress and found a bloodstain on the back, I started crying.

"I never thought I'd be so happy to get blood on my dress," I said, too ashamed to look over at Tabitha. "Owen Labrie took advantage of me and I don't think he used a condom."

"I'm so sorry," she said, her voice trailing off.

Neither of us knew how to say anything more.

Catie barged in and announced it was time for a frozen yogurt excursion downtown. That always made things better.

Catie was still worried that I might have an STD, so she made me FaceTime with her friend who had graduated earlier that day. I was mad that she had confided in him, but he gave me good advice and offered sympathy. He explained that I could go to the hospital and have a rape kit done and get tested for sexually transmitted diseases.

"You need to make sure you're physically okay," her friend said. "And you should talk to a counselor."

I was overwhelmed. Hospital. Rape kit. This was all too much. I didn't want to talk about this anymore. I needed to shift my brain to something else. Something not rape. Studying. I had math and science finals this week.

On Monday I hunkered down in a study pod—a windowless jail cell with white walls in the basement of my dorm. I took a break from geometry to change my Facebook cover photo to one of me and Lucy from graduation. We were standing on the chapel lawn, and Lucy had me in a semi-headlock and was holding a cigar in her right hand. Lucy and my friend Violet commented first.

> Lucy: aww love you chae
> Violet: so cute chessica

I was in the middle of inserting two red-heart emojis below Lucy's comment when a classmate typed Owen Labrie's name in a comment under the photo. My phone started ringing. The reception was terrible downstairs, but I could make out that Lucy was shouting. I ran upstairs through the common room, past Mrs. Hebra, and into my room.

"Why did you have to do this? Why did you go with him? It was so stupid to go and meet him," Lucy roared. "And then you apologized to Owen after I punched him? I was defending you. That's sister code. Don't you get it?"

"I'm so sorry, Lucy. I'm so sorry."

"Just tell your stupid friend to take down his tag of Owen."

"He's not my friend. I don't know why he would do this."

I was upset that Lucy was upset, but I wasn't mad at her. I was mad at me like she was mad at me. But I was also mad at Owen Labrie. He did this to me. I pulled up my bra straps. I yanked up my underwear, twice. I dragged his head up away from my vagina. I said, "No, no, no, let's keep it up here." I know I didn't kick. I didn't scream. I didn't run away. I froze. And I wasn't the only girl he did this to.

ooooo

Later that night Owen MacIntyre texted me a sickening manifesto.
I was so gullible to have believed that nothing bad would happen.
Why did he pressure me so much to go on that STUPID SENIOR
SALUTE?

> O. Mac: Chessy, I know what happened with you
> and Owen, and I just wanted to say I'm really sorry,
> and I know nothing I am saying will change that but
> I just wanted to let you know that as much as I love
> you I love Owen too. I know him really well and if he
> thought he was doing anything to hurt you physically
> or emotionally he would've stopped. I know that all this
> drama is probably wearing on you and you don't know
> how to handle everything that's happening to you, so
> I just wanted to let you know that you can talk to me.
> If Owen knew all the stuff that's being said about you,
> he'd do anything to stop it. It is my understanding that
> he didn't ask you if you wanted to have sex before he
> did that and that is 100% his fault, but I think that he
> thinks that because you didn't tell him to stop what he
> was doing was okay. So before you tell anyone names,
> I just want you to consider the circumstances. Owen is
> starting a new life in a new place, and next year will be
> a fresh start for you too. If anyone else says anything
> to you I'll deal with them, and if you need a hug I can
> be there for you. I just love you both and I know what
> he did hurt you, and maybe you didn't necessarily hate
> what he was doing at the time. I don't want to see
> either of you get hurt.
> Love,
> Owen

What was everyone saying about me? Maybe I didn't hate what he was doing? Was this some kind of threat? My body convulsed and I shrieked uncontrollably.

Dr. Theresa Gerardo-Gettens, a dorm adviser who lived next door, heard me through the walls and brought me into her apartment. I started to tell Dr. G. about what happened, using hypotheticals, because that's what we were advised to do at orientation when talking about serious stuff with adults.

I didn't understand back then how messed up that advice was, how it appeared to protect St. Paul's reputation, not the students in its care. It seemed like a well-designed loophole that allowed the school to get out of mandated reporting to the police. St. Paul's led students to believe that talking bluntly to adults was a bad thing, that it could get them in trouble rather than get them the help they needed, the justice they deserved.

"What if somebody had sex with me and I did not want them to and said no?" I sobbed.

"I don't want this to happen to anyone else. What should I do?"

"Call your mother," Dr. G. said. "How you handle this will inform the rest of your life."

On the night of my assault, I demonstrated on Ivy how Owen pinned my arms above my head so I couldn't move (below). The next day, I leaned on my friends for support (right).

After I posted this picture of me and Lucy to Facebook, a classmate wrote Owen Labrie's name in a comment under the photo.

EIGHT

The Police

walked out of Dr. G.'s apartment and ducked into an empty dorm room that three seniors had vacated after graduation. I sat on the threadbare carpet and hugged my knees to my chest.

Was I really going to do this? It was already after midnight. Mom was staying at Grandma Prusaczyk's house in Connecticut, and she was probably curled up in her childhood bed, cuddling Christianna. I knew I had to call; Mom always made things better. As soon as I heard her soft, sleepy voice, I lost it.

"Honey, are you okay?"

"Nooooo," I howled.

"Chess, what's going on?"

I could barely breathe, let alone speak. I felt my lips forming words, but my mouth released animal noises.

"Something . . . bad . . . has happened."

"What's going on?" Mom whispered urgently. "Tell me, honey, what's wrong?"

"A boy had sex with me and I didn't want it."

I expected Mom to freak out, but instead she spoke in a calm voice that flight attendants use when there's terrifying turbulence and everyone thinks they're going to die.

"It's going to be okay. Are you safe right now? Are you going to be able to sleep tonight? What can I do to help you right now?"

"I'm okay, Mom," I blubbered incoherently. "I'm going to sleep with Catie tonight. I'm safe."

"I'll come first thing in the morning," Mom promised. "When you wake up, go see Buzz at Clark House and I'll be right there."

I hung up the phone and looked at the floor. My T-shirt clung to my skin, a soggy rag soaking up tears. I could feel my clenched jaw slowly releasing, my shriveled lungs filling up with oxygen, the protective armor sliding off my skin. It was as if somebody had poked a hole in the hell bubble I'd been trapped in since Friday. I could breathe again.

I woke up on Tuesday and briefly considered ditching my geometry final and following Mom's instructions to go straight to Clark House. My brain had liquefied, no longer holding solid thoughts, much less math formulas. But I couldn't let some guy wreck my grades. I kept my head down and ignored Owen MacIntyre's attempt to talk with me before the exam.

I blew through the questions and bolted across campus to Clark House. Mom had called Buzz in the morning on her drive up to New Hampshire and told my counselor that I'd had an "unwanted sexual experience."

"Susan," Buzz responded, "that sounds like rape."

I wasn't ready to utter the R word when I sank into one of the navy-blue swivel chairs in Buzz's office. I inhaled some Hershey's Kisses from the candy bowl on the table and read one of the posters covering the lilac walls. It was a quote from Margaret Mead, a famous American anthropologist: "Never doubt that a small group of thoughtful, committed citizens can change the world; indeed, it's the only thing that ever has."

I was bawling again; crumpled white tissues were my new accessory. I finally looked up at Buzz, her eyes crinkled with kindness. We'd been meeting regularly since my health leave in November, and I was grateful to have a safe space on campus to unpack my feelings. I could talk to her with zero judgment. Buzz helped me learn how to be myself and not accept the status quo at St. Paul's.

Buzz asked me what happened on Friday night. I wrapped my arms tightly around myself and I eventually muttered some words.

"I felt manipulated by Owen, and I think he's manipulating another friend, who pressured me to go," I said.

"Chessy, because of what you and your mom told me, I'm obligated to call the authorities," Buzz said. "There are safe school zone laws that require me to notify the police and the Division of Children, Youth, and Families."

"Uh-huh," I said distractedly.

"When your mom gets here, we are going to head over to the hospital to get a rape kit done, and a detective from the Concord Police Department will meet us there."

I couldn't process most of what Buzz said, but I was relieved that an adult was telling me what to do. Navigating this on my own had been exhausting.

"Wow . . . okay." I sighed deeply.

While we waited for Mom, I saw another message.

Owen: . . . people have been saying some scary things considering we never had sex. since i'm not there i have to trust you've got my back and you make sure the right people know what's actually up.

I read it out loud to Buzz along with another note he had sent.

> Owen: a couple of my friends have called me tonight
> asking about some rumors they heard . . . we need to
> make sure people don't think the wrong thing.

"Oh my God." I froze. "What am I supposed to do?"

"Don't answer," Buzz instructed. "And you need to preserve the messages. Can you save them?"

"Okay, I won't answer. And yeah, I can take screenshots."

I frantically snapped photos of every communication between me and Owen: questions about condoms, ejaculation, and birth control pills; my apology after Lucy punched him; his subsequent denials that he'd taken my virginity.

I started to spiral when Mom texted that she had arrived. I ran downstairs and jumped into her arms like I had after the earthquake. This time I didn't care whether people saw my hot tears.

"It's all going to be okay, it's all going to be okay," Mom said as she wept and rubbed my back.

Mom and I followed Buzz on the five-minute drive to Concord Hospital. As we parked near the emergency room entrance, I began breathing rapidly and my heart pounded so hard it rattled my ribs. This was all getting too real. How bad was what happened to me that I needed to go to the hospital?

I despised anything medical, especially shots. I'd staged various forms of protest over the years. When I was a baby, I gave the doctor a death stare instead of crying after he injected me with a needle. At five years old, I refused to walk to the exam room to get my shot, so the nurse carried me *and* the chair I was sitting in all the way to the doctor.

I didn't see any immediate getaway options. Mom put her arm

around me as we made our way inside Concord Hospital. Thankfully, the emergency room was empty, and we didn't wait long before a nurse brought us into a spacious room with a private bathroom.

Everything was bright and white. When I sat on the exam table, the blood drained from my face so that I blended in with the walls. My nerves were eating me from the inside out but I wore my Japanese mask, trying to hide any emotion at all. I crawled inside my head while Mom and Buzz made small talk. I'd never seen a gynecologist before or had any doctor examine me down there. What were they going to do? What if I had an STD?

A woman wearing a black blazer and pink blouse knocked on the door and introduced herself as Detective Julie Curtin. She was with the Concord Police Department and had spoken earlier on the phone with Buzz. Detective Curtin had a no-nonsense attitude, a stocky build, and an intense stare. I immediately feared that she wouldn't believe me. She would criticize me for being a baby and for wasting her time.

"Chessy, we're going to talk a little now, if that's okay. I know this might be difficult for you, but tell me what you can," Detective Curtin said softly after Mom and Buzz left the room. "Don't worry about all the details, because we'll have the chance to talk more later."

I walked her through the night: the rooftop, the kissing, the bra straps, the underwear, the thrusting inside me.

"I have all of these emails and messages from him and I started grabbing screenshots," I said.

"That's very helpful," Detective Curtin responded, nodding in approval. "Why don't you finish taking screenshots and forward them to me."

"Okay, I'll do that."

Detective Curtin brought Mom and Buzz back into the room.

"Chessy, this is a serious matter. I'd like to have a more in-depth conversation at the Child Advocacy Center. It's a place in town where we conduct interviews with young people who have been through situations like yours," Detective Curtin explained. "It will be just the two of us talking, but our conversation will be recorded so that other people can watch it from another room."

"Who else needs to see it?" Mom asked.

"Usually we have people from the police department, the prosecutor's office, the advocacy center," Detective Curtin said. "This way, Chessy, you only have to speak with one person and not repeat what happened over and over again."

"Okay," I said. "I can do that."

"Do you have time tomorrow?" Detective Curtin asked.

I looked up at Mom and shrugged.

"Chessy has finished her exams so we're going to be leaving tomorrow afternoon," Mom said.

"We can try to schedule something for the morning," Detective Curtin said.

"Thank you. Thank you so much for helping me," I said.

An emergency room nurse named Samantha eventually arrived and explained that she specialized in treating victims of sexual assault as a sexual assault nurse examiner, or SANE.

Samantha was disarming and sweet. She launched into a lengthy checklist of questions before the poking and prodding began. My body was no longer a body. It was a cavity of potential evidence: my blood, my urine, my cheek cells, even my tampon. I shuddered thinking that someone would have to examine my tampon. Samantha showed Mom some fingerprint bruises on my back near my shoulders, something that never made it into her report.

When I told Samantha that I had physical pain in my vagina, she found redness and an abrasion where I had lost a layer of skin. Then she explained that she was applying a blue skin dye with cotton swabs so she could see the area better.

Blue. My vagina was blue. Blue was my favorite color. I didn't know if I could ever look at blue the same way.

Samantha stayed in the room while a male physician conducted the dreaded internal examination. I cringed when he inserted a speculum inside me. It was cold and hard and hurt. I squeezed my eyes shut. Why were there so many unwanted things in me? When had my body become a place occupied by other people?

The day had evaporated by the time we stepped outside. I slid down the seat of the rental car in a state of disbelief: I'd just spent five hours in the hospital going through the most intrusive, grueling probe of my body. My arm was throbbing from the shot I'd been injected with to prevent gonorrhea, and I felt light-headed from the antibiotics I'd taken to protect against chlamydia. I opened the car window to let the cool breeze sweep across my face, the first gentle touch that day.

"You did great, Chess," Mom said. "I'm so proud of you. We're going to get through this."

We sat in the hospital's hilltop parking lot and called Dad. He'd been in all-day meetings in New York and had a flight out of the country that night.

"I'm coming up to Concord now," Dad said. "I'll cancel my trip."

"I can handle it," Mom said.

"No, I'm coming right away."

I had initially agreed to stay with Mom and Dad at their hotel, but I changed my mind because I wanted to say good-bye to some friends and pack up my stuff. I'd also promised to meet Lilly for dinner. I felt bad that I'd been avoiding her since Friday.

The coast was clear at the Upper since all the seniors had left campus. I pushed the food around my plate—the medications had my stomach doing somersaults—and filled her in on the last few days.

"I'm so sorry. I should have told you what's going on," I apologized. "I just knew that if I saw you, I'd have to deal with what really happened."

"No problem at all. But know that you can talk to me anytime," Lilly said, running her hand through her dark brown hair.

"I just want to forget about it all for now," I said.

"Of course, I understand," Lilly said.

Later I walked down to the crew docks with Ivy, Catie, and a bunch of other third formers. We piled into a dinghy and jumped into the lake. The cool water numbed my skin and anesthetized my brain. I was just a normal kid, floating in water so deep that I couldn't feel the bottom.

Tabitha sat on her bed as I rummaged through my closet and debated whether to change my outfit for my meeting at the Child Advocacy Center. I still couldn't bring myself to tell Tabitha exactly what was going on. Instead I talked around it.

"What am I supposed to wear to a police interview?" I asked, my voice catching in my throat.

"You look fine," Tabitha said. "It'll be okay. Just breathe."

Mom and Dad were waiting in the car outside my dorm. Dad was usually the ringleader of fun in our house, always joking and finding ways to make us laugh. This was not the Dad who showed up in Concord. His eyes were red from crying, something that he unsuccessfully tried to hide. He gripped the steering wheel so hard his knuckles turned white.

"It's okay, I'm okay, Dad," I reassured him. "I'll be fine."

"Chessy, I'm sorry, I'm so sorry. We're going to do whatever we can to help you," Dad said. "Anything. Everything."

I sat quietly in the backseat with a small cloth bag in my lap that contained the underwear I'd been wearing on Friday night. Detective Curtin wanted it as evidence.

We pulled up to the Merrimack County Child Advocacy Center,

a blue Victorian home on a narrow street in a residential neighborhood. The walls inside were a pale yellow and plastered with children's handprints in all the colors of the rainbow. Stuffed animals and picture books crammed a small shelf near the entrance.

I couldn't imagine young kids having to share horror stories like mine with strangers. Or even friends like Tabitha. I swept the thought out of my mind before it could leave an imprint; it was too painful to think about.

Mom, Dad, and I never questioned whether it was a good idea for me to talk to the police. We were big rule followers in our family, and when law enforcement asked us to do something, we listened. We assumed everyone else did the same.

The gravity of what was going on—that I was the victim of a crime—hadn't sunk in. Things couldn't be that terrible, I convinced myself, because I was still alive.

Detective Curtin brought Mom and Dad to the back room and briefly introduced them to the people who would be watching me on the live video. Mom and Dad stayed in the waiting area while I followed Detective Curtin down a long hallway lined with photographs of children walking on grass, a ladybug crossing the sidewalk, and two llamas peering over a fence.

We entered a room on the right, with pumpkin-colored walls and two brown leather chairs. Detective Curtin showed me a small circle attached to the wall where a camera would record our interview.

"All right, just so you know, I think you already do know, everything in here is audio and video recorded, and the team of people that I work with, they watch us from the other room. And you'll hear me after check in with them to see if they have any questions."

"Okay."

Detective Curtin waited for me to pick a seat. I chose the chair closest to the door. I tried to make myself as small as possible in that chair. I was a vacuum sealing gross, dirty particles into a tiny compartment so that no one could touch me, no one could hurt me.

Detective Curtin perched on the edge of her seat and folded her hands in her lap. She looked me in the eyes and held my gaze. "The number one rule is that everything we talk about is the truth."

"Mm-hmm."

"Do you promise to do that today?"

"Yes, I promise."

My hands trembled as I laid out exactly what had happened in the mechanical room. I had nothing to hide. Yes, I was okay with kissing. Yes, I put my arms above my head when he stripped off my shirt.

"I said no to him pulling down my underwear, which I thought would send him the message that I didn't want him to do anything below there. And I thought it was going to be like, okay, she doesn't want me down there, I understand, I'm not even going to try to have sex with her, but he kept on trying. I said no twice, and then he just went on down and around anyways."

Detective Curtin asked me to explain the Senior Salute and the competition among the boys. I told her that senior guys are constantly targeting third formers, particularly those with older siblings. I mentioned the secret snuggle invitations I'd received from Andrew and Duncan. I shared that Owen was aggressive with other girls. Someone from the other room told Detective Curtin to ask me for names. I gave them.

After talking for more than an hour, Detective Curtin asked if I could take her to the top of the Lindsay building. Maybe they could find the flannel blanket Owen brought. Maybe he'd left behind a condom.

"Would you remember how to get there if we were in the building?" Detective Curtin asked.

"Yes, I think so," I said.

Dad drove me and Mom back to St. Paul's, and Buzz met us out front of Lindsay. I was sandwiched between my parents as we climbed the stairs—Dad up front, Mom following behind. Panic jumped up my ribs with each step.

"You only have to stay for a few moments so that we know where to search for evidence," Detective Curtin said.

As the school's security officer opened the door at the top of the stairs, we could hear the roaring machines. The police and security officer walked ahead and turned on the lights. I saw thin copper pipes, white PVC tubes, a red fire hose, and metal vents. The vents I'd stared at when he was inside me.

My feet were cemented to the floor. I couldn't go any farther. The harsh lights exposed what this was: a trap. A locked door with noisy machines. No one could have heard me even if I had screamed.

"Where did he lay down the blanket?" Detective Curtin asked gingerly.

All I could do was point to the ground before crumpling into Mom's arms.

"I want to go, I want to go," I bawled. "I can't do this."

I collapsed on the landing outside and faced the wall. Dad tried to hug me from behind, but my body went rigid.

"I just want to get out of here," I pleaded.

I couldn't wait around to see if they found any evidence.

"Yes, sweetie, let's go," Dad said.

Mom and Dad each took one of my shaking arms and guided me down the stairs.

"Let's get your stuff and leave," Mom said.

Back in my dorm, we quickly shoved clothes and posters into bags and boxes as if there was a ticking time bomb. Mom, usually an organization wizard, angrily hurled things into cardboard boxes. Dad tried his best to stay calm and dutifully taped up boxes and hauled them out to the car. Mom and Dad were like that—when one got upset, the other tried to keep their cool. No one stopped by to say good-bye or ask if I was okay or needed help packing.

I debated what to do with my furry white beanbag chair. It was too big to fit in the rental car, but I didn't want to have to buy a new one in the fall. It never crossed my mind that I wouldn't return. My parents still lived in Hong Kong. St. Paul's was my home.

"Maybe I could store it at Dylan's house, at the rectory?" I suggested.

Mom hissed something at Dad in the corner. I could barely make it out: "There is no way I'm letting her come back."

NINE

A House Divided

I was back in Naples, spread out like a starfish on my queen-size bed. A quilt of emotions covered me: confusion, fear, paranoia, sadness. I dug up my old turquoise-blue journal from my bedside table, the one I'd started after the earthquake three years ago, and began writing down the thoughts ricocheting in my head.

> *I also feel overwhelmed although the events that happened in Concord, NH are not always, vibrantly on my mind (I think because this area now has no constant +physical landmark reminders) ... I know I am doing the right thing, but am I really willing to ruin someone's life to prove a point to him or the school? Yes (yet my hands are still shaking.)*

I hadn't shared much with Lucy when we met up for a couple of days in New York City on the way back from Concord. She was coming from graduation parties in Block Island and heading off to Paris for a celebratory trip with her St. Paul's friends. She couldn't, or wouldn't, absorb what had happened.

We talked briefly in the hotel in New York one morning after she had brunch with a friend, Poppy, who'd dated Owen during the fall of senior year. He supposedly did something bad to her, too.

"Poppy said she hopes he gets what he deserves," Lucy recounted to me and Mom. "She's glad you're speaking out."

I didn't even know Poppy. Ivy texted me that the police had interviewed another third former about her encounter with Owen.

> Ivy: . . . she wanted me to pass on to you that she's here for you if you ever want to talk.
> Me: Oh my god. Okay. I was wondering if they were going to do that. Wow tell her thank you for reaching out, and that I am so sorry for putting her in that situation.

I was relieved that the girls seemed to be on my side. I felt guilty burdening them and their families with such an uncomfortable topic. I didn't want my classmates to hate me. I hoped the police would hurry up with their investigation. Owen still didn't seem to have a clue that he was in any trouble in his most recent message.

> Owen: hiii chessy so we just got back to the states from our absolute bender in montreal so I'm pretty dead but also hoping things have quieted down a little . . .

I forwarded the note to Detective Curtin along with the other messages he sent. The police were planning to interview him soon. I hoped he would be scared shitless.

In the meantime, my parents were on high alert. They treated me as if I was one of the orchids in our house, fretting that I would lose my delicate petals at any moment. Are you hungry? Are you tired? Are you lonely?

I was annoyed at Dad for violating my personal space—writing down my Facebook and email passwords and looking at both accounts while I was sitting right next to him!

Their worrying was now oppressive, even when it was warranted. My resentment built and I had a meltdown on a family bicycle ride to the beach. I barely made it across the street before the pressure of the hard seat between my legs became intolerable. Mom led Christianna away while Dad tried to console me as I curled up behind the large green garbage containers on the side of the driveway.

Once I calmed down, my panic converted into anger. Biking—a favorite family activity—was completely out of the question. Owen had stolen my virginity and now he'd taken this? And in one fell swoop, I'd managed to frighten Mom, Dad, and my little sister.

I was determined to prove to myself and everyone else that I was stronger and wiser because of all this. Later that day Mom and Dad brought me into the living room. I sat stiffly on the couch and focused on Dad's black lacquer table, which we'd brought over from Japan, and saw my childhood before me: slurping udon noodles on Friday nights, twirling around for dance parties, playing with Barbies. Would that little girl ever come back?

Mom interrupted my trip down memory lane.

"Chess, what happened out there?" she asked, her blue eyes burrowing into mine.

Silence. I had nothing to say. Nothing I could say. I used to tell Mom everything, but a new era had dawned. Detective Curtin had advised me not to share details of my assault with anyone in order to preserve the integrity of the investigation. I tried to keep everything bottled up inside, but a tear crept out. Mom came over to hug me. I pushed her away as my body turned to stone.

"Don't touch me," I snapped.

Mom sniffled and then wept softly. I felt horrible for hurting her feelings, but I didn't want to be touched. Especially without her asking first.

I talked plenty with Dr. Sloane. We reunited right after I came home to Naples. We met twice a week, sometimes for an hour and a half, double my usual sessions.

I wanted to let my best friend Arielle know what was going on, but I couldn't find the right time, the right words. I attempted to corner her during a birthday celebration at her house, but our friend Paige wouldn't leave the kitchen. Finally, I just blurted it out to the both of them.

"So . . . this thing happened at school with a boy. The police are involved and there's an investigation."

Arielle's jaw plummeted and her eyes went dead.

"I was sexually assaulted—raped—or whatever."

"Oh my God, I'm so sorry," Arielle said.

"Chessy, that's terrible. What can we do?" Paige asked.

They were kind and caring. I didn't think Arielle or Paige could actually help me, but it was too tiring to keep such a big secret.

My body was exhausted yet my mind never stopped wandering. I'd lie motionless in bed, questioning my faith. Why was this happening to me? What if I'd never gone out that night? I just wanted to be a normal fifteen-year-old riding my bike, going to the beach, learning how to drive.

I hoped to find my way back to God on a youth missionary trip to an orphanage in the Bahamas. Lucy had done some missionary work when we lived in Asia, and now it was my turn. A friend from North Naples United Methodist Church had encouraged me to join the excursions for teens she'd led over the last several years. I'd signed up months ago and had a ticket for the end of June. But Mom and Dad were so distressed that they suggested I cancel the trip.

"I don't want you to go someplace by yourself," Mom said.

"You need to be around your family right now," Dad agreed.

I understood their concerns. I was apprehensive about not knowing anyone, but I didn't have any fears about my safety. It was a chance for me to be my own person, not the girl who'd just been sexually assaulted. None of these kids knew anything about it.

"I've been looking forward to this. I made a commitment. Please let me go," I begged. "Besides, I need to fulfill my required community service hours for St. Paul's."

I started having doubts about the wisdom of the trip after boarding a prop plane in Nassau with fraying seat belts and a broken AC. It didn't help matters that I had to sign a legal document before I left, picking which funeral home I would want to be shipped back to in Florida in case I died.

I inhaled the stale, hot air and gazed at the ocean during our thirty-minute journey to Cat Island, a remote stretch of sand in the central Bahamas with a population of about 1,500 people. Here, the main attraction was Mount Alvernia, the tallest point in the Bahamas at roughly two hundred feet above sea level. It was topped by a stone monastery called the Hermitage, which offered a spectacular view of the lush island and aquamarine waters sweeping to the horizon.

When the plane door opened, a cool breeze settled my stomach. Ten of us loaded into a silver van meant for six people. By the time we arrived at the Old Bight Mission Home and Orphanage, my butt was covered in sweat. That would be a constant for the next week.

Old Bight takes care of children who have been removed from their families because of abuse, neglect, or other problems. I had envisioned sad, mopey kids. But as we pulled up to the home, a bevy of beautiful children chased our van into the gravel driveway and screamed with excitement. I felt like a movie star as I opened the door, with kids climbing all over me—a stranger—offering hugs and warm welcomes to their gorgeous island.

We woke up every morning at six thirty a.m. to Christian rock tunes and songs from Florence + the Machine. The sun boiled in those early hours, and hornets greeted me as soon as I rolled off my leaky air mattress. We prepared breakfast and kept tabs on the water. There was only one pitcher in the main house fridge for all eleven children.

We spent our days hosting different stations that combined arts and crafts and science projects with daily Bible lessons. We assembled in the sanctuary for worship after breakfast, before lunch, and after dinner. During free time in the afternoons, the girls braided my hair and then we jumped for hours with the boys on the black trampoline on the scrubby lawn.

Mark, one of the smallest boys, stole my heart immediately. He was seven years old, always wearing pants that were too big and falling down. I found a bandanna and fashioned it into a belt by tying it around his waist. During worship one day, he sat on my lap and fell asleep. I adored holding him. I was protecting him as much as he was protecting me.

The kids reminded me of the joys of human connection. They were filled with love and grace, and their spirits were as high as the Hermitage. I realized that nothing sticks to your soul like love. Everything else could be washed away.

I felt lucky to be there. Yes, I was doing volunteer work, but it was a privilege that my parents had to pay for. Cat Island provided a temporary escape, a refuge from the trauma that waited for me back home.

Each night I read stories from a Disney Princess collection to the girls and then gathered with the other volunteers in the living room of our house. We discussed Bible passages and answered questions about how the text had meaning in our lives. What do you worry about? Have you ever been in a situation where you were in need? What happened?

The topics couldn't have been more relevant, but I had my own set of questions. Did I want to tell them? How would this church community react to a sex crime? Would they blame me? I pondered these questions by myself at night outside the chapel as I searched for the Milky Way in the star-studded sky.

During the week, other volunteers confided deeply personal struggles with illnesses and being gay. Everyone offered compassion, which made me relieved and helped restore my faith a bit. On Thursday night, we sat in our usual circle and discussed a parable about how we should use what God has given us and provided for us. This time, the question had instructions: How has God gifted you personally? *Make sure everyone answers this one!*

I exhaled loudly when my turn came. I started out slowly, halting, hesitating.

"It's such a gift to be here on Cat Island and meet all these people and make all these relationships . . . I've learned so much from the kids at a time when I really needed to learn from them . . . and find a way to get back to God."

Silence. Deep breath.

"At my boarding school, I was assaulted on campus by a student there . . . I've been dealing with the aftermath of all that for the last couple of weeks . . . It's made me question what my purpose on earth is."

Then my words began flowing like the ocean waves around us.

"Being here and being able to see the kids and their raw, unadulterated faith and belief in God even though they have faced much worse than I have ever faced has made me realize that if they can get through it, so can I. Instead of saying why me, I can be thankful for what I have and be strong."

I glanced around and saw nodding heads, mournful eyes. There was a smattering of "I'm sorrys" and "Are you okays." I had done it.

On the seventh day, our last day on Cat Island, little Mark closed our worship service with a thoughtful prayer, thanking us for everything we'd done. With his eyes fluttered shut, the sweet Bahamian boy ended his prayer by saying, "And please bless Chessy on her way home. Please bless Chessy."

From my sweaty metal seat, I cried, tears sliding down my cheeks. After our group's farewell lunch of crab and rice and barbecue chicken—most likely the chicken we'd played with earlier—we undertook our difficult good-byes.

I searched for Mark so I could tell him how much I appreciated his prayer. I saw him making the rounds and heard him lovingly call each female leader by my name, Chessy. He had been praying for all the women on the team. He was using my name as a symbol for every woman who brought love, kindness, and relief. Now I knew I had something to live up to, especially when I got back to St. Paul's. I could be a voice for voiceless survivors. I could help others. I had found my purpose.

I returned to Naples with love bursting from my heart and mosquito bites destroying the backs of my legs. I scratched and scratched without realizing what I was doing. I couldn't feel my nails across my skin, the blood dripping, the scabs ripping open again and again. Nothing. I just kept clawing until the wounds got infected and Mom hauled me to the doctor.

My Cat Island glow quickly wore off as I found our house submerged in anxiety. Dad's boss seemed to be giving him a hard time for taking off work. I shriveled up whenever anyone tried to be affectionate. Our close relatives criticized Mom for considering my return to St. Paul's. One even told her to "act like a goddamn adult."

Mom and Dad were still trying to sort through the wreckage as I dug in my heels. The guy who assaulted me was gone, and so were his buddies. This was my education, after all. He couldn't take that away too. Lucy was biting her tongue so hard I thought it would fall off.

I hoped Lucy would come around by the time we left for Italy. We were headed there for the first time as a family since Dad's sister got married in Venice back in 2000. We'd long talked about spending summers with them in Italy, and Dad finally planned a trip around Mom's fiftieth birthday.

There seemed like no better time to flee the United States. We'd learned that the Concord Police had enough to pursue certain charges against Owen, but they wanted to question other potential victims and gather additional evidence. If he was getting arrested, I wanted to get the hell out of the country.

We stopped for a few days in New York City to see Grandma Prout, Aunt Frannie, and Aunt Cathy. Lucy and I were walking on the Upper East Side past the Guggenheim Museum when I told her that she needed to respect my feelings—my anxiety over what happened and my desire to go back to St. Paul's.

"Respect? Let's talk about respect," Lucy shot back. "Why did you go see Owen even though you knew I had had a relationship with him? That totally violates sister code."

"I know, I know, I'm sorry," I stammered. "I've wanted to apologize to you for a while, but I didn't want to bring it up."

"I'm furious at him, but I'm also upset with you. I told you what to expect, why you shouldn't engage in the Senior Salute," Lucy said. "They're gross, sleazy guys."

"I went because my friend told me he was different," I explained. "I felt special that he was giving me attention."

"Ugh," Lucy sighed. "I could have prevented this."

The guilt I felt for not listening to Lucy consumed me. I never should have changed my mind and agreed to meet Owen. I could have saved myself and my family so much pain if I hadn't gone to a secluded place with a guy I didn't know well. I was too trusting, too naive. I felt like it was all my fault. It would take me years to accept what now seems obvious: rape is not a punishment for poor judgment.

During our family vacation that summer, I'd stay up late and scour the Internet for any updates on the case. On our second day in Italy, news broke on Owen's arrest. The reports described him as a six-foot soccer player who studies at Harvard, a presidential scholar. I, on the other hand, was just a fifteen-year-old female student, a nameless victim. I was nothing. I felt sick. I read through the comments and saw anonymous posters referring to me as a liar, a scorned ex-girlfriend, a slut, an attention grabber. One person on a local CBS Boston website outed my name in the comments section.

I raced to the bathroom and threw up my spaghetti into the toilet. I banged on the door of my parents' room, sobbing. It was one a.m. Dad immediately emailed Detective Curtin and Mr. Hirschfeld. The CBS site eventually redacted my name, but who knew how long it was up there? And why were people spewing so much venom at me? I was the *victim*. Owen had done something to hurt me.

I hoped he felt as bad as I did. I wanted this to be a wake-up call for him and his family so he realized the seriousness of his actions. He needed to own up to what he'd done to me and to other girls. I pulled the covers over my head and slept with Mom and Dad. So much for their romantic getaway.

Mom carted us out of bed the next day. She wasn't going to let this wreck our family vacation. Later that night, as Christianna and I got ready for dinner, I heard loud voices coming from Mom and Dad's room. Christianna was only eight, but she knew that something bad had happened to me that made everyone sad and angry. I tried to distract her while eavesdropping on the yelling next door.

"Why would you let her go back to the school where that happened?" Lucy shouted. "You don't understand the culture there."

"Luce, how is it that bad? I never saw this stuff when I was there," Dad said. "Besides, if Chessy goes back, there will be lots of adults looking out for her."

"I don't care how many teachers are watching over her. She is going to get chewed up and spat back out," Lucy hollered. "If I was treated so badly just for breaking up with Brooks, she is going to be treated a million times worse for getting someone arrested."

"But she's a victim," Mom said. "The police clearly found enough evidence against him."

"You don't know St. Paul's like I know it. Do the math. He was a popular guy and this was a school tradition," Lucy warned. "If you let her go back, I'm never going to talk to you again."

Lucy barged into our room and glowered at me. Christianna twisted herself around me like a cobra. Maybe if she squeezed hard enough, she could keep me there forever.

We then traveled on to Hong Kong to pack up my family's apartment on the twenty-ninth floor overlooking Repulse Bay. I hated that Mom and Dad lived so far away, but I loved visiting Hong Kong's vibrant markets. Where else could you eat a bowl of ramen and then get a foot massage at ten p.m.—all in the same building?

Dad was filling out paperwork so that he could take a formal unpaid leave of absence from his job. He wanted to stay close to New Hampshire to support me and the legal process. Mom and Christianna would move back to Naples and start over again there.

Dad assured me repeatedly that it was his decision and it was no burden at all to the family. Things had been strained at work since he'd spoken up a few months ago about a colleague who he believed was misusing funds. Instead of thanking Dad, his boss ostracized him. It went from bad to worse after I was assaulted. When Dad explained why he couldn't return to work immediately, his boss retorted, "I certainly hope your daughter gains better judgment in the future."

His boss was a jerk. But he wasn't a lone real-life troll. I knew there were classmates at St. Paul's who would judge me. I assumed that the worst they would do was ignore me. Mr. Hirschfeld sent several letters to the school community over the summer, and I hoped his words like "alarming" and "serious breach" resonated with them. At first, I felt comforted by his August 7 email, which stated:

> Dear Students and Parents,
> . . . While the allegation and the people it involves will not be a topic of conversation at the School, the broader issues it raises—the use of social media to perpetuate unhealthy relationships, the "hook-up" culture and unsanctioned student "traditions"—will be. Students will be supported in these conversations when they return to the School. . . .
> Sincerely,
> Rector Hirschfeld

All I wanted was support. When we arrived back in Naples, Mom scheduled a group session with Dr. Sloane. Mom and Dad were still very reluctant to send me back to St. Paul's.

Dr. Sloane was a New York transplant with dark curly hair that came down to her shoulders. She was a no-bullshit therapist who had a potty mouth just like me. I usually sat on her charcoal-gray couch while she settled into a chair in the corner of the room. I'd study the books on her shelves—*Yoga for Depression, Feminist Family Therapy, Staying Sober*—and admire her small golden figure of Ganesha, the Hindu god with an elephant head who is revered as the remover of obstacles.

For our group session, we met in a different room with cushioned black chairs arranged in a circle. Dr. Sloane got right to the point: "So the purpose of this meeting is for Chessy to talk about why it's so important for her to go back to school and how she is prepared to deal with the various issues that may arise. Chessy, why don't you start?"

"I want to be there. I deserve to be there," I said. "He's taken away so much from me, so much from us. I don't want to him take away my education, too. St. Paul's is my school. I trust my friends to know that what happened to me was wrong and to help me through it. Everyone was so supportive after my health leave last year."

"But what if that doesn't happen, sweetie?" Mom asked. "What if there is backlash from other students? I want to make sure you don't turn your anger inward."

"I know it's not going to be perfect there. But I have Buzz. And Catie," I insisted. "There are just so many goals I have with piano and singing and Japanese. I can't give that up. I can't run home to Mommy and Daddy. I want to show people I'm strong. I'm stronger than this."

"We know you are. But we want to make sure you stay strong if it gets tough," Dad said. "You need to be able to wave the white flag if things aren't going well."

"I will. I'll get help if I need it," I said. "I won't try to hurt myself."

"We're going to visit every week, but we can't be there every moment," Dad said. "How can we get you a larger support network at the school?"

"Are there other adults who can support you besides Buzz?" Mom asked. "Is there a way to have another adviser? Maybe Mrs. Hebra? Or Lucy's adviser, Ms. Carter?"

"Maybe," I said.

"That's a good idea to build up the support network," Dr. Sloane said. "You can hear how important it is for Chessy to go back and to feel like she has control and power over her life. If she doesn't return, she'll always wonder what it could have been like."

Weeks after my assault, I went on a mission trip to Cat Island in the Bahamas. The kids there taught me that I could survive and fight for justice.

TEN

Shunned

I vy wouldn't even look at me. It was late August and we were standing in our wood cabin at Team Prep, a volleyball training camp near Sebago Lake in Casco, Maine.

The girls were scrambling to find bunkmates and flinging knee pads and spandex onto beds they claimed as their own. I tried to catch Ivy's attention, but she locked eyes with Haley, whose older brother was best friends with Owen. The last time I saw Haley during graduation weekend, she had her arm around my shoulder and promised me everything would be okay. Now I felt a chill sweep across the room.

I glanced down at my red toenail polish and waited for the girls to finish pairing up. I was left a sagging bottom bunk below Erin, a sweet girl who had been unfairly deemed worthless by the social climbers because she was a little overweight and spoke her mind.

I HAVE THE RIGHT TO

We headed over to the volleyball courts, where things actually mattered. The coach greeted us and instructed us to do warm-ups, passing the ball back and forth with a partner.

Ivy had been my bump partner for most of last season. We'd sing loudly to "Reflections" by MisterWives, a Kygo remix of "Younger," and other music on the practice playlist. We'd do silly moves like setting the ball backward and then laugh hysterically.

But this time, when I turned around to find Ivy, she already had a partner. All my good friends had found someone. Someone who wasn't me. I wished Lucy was there.

I tried to stay upbeat when Dad picked me up a few days later. I gave my friends and teammates the benefit of the doubt. Maybe I was just being overly sensitive. Either way, I didn't want Dad to worry and have second thoughts about letting me return to St. Paul's.

"How was it, sweetie?" Dad asked.

"Good," I said.

I knew Mom and Dad hated when I gave one-word answers like that.

"Things were okay with the team?"

"It was fine," I said.

"You sure?" Dad asked skeptically.

"Yeah, some of the girls didn't really talk to me that much, but it's okay," I said, before changing the subject. "So what music do you want to listen to?"

I settled in as copilot for our journey across Maine, New Hampshire, and Massachusetts to meet up with family in Hillsdale, New York. But first, and most importantly, was food. Dad and I shared a passion for eating. We planned our days, our trips, our lives around finding delicious meals.

We needed the best lobster roll—we were in Maine, after all—and our destination was Clam Shack in Kennebunk. After I plugged the address into the GPS, Dad fed me his music requests and we jammed to "Lady" by the Little River Band and then rapped to "Ice Ice Baby." Dad got so into it that he pumped both fists in the air, forgetting he was driving.

About an hour in, Dad turned down the volume and put on his serious voice. He told me he had met the day before with the Merrimack County district attorney's office about my case. They hoped to reach a plea agreement, but they needed to wait until Owen completed a psychosexual evaluation.

"Okay," I mumbled, not processing any of it.

"And there's another thing," Dad said softly. "They did some testing and found traces of semen on your underwear."

"Oh my God," I gasped. "Dad, now they have to know I'm not lying! It's not just my word against his."

"Chess, we've always believed you. That was never even a question."

"Yeah, but this is so much more real now," I sputtered. "All those lies he was saying that he didn't have sex with me. He's a hundred percent lying. This is indisputable now."

"Absolutely, and he's going to pay the price and get in big trouble," Dad said.

"Yeah, but those people who commented online and called me a liar and slut . . ."

"Those people are ignorant assholes and don't know the truth." Dad turned red with anger and his voice rumbled like thunder. Then he got quiet. "You know the truth. We know the truth. The police know the truth. And that's what matters."

But Dad's attempts to comfort me didn't make me feel any better. It was another reminder that I was not okay, that this thing had happened to me. It was as if I was being violated all over again, like somebody was trying to get inside of me. I crossed my legs to protect my private parts. I wanted to roll out of the car.

When we finally pulled up to Clam Shack, overlooking the water and Dock Square, I had no appetite for juicy lobster meat. I just wanted one thing: to be believed. And now we had proof. It all seemed so simple.

Dad drove me back to St. Paul's in early September for volleyball preseason. All the athletes arrived a few days early to move in and start practice. Dad planned to stick around for the rest of the week to talk with Mr. Hirschfeld, Buzz, and the security team at the school to make sure I would be safe.

We had a brief meeting together with Mr. Hirschfeld in his office, where he called me an inspiration. I wasn't sure who I was inspiring, but it was nice that he said it.

I hoped things would return to normal with Ivy and my other teammates now that we were back on campus. I was terrified of walking around by myself, especially going to the Upper and facing the senior couches on my own. The last thing I wanted was attention.

Catie and the rest of the students wouldn't show up for several days, so I needed the volleyball girls by my side. During practice, I asked Ivy and another teammate if they could pick me up on their way to dinner so we could walk together.

"I definitely can't see those guys alone," I explained.

"Yeah, of course! No prob," Ivy replied.

Around six p.m., I saw Ivy slip outside the front door of the dorm and walk past my window facing the chapel. Maybe she'd forgotten me. I couldn't chase her across campus. That would look ridiculous. Maybe she would come back if I messaged her.

> Me: Did you guys head to dinner already?
> Ivy: Ooff ya we are getting to the upper now Haley was
> calling me

At first I tried to make excuses to protect myself and my friendship with Ivy. As I sat in my room and peeled open a tangerine, I felt more alone than I ever had before. For the next few days, I subsisted mostly on Luna bars for breakfast and tangerines for dinner when it became clear that plans we made were not plans Ivy intended to keep. I started to get mad and had silent fights in my head: Why was she ditching me? What had I done to her?

Whenever I saw Ivy, she gave me weird looks—if she even looked at me at all. The next night, I tried to find common ground with treats.

> Me: Hey, my dad just brought me a ton of snacks, if you
>   need some tonight come by! ☺
> Ivy: Awesome! I actually have some too but that's sweet

I don't think she had ever rebuffed a snack before. Thankfully, Dylan and Lilly were around. They invited me to get ice cream in town with Mrs. Hebra and her daughter Reese, who was in my grade. I girded myself for the two-minute walk from Con20 to the flagpole. I stayed hyperalert, my head spinning in all directions like in *The Exorcist*. What was in front of me? Who was behind me? Was I in danger?

I noticed the hockey boys up ahead congregating on benches outside the post office. As I got closer, about half a dozen guys stood up in unison and turned toward me, including some of the boys who had aggressively pursued me and Ivy the year before.

One hockey player who stood near the front pointed in my direction, and the rest followed his lead. I looked behind me, thinking there was another hockey bro. But there was nobody. The team was staring me down, trying to intimidate me. I was shaking by the time I opened the door to Mrs. Hebra's car.

"Did you guys see that? Or was it just me?" I said. "Those hockey boys all just stood up and pointed at me. It was crazy."

"I'm sure it's nothing," said Mrs. Hebra, the vice rector, who now worked as a dorm adviser in Simpson, where many of the hockey boys lived. "But if you want, I can talk to them."

"No, it's fine!"

I was petrified of making waves. I held my breath and pressed my lips together in the backseat. Dylan gave me a knowing smile and filled me in on his summer vacation. I told him that Ivy bailed on dinner plans and Dylan suggested we order in sushi that week and eat at his dad's house.

"We can go over to the rectory anytime if you want to escape the Upper," Dylan offered.

"Thanks," I said. "I'll definitely take you up on that."

I tried to forget the hockey boys as we pulled up to Arnie's Place, an old-school ice cream and burger shop with red-and-white checkered floors. I rested my elbows on the sticky countertop and ordered a small cup of vanilla Heath bar crunch. It immediately brightened my mood, and I smiled in the pictures Reese, Dylan, Lilly, and I took together, posting some to my Snapchat story in hopes of seeming fine and normal.

The sugar rush—and the temporary courage it fueled—wore off when Mrs. Hebra dropped me at Con20. My breath quickened and my hands trembled as I searched for the red high-heel door stopper Mom had bought to keep my door propped open. Instead I slammed the door shut and jammed the shoe between the bottom of the white door and the carpet so that no one could open it from the outside. Especially not the hockey boys.

I didn't tell Dad about barricading myself in my room. I figured that wouldn't happen again once Catie arrived. Besides, he had more important things to focus on. We had our first meeting with the attorneys working on the criminal case coming up.

A couple of days later, Dad and I pulled up to a redbrick building across the street from the Merrimack County Superior Courthouse. A woman with long dark hair and thick glasses introduced herself as

Barbara, a victim advocate. She led us to a conference room, where Catherine Ruffle, the deputy county attorney handling the case, stood up and shook our hands.

Back in June at the Child Advocacy Center, Dad had met a different lawyer, David Rotman, who frequently prosecuted sex crimes. But Catherine seemed really smart and approachable. She and Barbara spoke in soft, comforting voices but didn't try to sugarcoat anything.

"Don't compare this to what you see on TV or you'll end up being disappointed," Barbara said. "The criminal justice system is not user-friendly."

Catherine explained that there were two paths forward: a plea or a trial. It could take several months to negotiate a deal in which Owen would plead guilty to certain charges and receive some form of punishment. If that failed, the case would go to trial, and that process could take a year.

A year? The gravity of all this was sinking in. I played out the worst-case scenario in my head.

"Will I have to see him again? Will he be in the courtroom?"

"If there was a trial, you would see him," Catherine said.

My stomach lurched.

"What if the jury doesn't believe me?" I asked.

"Juries are unpredictable," Catherine explained. "It's our job to convince them beyond a reasonable doubt. We believe you and that's why we're here today."

I nodded.

"Hopefully we can reach an agreement and avoid a trial," she added.

"How are things going for you at school?" Barbara asked.

"Some of my friends are distancing themselves and it's hurtful," I said. "No one is talking to me about what happened, and I guess that's okay."

"These kinds of cases can polarize people," Barbara explained.

"I'm here to help you, and I want you to reach out to me and use me as a support if something is going on beyond your control."

"I just don't want to be an alleged victim," I sighed. "I want people to believe me."

"Chessy, 'victim' is the wrong word. You're a survivor," Barbara said. "You've made it through a terrible experience, and we're here to help you get justice."

Survivor. I liked that word. I wasn't a faceless, nameless victim. I was a survivor seeking justice.

I had no interest in reconnecting with Owen MacIntyre, but he kept messaging that he wanted to talk.

> O. Mac: Hey Chessy just wanted to say sorry again for what happened and that I hope we can talk when we get back to school when you are ready. Miss you ❤

I was furious with him for convincing me to go on the Senior Salute and then pressuring me not to tell anyone what happened. I had heard rumors he might get kicked off campus for "pimping" me out.

I would have preferred to curl up in bed, but I didn't want to be rude and lose all my friends. Besides, I was warned that Mr. Hirschfeld told O. Mac he had to apologize to me, so I didn't really have a choice. The pale sun was falling in the sky when O. Mac met me in front of my dorm. We walked up the brick path past Nash and toward the Upper.

"Look, I'm supposed to apologize to you. I'm really sorry for pushing you to do something you didn't want to do," he said.

"Thank you," I said. "I appreciate you saying that. I wish I never went."

"Yeah, so much has happened."

"Honestly, it's been really, really hard with the police, the hospital, school. It's hurt me a lot. Some of the girls are ignoring me," I said. "None of the guys are talking to me either."

"That's just like the way boys are," O. Mac said. "We stick together." Jeez, how archaic.

"It's been hard for me, too," O. Mac whined. "I'm catching so much shit for this. Mr. Hirschfeld called me into his office and he contacted my parents. I was so scared when the police came up and knocked on my door and, like, started asking me questions."

We turned left on the road behind the Upper and headed toward Kehaya. I looked up at the indigo sky to try and calm myself. I floated up there on top of a pile of clouds as the sun warmed my face.

"Yeah, I really turned my back on Owen by talking to the police," he said. "I think I should apologize to Owen, too. I should call him."

"What? Why would you do that?" I said, choking on my own breath. "You want to apologize to him for not lying to the police?"

"Yeah, I turned my back on my friend."

"Why are you telling me this?" I hissed. "He's the one who did something wrong. You should never feel bad about telling the truth."

"But yeah—"

I cut off O. Mac before he could say something stupid again.

"Thank you for coming here and talking to me," I said. "I hope things can get back to normal."

I waved good-bye and stormed inside Con20. Was he expecting me to have sympathy for him because he felt guilty for being disloyal to the person who'd assaulted me? O. Mac was being disloyal to me! Did he have to have an internal examination done? No. He should shut the fuck up.

These kids cared only about themselves. Ivy and my other volleyball friends had glommed onto Sally, the bully who months earlier had tried to block me from dinner conversation before our winter formal. Now Sally was the ringleader of my "haters," calling me a liar and telling girls on the field hockey team that I was to blame for Nash Bash getting delayed a week. Faith, as usual, was following Ivy's lead and giving me the cold shoulder too.

I wished I could turn to Tabitha, but she had fallen away. She lived in a different dorm and had new friends. And to be honest, I was avoiding her for fear of ripping open old wounds.

I hid under the covers and sulked to Catie that I didn't want to hang out with Ivy and Faith anymore. Catie said she would go talk with them and find out why they were being such bitches. She headed down the hall with a fierce look on her face. A little later, Catie returned to our room and cackled.

"So apparently the two of us are no longer going to be invited to any gatherings, because they feel like you're a liar and have no integrity," Catie announced. "Sorry."

"What?" I winced, completely dumbfounded.

These were the girls who'd seen me moments after my assault, who'd helped me compose the brutal messages to Owen, and who, I'd later learn, told the police that I was shaking, in shock, and had pulled Owen's head away from my vagina. I was the victim, not the villain.

But none of that mattered when I became a liability and threatened their rise to the top of the social stratosphere at St. Paul's. The betrayal cut deep.

"What do these girls know about integrity, or self-respect for that matter?" I exploded.

I looked over at Catie, and my outrage morphed into guilt when I realized that my best friend was getting iced out because of me.

"I'm so sorry, Catie. This is all my fault," I said. "You don't have to be friends with me. I don't want your life to suck because of me."

"Are you kidding me, Chessy? This is stupid of them," Catie said. "You'll always be my friend. Those girls aren't worth it."

"Thank you," I said, biting my lip. "I couldn't do this without you."

The next morning I raced into Buzz's office, a typhoon of tears.

I'd been stopping by twice a week, reduced to a ball of misery in a blue swivel chair. I rocked back and forth as I gave the latest headlines about Ivy.

"Am I really that terrible of a person? Why are they acting this way?"

"You're a good person, Chessy," Buzz said. "This is not okay."

"I might need to go home for good if this continues." I sniffled.

We called my parents together. Buzz did most of the talking as I blubbered in my chair. Dad booked a ticket to fly up that night. Before I left, Buzz reminded me that I could come to Clark House at any time, even just to eat meals.

I lumbered back to my room and found Catie. God, what would I do without her? I felt awful that she was losing friends because of my shit, but she didn't seem to mind. Her full attention was on furnishing our room. She was still receiving guilt money from her dad. Catie had bought a new couch cover, a shelving unit, chalkboard tape, and a large computer monitor that we plugged our laptops into to stream Netflix. It was a creative work-around for the no-TV rule.

She charged pizza after pizza from Domino's and Checkmate's and had them delivered to school. Her dad, who sat on St. Paul's board of trustees, was in the middle of a messy divorce from her mother. Catie and I commiserated about our crappy lives while shoveling slices into our mouths.

We nested together, shutting all the shades and hiding on the couch. We put on movies like *The Fault in Our Stars* and binge-watched episodes of *America's Next Top Model*. I didn't need anyone as long as I had Catie. But then I got a weird text from Ivy. Some adult must have talked to her.

> Ivy: Hey I know this is gonna sound really scarry but can
> we please talk tonight because i know it's been weird
> and I've been weird and it may have come across badly
> and I know you're going through hell right now and I

should be there for you and I'm sorry but I really just
want to talk to you and appologize and like tell you why
I've been so weird cause I want to move forward
Me: Yes, I agree it's been an elephant in the room.

Later that night, Ivy swung by and awkwardly asked if she could come inside. She sat on my red trunk and shed crocodile tears.

"I'm sorry, but you don't know how hard it's been for me to know you, to know that this happened to you. People ask about it and talk about it." She trailed off.

My eyes widened in disbelief. Of course I knew "how hard it's been." I was living it firsthand! I laughed inside and felt sad that she was this self-centered. And I realized in that moment that there are some people in your life who just don't belong there. Ivy was one of them.

When I got back to St. Paul's in fall 2014, many of my volleyball teammates and other classmates ignored me. I'm in the back with jersey number thirteen.

ELEVEN

Numb

I couldn't stop the nightmares. I tried building a fortress of happy thoughts before I went to bed each night: Florida beaches, dressing up with Christianna, slurping noodles with Dad.

But as soon as my head hit the pillow, the castle walls came tumbling down, revealing the mechanical room, my underwear, his face. Sometimes I kicked and screamed. Other times I froze. Most nights, I woke up soaked in sweat. Catie couldn't believe how often I was doing laundry. I cleaned her clothes too—a small consolation prize for sticking with me.

Getting through the days wasn't any easier. My chest tightened whenever I was near the Lindsay building. My physics class was right outside the staircase that led up to the mechanical room.

One day while we were working on an assignment about the composition of pennies, I thought I saw Owen's face in the window. I couldn't talk. My limbs started to shake. My teeth chattered. A tear dripped down my cheek. I really wanted my teacher to notice. I wanted somebody to notice, somebody to care. Nobody even looked at me.

Buzz taught me coping skills to chop down the negative thoughts growing like weeds in my brain. Journaling. Playing piano. Taking deep breaths. Breathing into a paper bag to stop the panic attacks.

I roared through her door one morning after listening to a speech about forgiveness in chapel. The rabbi talked about how she brought books to prisoners, talked with them, and forgave them.

"All I can do is forgive them," the rabbi said.

I fumed to Buzz, "She can't forgive people when she doesn't know what they've done! She doesn't know whose lives they've destroyed or who they've hurt. It's not her job to forgive them!"

The idea that this rabbi or someone else could forgive Owen and set him free made my blood boil. He hadn't shown any remorse or acknowledged any responsibility for his actions.

"I don't think I'll ever forgive him," I declared.

"You might never forgive him," Buzz said. "But have you forgiven yourself?"

I twirled that question around in my brain for a while. If I was truly honest, I still blamed myself for not screaming or kicking. For going there in the first place. But now, raw anger was displacing the shame. I was livid at Owen for doing this to me. I was enraged at my classmates for shunning me and calling me a liar. No one blames people who are beaten up and have their wallets stolen, but somehow my peers believed I was at fault for having my virginity stolen.

Mom and Dad tried their best to support me, taking turns flying to New Hampshire every week. Mom wrote emails to administrators and gave suggestions to help improve St. Paul's culture. She shared books with Mrs. Hebra about empowering women, like *The Invention of Wings* by Sue Monk Kidd.

Mrs. Hebra politely accepted the materials but tempered Mom's expectations. "Susan, change needs to be organic."

Whatever the hell that meant. Dad planted himself in the rector's office and even offered to become St. Paul's head of discipline. He was used to running a business with billions of dollars at stake. All he wanted now was to make the school he loved safe for me and for all the students there.

But the culture at St. Paul's was too strong to dismantle alone. He tried to help me not lose sight of who I was and what I was fighting for. We'd sit together in his rental car and call Ron Bard, a family friend who was Tokyo's soothsayer and a psychic who helped solve police cases. He'd been written up in *Forbes* magazine and had supposedly advised celebrities like Brad Pitt. I'd only met Ron once, but we called him Uncle Ron and I'd heard tons of stories about the things he foretold in our extended family.

"Chessy, the assault isn't what's going to hurt you the most. It's the betrayal from friends and people you trust that will have the biggest impact on your life," Uncle Ron explained.

I wanted to believe that the pain from the assault itself would ease over time. I still couldn't be touched by my family. I wouldn't let Dad hug me, and I almost threw Christianna over the side of my lofted bed after she tackled me during a visit with Mom.

"Please don't do that, it really hurts me," I scolded her. "I get scared when other people touch me. It's not your fault."

Christianna looked up with wounded eyes. My poor little sister was clueless. Sometimes I had no idea what was going on either. I had more and more trouble concentrating, not just with my mind but with my body.

I'd scratch an itch on my arm but feel nothing. I'd bang my leg against a table without it hurting. I fell during volleyball practice and it was as if it never happened. I dragged a brush across my scalp, but it seemed like I was brushing someone else's hair. Why couldn't I feel anything? I was so scared and thought I was truly losing it. It took weeks to muster up the courage to tell Buzz about the numbness.

"This is your body's way of protecting you. It's what your body did during the actual attack to get you through it," Buzz explained. "It's a common symptom for PTSD."

During the summer, Dr. Sloane had explained that my panic attacks were related to my sexual assault, but she didn't give a definite label. It was a relief to hear that the numbness was also typical. I wasn't going crazy.

"Sometimes I feel like I'm floating," I said to Buzz. "Like right now, I don't feel like I'm here."

"Okay, Chessy, we're going to do some techniques to regroup and become present," Buzz said. "Let's look around the room. Over there, there's a blue picture on the wall. Do you see what day it is on the calendar?"

"Yes."

"And do you see sunshine coming through the room from the window over there?" Buzz asked. "Do you see I have both feet on the floor and a cold drink in my hand?"

"Yes."

"Now, let's do some tapping of our feet on the floor. First let's tap our right leg, then our left. Now let's tap our left hand and then our right hand."

Slowly I reinhabited my body. I was relieved to be back, at least for now. Dad and Lucy were visiting for the weekend, and I hadn't seen Lucy since she started at Georgetown.

She showed up covered in Sharpie marker from some kind of volleyball party the night before. I didn't ask too many questions—I was just glad she was there. Dad and Lucy cheered from the bleachers during my volleyball game. At halftime, Lucy and I passed the ball on the sidelines for old times' sake. Then we all got Thai food at Siam Orchid for dinner.

"I don't want to go back to the dorm," I said to Dad. "I'm staying with you guys at the hotel."

Lucy and I hijacked the bed and watched episodes of *Scandal* as Dad snoozed on the couch. The next day was Ecofest, and I was reluctant to go.

"It's all about taking photos, and I know it's going to be people not asking me to take photos," I said to Lucy. "I don't want to be in a place where nobody wants me."

"Just try it for a little. There are people who want you there," Lucy insisted.

I put on a blue-and-white-plaid flannel and tried to look the part of a happy prep-school kid. While I was listening to the musical acts at Ecofest, my friend Harry came over. He was one of the few guys besides Dylan who hadn't ditched me.

Harry sat down between my legs, leaned his head backward onto my chest, and stuck out his tongue as he snapped a selfie. I was uncomfortable and squinted my eyes so they almost closed shut. I tried to scoot back without him noticing.

In recent weeks, Harry had been dropping by our dorm room a lot, especially when Catie wasn't around. We'd do homework together and sometimes he'd ask how I was feeling. I'd share how hard it was to adjust to school and how scared I was that everyone at St. Paul's hated me.

During one vent session, Harry listened sympathetically, then slid closer to me on the couch and wrapped his arms around me. His hand lingered on my back longer than it should have and his hug felt suffocating. He'd done this a couple of times. I needed him gone and now.

First I messaged Catie and asked where she was.

Then I turned to Harry. "I really have to do my chem homework on my own. But thanks for stopping by."

I liked Harry but not in *that* way. I didn't know if I'd be ready for *that* way ever again.

○○○○○

I took Buzz's advice and played the piano to try and lift my spirits. I loved practicing music from my childhood, or learning pop songs by ear. Catie had invested her dad's money in a big pair of speakers, so I continued my music therapy in our room, belting out Broadway tunes with Catie, or losing myself in melodies from Cat Island.

I missed those kids so much. Sure, it was draining at times, but I had never felt more at peace. I had found my own version of heaven. It was a feeling so inexplicable that I didn't try to share it with others because I could never do it justice. I needed to work harder to find that peace here at St. Paul's.

I was grateful for my family, Catie, Lilly, Dylan, the authorities, Buzz, and Dr. Sloane. And I was thankful for my determination and strength. I was breathing, walking, eating, and living comfortably. I was learning Japanese, singing with the Madhatters, and playing piano.

I felt especially Zen after a late-night piano session and went to fill up my water bottle in the lobby of the music building before heading to my dorm. Suddenly I heard a guy snarl loudly, "Get out of here!"

I saw Jake, a senior football player, lying on the couch getting a blow job from a girl with bleached-blond hair. I froze.

"Yo bitch, what the hell! Get outta here!"

I couldn't speak. I sprinted to my dorm, clutching my half-filled water bottle. I was so pissed. I should have flipped on the lights or alerted security. Instead I called Mom.

"They've ruined every place. Now even the music building isn't safe."

Dad lost it when he heard about the football player yelling at me for interrupting his blow job. Each day was a new, horrifying revelation for Dad that he had sent his daughters into danger. The adults were nowhere to be found, and the boys were running wild. He didn't understand how the community he trusted, the school that helped shape him, had completely lost its way.

○○○○○

I turned sixteen at the end of October, but I was in no mood to celebrate. I called Mom crying, utterly defeated by the coldness I felt from my classmates.

Mom knew I needed a pick-me-up, so she spilled the beans: Arielle, my best friend from Naples, was planning a surprise visit for my birthday! Mom placed a giant pink bow on Arielle's head so I couldn't miss her in the audience of my Madhatters a cappella concert. Mom kept trying to surround me with love—the week before she'd given Catie her credit card to throw me a surprise dinner at Siam Orchid. Even Ivy came.

They were decent distractions, but a court date scheduled shortly after my birthday overshadowed everything. I was terrified that Owen would hunt me down while he was in Concord, especially after Harvard had rescinded his admission. Buzz promised me that he was banned from St. Paul's and there were safety measures in place.

The next week Dad spent hours with the prosecutors hammering out a plea bargain that involved minimal jail time for Owen and no registration as a sex offender. I would receive an apology and Owen would have to go to counseling. Dad spun this as a positive development, one that would allow us to avoid a trial and focus on healing. All I really I wanted was for Owen to acknowledge what he'd done and to get help so he never hurt another girl. And I needed everyone else—especially the kids at school—to know the truth.

Mrs. Hebra sent me a sweet handwritten letter the next day.

Chessy Dear, Just a quick note to remind you of how many of us are thinking of, praying for, and celebrating you. I am sure it doesn't feel this way at the moment, especially when doubt and scary thoughts enter your

mind, but you are a hero. You are __my__ hero, and for as
long as I live I will think of you as such.
Much respect,
Mrs. Hebra

She invited me to her faculty house so I could have a quiet space to work on my victim impact statement. I had to have it ready by the next court date in mid-November. It was my one chance to explain to the judge how the assault had changed my life.

I stared at a blank sheet of paper for hours at Mrs. Hebra's house. I had tried so hard to avoid thinking about these painful things, how I was no longer that innocent girl. And I never would be again.

I scribbled some notes during humanities class, but I couldn't string together full sentences. Dark circles cupped my eyes and anxiety smothered my brain. I stopped returning Mom's calls as the court date drew closer. She knew that was my silent cry for help, so she flew up to New Hampshire and took me on a road trip to the coastal town of Portsmouth.

We wandered around the cobblestone streets along the Piscataqua River and stumbled into a historic inn with a beautiful garden. Mom thought surrounding me with nature would cure my writer's block. It wasn't until four a.m. that I ripped out the jagged blades of anger, despair, shame, and panic tearing through my body and laid them out so that the judge could feast on the bloody carnage.

Lilly wanted to attend the hearing to support me, but shortly before we got word that Owen had fired his lawyer. The plea deal was off. I had numbed myself of all expectations, but I could tell that Mom was devastated. Dad got riled up, saying this was all part of a game to mess with us, to wear us down, to make us go away.

We met at the prosecutor's office with Barbara, Catherine, and Joe Cherniske, an assistant county attorney working on my case.

"It's a difficult process and, again, it's not user-friendly," said

Barbara, the victim advocate. "We're very sorry that you and your family are experiencing this."

"I'm not going to give up. He is not going to intimidate me," I said. "I know this is wrong and I want justice."

"We'll keep pressing ahead, then," Catherine said.

My shoulders sank. My head hung down; it felt so heavy that it might roll off my body and down the gravel street. I couldn't bear to resume a "normal life," so for the second year in a row, I left St. Paul's without completing my midwinter exams.

Back in Naples, I burrowed in the Prout cocoon. Lucy cuddled with me on the couch and watched rom-coms. Christianna and I buried each other in velvety sand and held hands as we crossed the finish line for the annual Turkey Trot.

For the first time in months, I felt safe and free. I didn't have to look over my shoulder or worry about sleeping in my room. We were back together as a family again. My heart ached. I had missed this so much.

Mom held a post-Thanksgiving party to clear out the leftovers. Soft jazz music flowed throughout the house while my friends devoured the apple pie I had baked. I ducked into the kitchen to get a few minutes of alone time and found Mom standing by the water cooler. I perched on a white breakfast stool and exhaled deeply.

"Would it really be okay if I came back home?" I asked, looking her straight in the eyes. "Would it be a big hassle?"

"You're always welcome to come home, darling. We've talked to the headmaster at CSN, and he said he'd hold a spot for you in case you want to return in the new year," Mom said. "We'd love to have you back."

"I just don't know how much more I can handle," I said.

Mom held my gaze for a moment before saying, "I don't know if they deserve you anymore."

We agreed that I'd finish out the semester and decide over Christmas break whether I would return next year. All I had to do was make it through a few more weeks.

Back at St. Paul's, I had trouble sleeping and I barely made it to chapel on time in the morning. I scooted into the pews and stared at the wrought-iron light fixtures hanging from the ceiling, imagining them crashing to the ground. The chapel had tiered seating with faculty in the back and freshmen in the front. Each year, the students ascended to a higher level. Would I ever make it to the top?

The dim lights and monotonous drone of the speakers created a powerful sedative, especially for the sleep-deprived. My eyelids started drooping as two seniors made the morning announcements from the wooden lectern in the aisle separating the facing rows of pews. One of them was Jake, the guy who'd yelled at me after I saw him getting a blow job in the music building.

They announced a powder-puff football game taking place on campus but only invited girls over the age of consent to participate. My eyes popped open in time to see classmates turn and face me. My friend Reese's mouth hung open. "I can't believe they just said that," she gasped. "That's so insensitive."

The rest of the students erupted in laughter. My eyes darkened like a monsoon. My insides were gutted. How could they joke about something so serious? I scoured the upper rows, searching for my teachers. Some of them were laughing, too. None of the adults stood up and said anything. The chapel had been my last refuge on campus.

When the announcements ended, I stormed out, shattering the facade I had promised myself to keep up. I walked hastily past the older students, not caring if I bumped into them. I glared at both of the reverends for allowing this to happen in a holy place.

Before I could get to the main road between the chapel and my dorm, my body started heaving. I was having another panic attack.

Back at Con20, I slammed my door shut and called Mom, incensed: "I'm done with this place. I have to come home. It's not healthy to be here anymore."

Mom told me to go see Buzz while she made arrangements for Uncle Bernie to drive up from Massachusetts and get me out of there that afternoon. On my way into Clark House I saw my adviser, Mr. Callahan, who served on the disciplinary council, walk the two boys from chapel out of the health center. It took all my self-control not to give them a piece of my mind.

Buzz had me do breathing exercises to calm down after I closed the door to her office. Then I explained the powder-puff fiasco.

"This environment is not supportive of or respectful to girls," I said. "I'm reminded of the assault every day. I want to go home and never come back here."

Buzz looked at me hard, her blue eyes brimming with tears. "I understand."

Then she brought me back to the dorm so I could pack up.

My room suddenly became a gathering place for people to either say good-bye or attempt to feel better about themselves. Some girls who hadn't talked to me all semester finally chose now to communicate, but it was way too late.

The dean of students, Chad Green, stopped by and began to bawl. "I'm so sorry we failed you here," he sniveled.

Mr. Hirschfeld knocked on my door next and awkwardly promised that there would always be a place for me at St. Paul's if I wanted to return. There was zero chance of that happening.

"Thank you, but I am never coming back. I just hope it gets better for other girls," I said, attempting to shroud the anger radiating off my skin.

When Uncle Bernie arrived, Buzz handed him an apology note written by the two boys who'd made the announcement in chapel. I refused to look at it. I knew it was all bullshit.

As Uncle Bernie waited in the hallway of my dorm, a man, maybe a teacher, told him that if I was this sensitive, perhaps it was a good idea that I was going home.

I walked outside without a jacket. The blustery December air burned my face. Catie, Lilly, Faith, and Ivy followed me out, and we embraced in a group hug with my back to the chapel. Ivy cried the hardest and kept apologizing, but I was so tired of these delayed reparations. I was done with being the person that other people wanted me to be. I followed Uncle Bernie to the car, my knee-high black boots trampling over gritty salt and dirty St. Paul's snow for the last time.

Mom tried to cheer me up with a visit from Christianna and Arielle, my best friend from Naples.

Lucy came up one weekend (below right) and passed the ball with me during halftime (below left).

Eventually the bullying got so bad that I had to leave the school. Catie, Ivy, Lilly, and I embraced in a group hug on my last day at St. Paul's (top).

TWELVE

Betrayed

When I returned home to Naples, Mom wasted no time in making sure I was back in the family fold. She put me to work helping Christianna's Girl Scout troop for an upcoming Christmas parade. Mom had trouble finding enough parents to chaperone—obviously, the adults had all been smart enough to get out of it.

"It'll be good for you," Mom said in her there-is-no-negotiating voice.

Suddenly I was chasing eight-year-olds wearing red-and-white Santa hats along Fifth Avenue in downtown Naples. They threw candy canes and lollipops into the crowd. A few of my little girls dove for the pieces that scattered on the street.

I couldn't believe this was my life now. All the independence I'd had at St. Paul's had vaporized overnight. Now I had no choice but to chaperone a bunch of little kids. I was also back to eating meals on my family's schedule, cleaning up after Christianna, and relying on Mom and Dad for rides.

But after a week at home, I relished the one privilege desperately missing from boarding schools: letting someone else take care of me. Instead of eating Goldfish crackers alone in my dorm and drowning my sorrows in TV, I fell asleep with my head on Mom's lap, drooling all over her. Dad cooked my favorite Japanese dish, katsudon—a flattened chicken breast fried in panko and topped with an egg and onions—while I played Marco Polo with Christianna in our backyard swimming pool.

"Five games of Marco Polo and then you can go inside," Christianna demanded.

"Three," I responded.

"Seven," she countered.

"That's not how it works," I giggled. "You're supposed to compromise and go down."

I was allowed to be a kid again. And I was starting to appreciate that.

A few weeks earlier Lucy had sent me the sweetest birthday gift. It was an orange journal with the words LIVE INSPIRED etched in gold on the front. She'd filled the pages with photos of us, one for each of our sixteen years together: arm in arm on the beach in Naples, parasailing in Miami, beaming on the volleyball court in our red St. Paul's jerseys.

She wrote a beautiful letter inside the front cover:

> To my dearest Chester,
> . . . There is so much love in our family, and I hope you will be able to find and take refuge in that. Remember, Prout sisters are the best kind of sisters out there.
> —Lucy

I was floored. It was so sentimental, so un-Lucy. And yet, as Lucy arrived home from Georgetown for Christmas break, I was nervous. I worried she was still mad at me because I hadn't listened to her about the Senior Salute.

I walked gingerly by her side down the beach in Pelican Bay, letting the gulf water lap at our feet. Without warning, she turned and embraced me. That's when I knew everything was going to be okay.

"You never hug me first." I chuckled.

Lucy smiled mischievously and then put me in a headlock.

I was sitting in the office, waiting for my new schedule at the Community School of Naples, when my ex-boyfriend Dean walked in.

"What are you doing here?" he asked in a deep voice that I hardly recognized.

I hadn't seen him since eighth grade. He was taller and had lost his braces.

"Well, I'm coming back," I said casually, hoping he didn't notice my flushed cheeks. "But don't tell anyone. I don't want it to be a big thing."

Only a few close friends knew the truth. For everyone else, I pulled the quintessential teenage move: I blamed Mom and Dad.

"My parents moved back to the States so we could all live together," I said. "I'm really happy to be home."

Over time, my friends figured out that something bad had happened, but they didn't probe for details. Instead they offered tenderness: "We are your friends. We'll listen when you're ready." It felt like a giant leap into a world of decency, something I had forgotten existed.

As much as I wanted to purge my brain of anything St. Paul's, I still felt strong ties to the place. I got together in January with Violet, a friend who had sung with me in Madhatters and was visiting family in Naples. I'd never had the chance to say good-bye to Violet, so I put on my best fake smile and pretended everything was fantastic, totally fantastic.

"Tell everyone I miss them," I said as we hugged good-bye.

Harry, one of the few St. Paul's guys who'd talked to me during the fall, texted that he was in Miami over break and wanted me to come visit. I tried to convince him to bring his family to Naples. I thought Harry was one of the good guys.

The adults at St. Paul's hadn't forgotten me either. I received several letters in the mail, including one from Mrs. Hebra. She felt bad about how I was treated but bizarrely likened me to a football.

> *Dear Chessy,*
> *. . . I am deeply disappointed in the SPS student body—*
> *in the entire community, actually—for fumbling this*
> *one. It's unfortunate that we were not able to support*
> *and protect you in a manner that you deserved. You are*
> *stronger than us. . . .*
> *Always your friend,*
> *Mrs. Hebra*

Ms. Carter, who was head of Lucy's dorm and had a daughter in my grade, also apologized.

> *Dear Chessy –*
> *. . . I want you to know, Chessy, that I will continue*
> *to push so that SPS becomes a better place, especially for*
> *girls. Your strength in coming back to school has inspired*
> *a lot of us and I know there are a lot of faculty—*
> *especially female faculty members—who want SPS to be*
> *a safer place for girls. You know that we are facing an*
> *uphill battle because many strange "traditions" exist at*
> *school but we will try. . . .*
> *- Ms. Carter*

I appreciated their letters, but I didn't understand why the rest of the adults didn't try harder to stop the traditions or the victim blaming. I was furious when Catie told me that the school gave her an ultimatum after I left: she had to accept a new random roommate or move into a smaller space. It was so disruptive to do that in the middle of the year, and it seemed like another way to punish the people who'd supported me.

On Valentine's Day I was getting ready for softball practice when I saw a Facebook message from Allie, a dancer from St. Paul's. I'd only talked to Allie once before, so it seemed strange to me that she was reaching out about a problem with her boyfriend, Hopper.

Hopper was a senior football player and the older brother of Sally, the girl who'd bullied me. He had a reputation for being intense, and even his own sister admitted in the student newspaper that he was "very protective" and "set many rules." One time he found Sally at the end of Nash Bash and held her arm as he walked her back to the dorm. It sounded controlling and possessive to me.

Everything became clear in Allie's messages.

> Allie: Hi Chessy, I know we don't really know each other but I really wanted to reach out to you and say how much I admire you for your strength and endurance during everything you had to go through. I'm not sure how much you know (if anything) about the situation I am currently in . . . Basically, a couple of weeks ago at the BC dance Hopper put a strobe light against my thigh which had been plugged in for hours and it gave me 2nd degree burns. It wasn't the first time he had been physically aggressive with me—he had pushed, slapped and hit me before a lot. So after the burn, I finally was able to stop being in denial and ended things as well as reported them. The school wasn't very quick to act and it

took 4 whole days to report it to the police . . . Hopper
has been on health leave since the burn incident claiming
that he was unable to bear the "false allegations"
against him. The school is allowing him back on campus
next week, so I have been left with no choice but to
leave. It's really awful and unfair that I have to, but I just
don't feel safe being on campus if he is also going to be
here. The administration is being pretty unhelpful and
unsupportive and, although Hopper is facing a DC for
"failing to respect the rights of others," it seems as if he
isn't really seen as being guilty. It's hard because I feel so
betrayed, not only by adults I trusted, but also some of
my close friends who have turned on me because they
can't believe that hopper (who on the outside seemed
like an honest, gentle guy) could do something like this
to me. . . .

Then she sent pictures of the gruesome burns, skin melted away,
leaving raw red flesh and a deep pink crater. My stomach churned
and my hands balled into fists of anger. I ran to Mom and held up
the phone with the pictures. Then I wrote back to Allie.

Me: You are so brave. Because of what you are doing
right now, you are preventing this from happening to
someone else, which first of all is amazing . . . Aggression
is assault, and I wonder how many educations will have
to be taken away for st. Pauls to learn that. Through all
of this i've also been able to weed out terrible friends, so
I know where you're coming from. My two best friends,
and Sally, spread nasty rumours about me which made
me feel so small until I realized that I was doing the right
thing no matter what is happening around me. You are

> doing the right thing. . . . I know this may sound crazy or
> paranoid, but all of this is so connected. These boys the
> school breeds all have these similarities which they have
> to realize at some point.

I was horrified but not surprised by St. Paul's response to Allie's assault. I connected Allie's parents to Mom and Dad so they could share their experiences and support each other. Allie's parents said that a local attorney, Phil Utter, who Mr. Hirschfeld had recommended to help us during the plea negotiations with Owen last fall, was now representing Hopper. Mom called up Mr. Utter and told him where he could shove his new client's retainer check.

We united in fear and fury over the justice system and the St. Paul's community. It was hard to decide who or what was worse: the perpetrators or the people and institutions that protected them.

Allie reached out again once she returned to school, distraught that Hopper seemed to disregard instructions to stay away from her and that students at St. Paul's were rallying around him. I shook my head as I read her message.

> Allie: he seems more popular than ever and I just can't
> understand why they want to associate with him?

In late February, Dad got a call from one of his inside sources at St. Paul's. Owen had emailed current and former students trying to raise money for his defense, and his letter was spreading quickly across campus. Someone read Dad the email over the phone: Owen claimed he was "falsely accused" and was seeking $90,000 to keep fighting for his "innocence." He had just fired another lawyer and backed away from a second plea offer.

Dad worked his network and got his hands on a copy of the letter and forwarded it to Catherine and Detective Curtin. Not only was it offensive that Owen was trying to manipulate sympathy for himself, but it also appeared to violate the judge's order for Owen not to have contact with the St. Paul's community.

Nothing could have prepared us for what happened next. Joshua Abram, the father of my friend Harry—the one who'd hugged me and promised support—forwarded Owen's request to parents and alumni. Dad was conveniently left off the list, but his source emailed it along.

Mr. Abram asked for the St. Paul's community to join him in donating money to hire J. W. Carney Jr., a high-powered criminal attorney who had recently represented Boston mobster Whitey Bulger and convicted terrorist Tarek Mehanna.

> Dear fellow SPS parent,
> . . . I feel that this star SPS student---recognized by the faculty with the school's character award---deserves a robust and competent defense. . . . Cristina and I have already pledged $10,000 towards the $100,000 that is required to secure the very well regarded and experienced Boston lawyer, Jay Carney, that Owen would like to engage. . . . In speaking with fellow SPS families over the past 48 hours we already have commitments for about half of the required amount. . . . We hope that you will join the many other SPS families who feel that while the facts of this case can only be decided by a judge and jury, we can be united in the bedrock principle that Owen has the right to his day in court with a proper defense. . . .
> Best,
> Joshua

Ballistic. Mom, Dad, and I went ballistic behind the glass doors of our family office, curses flying out of our mouths like sharp knives.

This was so outrageous, an unfathomable betrayal, the ultimate symbol of rape culture.

"Where are these people's moral compasses?" I yelled. "How can they live with themselves, supporting this psychopath who RAPED ME!!!"

Jeez. I had finally said it. That was the first time I had uttered the word out loud.

"He raped me," I whimpered as I collapsed into my parents' arms and onto the couch.

I knew I had lost most of my friends, but now I felt like the entire St. Paul's community was turning against me. And this was being spearheaded by my friend Harry Abram's dad! It made no sense—especially after we'd just gotten news that Owen's DNA was found in my underwear.

Mom and Dad fired off emails and texts to the police, the prosecutor's office, and school officials.

While sitting in church on Sunday morning, Mom wrote an email to Mr. Hirschfeld. She and Dad had been pressing him for months to rescind the Rector's Award and the diploma that Owen had received last year.

> Mike,
> . . . It is time to set the record straight. . . . In the absence of doing that thus far, you have let Owen Labrie wrap himself in the cloak of St. Paul's school's honors, and allow other people -- Mr. Abram and the coterie of parents defending a way of life that threatens their seedy world . . . to ignore what is known: that Owen Labrie was not deserving of the school's highest awards and distinctions. . . . While you did not protect Chessy from circumstances in which the heinous acts Owen committed on May 30th, she deserves at the very least not to be abandoned by her now former community,

but reached out to, and lifted up through this process,
none of which has happened in any tangible way. . . .
Sincerely,
Susan

The next day Mr. Hirschfeld responded as usual: opaquely unsatisfying.

Dear Susan and Alex,
Yes, it's time. We are working hard here with many to
think through about how we can best show our support
of Chessy and your family.
Sincerely,
Mike

Oh yeah? By doing what?

I never wanted to see or hear from Harry ever again, and I thought
he wouldn't have the audacity to reach out. I was wrong.

Harry: Chess
Me: What. What do you have to say that hasn't already
been said by your father?
Harry: Chessy i dont know what my dad has or hasnt said
but i dont have anything to do with it. If you want to
turn your back on a friend who loves you and has had
your back through all of this, go ahead. I wont stop
you.
Me: Are you telling me you haven't seen your parent's
letter? I can send you a copy if you would like.
Harry: Of course i have chessy but explain to me how im
responsible for what they say

Me: Your father, mother and brother have hired the
fourth lawyer for the man who raped me. I cannot
communicate with you any more.
Harry: Hello and goodbye mr prout.

That last line whipped me into a frenzy. He assumed Dad was writing him? Did he not think a girl could stand up for herself or be serious, God forbid?

"Look at this shit," I said to Mom and Dad as I handed them my phone.

"Enough is enough. I'm calling Harry now," I said. "Then he'll know who he's really dealing with."

Mom and Dad made me write down a few bullet points, because they knew anything I said could end up in court. And they insisted on staying in the room in case things got heated. Mom and Dad perched on the couch in the office while I stood with my back to them in the corner by the cabinets.

I gritted my teeth as I dialed. The coward wouldn't pick up—he let it go straight to voicemail.

My message was clear: that was not my father. I was capable of writing those words, of feeling betrayed by Harry and his whole family. Harry texted back. Was he too scared to hear a human voice? Would that make me too real?

Harry: You want to know what my first thought when i
heard that message was? Not 'fuck' or 'damn shes mad,'
it was 'wow, its good to hear her voice. No matter the
situation bc you were my friend and i love you. And i
miss you. I understand your side of the story chess, I
completely understand why youre upset at me but im not
going to compromise my morals by just presuming hes
guilty because you say so. I dont have the facts and i cant

make that judgement, im neither god judge nor jury. Im your friend and the son of someone who believes that everyone has the right to a fair trial. I cant say i disagree with him, because when its your family's 6 digit lawyer vs a public defender, the courtroom is no longer an even ground for facts to be presented . . . For you to penalize me for this is your choice and if thats what you want to do fine, but i wont apologize for my belief in the right to a fair trial, nor for parents vocalization of their similar views. I love you chessy, stay strong.

That was some seriously ignorant ass-backward mumbo jumbo. Our "6 digit lawyer"? You would've thought that someone would do his research before writing with such certainty. I had to set him straight for the last time.

Me: Harry, you are so far off base, I don't even know where to begin. Our lawyer is called the district attorney. But i'm glad that your father got an Al Qaida and murder defender to defend this man, who, through all of this, has shown that he is on those criminal's caliber. There is so much everyone is ignorant to, and it makes me sad that you are part of that group. I am asking respectfully, please do not communicate with me, because I have nothing left to say to you.

Harry sounded like a scorned little boy who hadn't gotten what he wanted. I was sorry if my friendship wasn't good enough for him. This was not the Harry who I'd met freshman year. St. Paul's had done to him what it did to most of the boys: turned them into aggressive, possessive jerks who never had to take accountability for their actions.

ooooo

It soon became clear that there was no more negotiating with Owen. This case was going to trial. Catherine had warned us that the time between setting the trial date and the actual trial date was the period of hell. That's where we were living. We had anticipated a spring trial, but the almighty Carney was too busy and asked for a delay. The judge granted the request and scheduled the trial for mid-August, timed precisely for the first day of my junior year. Perfect. Owen would ruin every year of high school so far.

Mom and Dad constantly huddled in the office, speaking in hushed voices so that Christianna couldn't hear. I wanted to know everything and nothing at the same time.

I couldn't stop thinking about Allie and the backlash she was facing at St. Paul's. She reached out in April to let me know that Hopper had been arrested by the police. Finally, a bit of justice. But then she confessed that his arrest had only made matters worse at St. Paul's.

> Allie: the general consensus amongst the students right
>   now is that I have lied about the whole thing . . . so a
>   lot of people are very angry at me . . . But the only good
>   thing that has come out of this is that he will no longer
>   be on campus.
> Me: I'm so glad that he is finally getting what he deserves.
>   I hope that will serve as a reminder to people about how
>   serious this stuff actually is . . .

The news of Hopper's arrest broke a few weeks later in the *Concord Monitor*. As usual, the attacker was described in glowing terms: "a reported honors student and active member of the rowing team."

I read the story while sitting in French class and scrolled to the bottom for the comments section. It infuriated me the way that the perpetrators were always portrayed as perfect, personable boys. And then the commenters consistently bashed the girls. I thought it was time to give readers some real facts. So I posted my own anonymous comment.

> *update: Ronald "Hopper" Hillegass is not a beloved member of the St. Paul's community; he was noted as a "strange, possessive" student by underclass and upperclass girls, and is rumoured to have suffered head wounds causing erratic violent behavior.

As soon as I clicked submit, my full name and Facebook photo appeared.

"Fuck, fuck, fuck," I muttered under my breath.

I hadn't realized that my log-in for the *Concord Monitor* was connected to Facebook. I took a screenshot of my mistake before scrambling to delete it from the website.

Then I warned Allie about the online haters.

> Me: I hope this brings some sort of "public justice" to you, although at the beginning of the press stuff, the comments don't usually go our way. I hope the supposed "intellectually adept" student body is respectful towards you . . .
>
> Allie: Hi Chessy! Thank you for your message. Things have been very difficult on campus—a lot of people are angry about the two articles and keep talking about how our two cases aren't at all related and are not a reflection of the culture here, but instead are apparently a result of us being "attention seeking." It makes me sick to my stomach that people can be so ignorant and say such hurtful things . . .

We had fallen into a pit of vipers. Getting second-degree burns from her boyfriend made Allie attention seeking? Reality check: Hopper would eventually reach a plea deal under which he was found guilty of a single violation of simple assault.

Allie wasn't attention seeking. And the last thing I ever wanted was attention. Every single day, I desperately wished to return to the fifteen-year-old I had been on May 29, 2014. How could these people be so cruel?

THIRTEEN

Spring 2015

I pulled my covers tightly around my body each night, protecting myself from the pain and betrayal nipping at the edge of my cool white sheets. I had trouble getting out of bed in the morning. Why should I bother leaving my room when I didn't know who I could trust anymore?

Mom and Dad always had my back, but I felt isolated from them, too.

I'd never explained to them about what had happened inside the mechanical room that night, the images that infiltrated my nightmares and haunted my days. The reasons why I sometimes recoiled from their touch and why no amount of showering ever made me feel clean. I didn't feel like I could ask them for help. All I had was Dr. Sloane, and we had resumed our usual schedule of seeing each other once a week. I felt so alone.

Whenever Detective Curtin had questions for me in the middle of the day, Dad would drive down to my school and get permission for me to leave class. I'd sit in the car answering questions about my underwear while he paced the parking lot and plotted softball exercises.

Dad was now an assistant coach for the CSN girls' softball team. He had planned to return to Invesco at the end of his unpaid leave, but the company fired him instead. I was so self-absorbed I didn't realize it for months until I overheard Mom and Dad arguing over Invesco's attempts to withhold years of earnings. How could Invesco do that? It seemed like Dad was being punished for taking time to be with his family. I felt sick thinking about how much everyone had lost because of me.

Dad insisted his unemployment was a good thing. I couldn't digest how this was anything but terrible—and all my fault. Dad told me that there was nowhere he would rather be than with me on the grassy outfield of CSN's softball diamond. To be honest, I didn't want him anywhere else.

The girls on the softball team loved Dad. He had such an upbeat and encouraging approach that his suggestions never sounded like criticisms.

"You're doing awesome," he told Tia during batting practice. "Why don't you put your elbow up a little higher and you'll get so much more power?"

I felt like I had traveled back in time to my utopia in Hiroo, where Dad used to coach our T-ball league and Mom showed up with cucumber rolls and inarizushi in bulk to make sure no one went hungry. Sometimes I could forget about the assault for entire afternoons. Other days I pictured my attacker's head on the ball as I smashed it with the bat.

During our drive home together, Dad let me swear freely, so I'd vent about everything from the assholes raising money for Owen to the ignorant kids at school who made jokes about rape.

Mom was more offended by my potty mouth and worried when I raged. She was the one I turned to for comfort. She helped me get through each day, rolling me out of bed, making my lunches, and gently pushing me out the front door. She tried her best to take my mind off the case by inviting guest after guest to stay with us in Naples.

Sure, it was a great distraction, but it was exhausting being "on" all the time. And how much was there to talk about with the adults, especially Mom's friends? They were great people, but every question felt so loaded. How's school? How are your friends? If I answered them honestly, I'd have to scrape their jaws off the floor.

"Everything's great," I'd say in a high-pitched voice, cocking my head to one side.

Some people can fake it until they make it. I couldn't do that anymore. Pretending everything was fine made it worse, and no one knew that more than sweet Christianna. Ever since I'd come back to Naples, she wouldn't let me out of her sight. Mom and Dad gave her a Disney version of what was going on: a boy hurt Chessy, and now she was home.

Christianna was always the first one to notice when I disappeared into my walk-in closet in the farthest corner of the house. That was my hiding spot when my muscles lit on fire and blinding white energy froze my veins. I'd squeeze my arms around my legs to keep my body from blowing apart. I'd try to make the panic stop by punching my legs or hitting my head with wooden hangers, the floor, whatever I could find. I needed to move the pain outside my body.

I was mid-punch when Christianna flung open the closet door after hearing my sobs from the other side of the wall.

"I'm sorry, I love you," she said as she wrapped her arms around me. I couldn't respond.

"You're going to be okay, Che Che," she whispered, using one of our nicknames. She was my Nan. I was her Che Che. But when I was in that closet, I was nothing.

"I'm okay. I just need some space." I gagged and rolled into a ball on my knees. She lingered by the door, afraid to leave me alone.

"Please!! Go!!" I screamed. I instantly regretted it as she ran away. My poor little sister, one more person hurt by Owen Labrie.

I tried my best to keep it together when Lucy came home for spring break with four of her friends from Georgetown. They seemed genuinely nice, and I was happy for Lucy. But seeing her move ahead with her life reminded me of how stuck I felt, how my world kept shrinking.

We never could just talk about what happened that night, so small issues smoldered—like my anger over her dirty laundry piling up in my room—until everything exploded and we found ourselves standing in a burning field of regret and shame.

I felt like I had betrayed Lucy. Making my own decision was the worst thing I'd ever done. How could I make it up to her?

"I'm so sorry, Lucy," I pleaded. "I'm so, so sorry."

"It's not your fault," Lucy said. "Stop apologizing."

Lucy was getting angrier by the second and that just made me apologize even more. I couldn't stop the vicious sorry cycle, so Lucy stormed off.

With the trial fast approaching, Mom and Dad searched for people to help guide us through the process. Detective Curtin suggested reaching out to a woman named Laura Dunn, a lawyer who'd recently spoken at a conference at the University of New Hampshire School of Law. Laura was a pastor's daughter who reported that she was sexually assaulted in 2004 by two students at the University of Wisconsin-Madison. She later filed a Title IX complaint against the college for mishandling her case and had recently started an organization, SurvJustice, to provide legal help to survivors of campus sexual violence.

Laura arranged for us to meet in Washington, DC, during a family visit to Lucy at Georgetown. She brought along an attorney she had worked with, Steve Kelly, who had spent his life fighting for victim rights after his eldest sister, a young mother of two, was brutally raped and murdered when Steve was fourteen.

Mom gave me some articles about their careers to peruse on the plane. I was overwhelmed; they seemed like such impressive people, who had endured way more than I had. Why would they want to help me?

My hands began sweating, an annoying family trait, as I walked into the hotel room. I spotted Laura, a petite brunette, and Steve, a boyish-looking lawyer in a suit. I stuck out my hand but Laura asked me for a hug. We both started to cry. This was the first time I had met another survivor in person. My family always tried their best to be supportive, but they didn't know what it was like to be a victim of sexual assault, particularly acquaintance assault, and to live each day battling guilt and shame.

I could see by the look in Laura's eyes that she understood me and the messy aura surrounding me. Finally, I was not alone. Laura had trouble getting out words, so Steve took up the mantle.

"Chessy, we're so incredibly impressed by your strength and your willingness to come forward," Steve said.

"Thank you," I said. "Thank you for all that you do. I'm so grateful that you might be able to help."

I let Mom and Dad discuss details while I took Christianna to the Georgetown Waterfront Park, where we galloped along the Potomac River and then admired cherry blossom trees near the Lincoln Memorial. It reminded me of how we used to dance on the carpet of pink petals at Shinjuku Gyoen National Garden in Tokyo. After being failed by so many adults at St. Paul's, it was uplifting to see Laura and Steve willing to fight for me and my family and this cause. It was an introduction to a new world. And it inspired me.

○○○○○

I was sitting in Mr. Rochette's classroom at CSN, surrounded by giggling, gabbing freshmen. I had missed the required freshman health class while I was at St. Paul's and had no choice but to take it as a sophomore. The course was intense, focusing on drunk driving and sports medicine. But it barely scratched the surface on issues that kids really needed to talk about, such as consent and healthy relationships.

Some days I felt like my education was going to shit. I was pissed that I couldn't take Japanese or music anymore. It sucked changing courses and schedules halfway through the year. I felt like I was being punished for being a victim. And I was going full angsty teenager about it.

The assignment that day in health class was to write a letter to our graduating selves. I rolled my eyes and looked around at the fourteen- and fifteen-year-olds. They laughed so easily, so carefree. I wished they could appreciate their innocence. I put my head on the desk. Eventually I picked up a pen and started writing a mix of questions and advice for my graduating self.

> Dear Me,
> . . . No matter how much you might feel the world would be better without you, you are wrong. I hope I never have to feel that way again. I also hope to be a size 2 and under 135 pounds but living is a gift in itself. . . . Did I have to go to trial? Was I as sturdy as I hoped to be? Well if I made it here to read this today, I must have done/followed something right . . . Make a difference. Be sure of yourself, be kind and compassionate and <u>patient</u> with others, but also let others see and respect you for who you really are. . . . Is my momma a published author yet?

Am I a published author yet? . . . Have I burst out of my bubble yet?
Love,
Chessy of 2015

I folded the letter with two creases and slid it into an envelope with CSN's circular blue logo on the upper left-hand corner. I put my name and phone number in the front and got chills down my spine when I wrote *Class of '17.*

I wanted to return to Cat Island in the summer, but Mom and Dad encouraged me to enroll in a language immersion program in France. They worried Cat Island might be too intense.

I had studied French in middle school and picked it up again when I returned to CSN. It seemed easier than starting over with a new language. But I didn't anticipate how gross it would feel to speak it. It transported me right back to the assault: using Google Translate to understand Owen's stupid messages and to help with the dumb notes I wrote back.

Chessy, French is a language, for God's sake, I scolded myself. *He can't take away something as universal as a language.*

I decided to reclaim something that had once been mine. I signed up for a monthlong excursion. I'd get home two weeks before the trial.

Mom and Dad planned a visit to New York City so we could spend time with our extended family before I left. Mom was most excited about taking us to the French bistro where she'd met Dad for their first date. We sat at a cozy table upstairs on an indoor balcony and devoured endless baskets of crusty bread. I had a bad habit of ignoring my gluten allergy.

Mom and I spent a few hours touring Barnard College and Columbia University. I didn't have much interest in Columbia after reading all the stories about Emma Sulkowicz dragging her mattress around to protest the university's failure to expel the student she reported had raped her. The news was saturated with scary accounts of sexual assault on colleges and institutions that turned their backs on victims like St. Paul's did to me.

I really liked the idea of an all-girls school such as Barnard, but I needed to make sure that the empowerment they promised was a reality and not just a selling point in their brochure. I'd had enough broken promises at St. Paul's.

"Are you certain you won't consider Georgetown?" Dad asked. "Lucy loves it and I had a great time there."

"No way in hell," I said. "Sorry. But I followed you guys once, and look where that left me. I'm going to make my own way."

I didn't mean to sound so harsh. I was about to apologize when I looked up and saw Dad smile with a twinge of sadness behind his eyes. He understood.

Uncle Ron was in New York City and wanted to do a reading for me before I left for France. I was nervous. What would he say? Would it make me feel better or worse?

I hadn't seen Uncle Ron since I was six, when he came over to our house in Tokyo for dinner and gave me and Lucy an iPod Nano to share, our first piece of technology. I remembered him being larger than life: big with a huge grin and a loud bellowing laugh, always dressed in black from head to toe.

He hadn't changed a bit when he walked into the Grand Hyatt Hotel. We chatted downstairs with Dad before Uncle Ron took me up to his room for the reading. I had barely spent any time with this man, but I felt safe with him. He knew more about my struggles at St. Paul's than many of my blood relatives. I didn't think Uncle Ron could help necessarily; I just wanted something to hope for—a reason to care about my future.

Stale cigarette smoke wafted over me as I followed him into a dimly lit room. We sat down in chairs facing each other, and Uncle Ron placed a deck of cards on the wood table between us.

"Oh, we're not going to use these. That's not what I do." He chuckled, and pushed the cards to the side.

Then he pulled out a pack of Marlboros. "Do you want one?" he asked as he lit a cigarette.

"No, thank you," I said as I folded my hands on the table.

"Good girl. But I won't tell your dad if you want to smoke."

"That's okay," I laughed. "I don't smoke."

Uncle Ron and I talked for an hour about everything from health issues to job prospects. He saw me doing writing or acting in the future and said I could use my story to change the world. I would be more than a victim or a survivor.

"Look for a bigger meaning, Chessy. Push out of your frequency," Uncle Ron said. "You're going to change millions of lives."

Millions of lives? No way. Besides, I had *no idea* how to make a difference. But I took his words as a sign to keep fighting for justice.

When we met up with Dad in the lobby, Uncle Ron repeated an offer he had made during the reading: "Alex, I know people who can make certain people disappear. Just let me know and I'll make the call."

"Okay, we'll keep that in mind." Dad chuckled. "But for now, we're putting our faith in the court system."

Dad and I couldn't stop giggling as we walked arm in arm uptown toward Grandma Prout's apartment. Mom was going to get such a kick out of that.

FOURTEEN

August 2015

I returned from France with a few new pounds of Nutella weight but I felt lighter in my heart. C'était très magnifique to be by myself in a foreign country and learn the language. I was able to study, to accept, to be unsure at times, and to keep trying again and again. My confidence soared.

I hoped it was the boost I needed to get me through the trial. But then Mom knocked on my bedroom door. She sat down on my white comforter and fidgeted nervously with her diamond engagement ring.

"Chessy, I'm not sure how to say this, but a private investigator visited Christianna's third-grade teacher and he came back to visit Arielle's house today."

Nerves sliced my stomach. This couldn't be good.

"Why? What did he say?"

Mom hesitated.

"He asked some pretty terrible questions," Mom said without looking up. "Like, are you promiscuous? Do you lie a lot? Are you a drama queen?"

The investigator told Arielle's father that he was an ex-police officer from New England and was working on an out-of-state criminal case. Arielle's father took his card and also snapped a photo of his blue pickup truck before telling the sketchy bald dude with a hoop earring to get lost.

"You've gotta be kidding me," I groaned.

"No, sweetie, I'm not," Mom sighed.

I mashed my face in the pillows and tried to suffocate the thought.

Naples had been my last remaining haven. Now Owen was injecting his toxic venom where we lived to poison what community remained for us. His message was clear: you're not safe anywhere.

I saw these as dirty tactics meant to intimidate me days before the trial. This intrusion violated me over and over again. Every time I walked past a window, I worried somebody was watching me, hidden behind a bush with a giant zoom lens.

I was afraid to leave the house, but Mom had scheduled a meeting at CSN to tell my teachers and volleyball coach that I would be missing the start of school. I shuffled into a conference room with Mom and Dad and peered out at the circle of adults facing me. We had talked about this moment, about how I would explain that I had to return to Concord for a trial because I was the victim of a crime. But I kept my lips sealed. Dad sat quietly by my side as Mom filled the awkward void. Her words pierced me like icicles.

"Chessy was sexually assaulted last year by a senior boy at St. Paul's. It was part of a horrific school tradition known as the Senior Salute," Mom said. "And now she is testifying against her attacker in a trial in New Hampshire."

I'd never agreed to share that I was a victim of a sex crime. I was desperate to keep those two worlds separate. But the words flew out of Mom's mouth faster than I could process: the assault, the bullying, the rejected plea offers, the fund-raising for Owen's defense, the private investigator.

Mom had sucked all the air out of the room; everyone sat in stunned silence. Two of my female teachers teared up. Mr. Phimister, an English teacher who I'd never met before, couldn't even look at me. *Oh my God, these men aren't going to understand anything. This is the end of me here and now I'll be ostracized just like I was at St. Paul's.*

I glared at Mom and cut her off before she could do any more damage.

"I don't want this to change anything for me in the classroom. I don't want any special treatment," I said, trying to remain calm and collected. "The reason we asked for this meeting is so I can get all my homework for the next couple of weeks."

I refused to speak to Mom until we got near the car.

"Why did you have to say 'sexual assault'?" I lashed out. "You're being overly dramatic! Why would you tell them? You knew I didn't want to tell them!"

Mom began to cry.

"Chessy, why are you saying this? Why are you being so rude?" Dad demanded.

"I thought you wanted me to tell them." Mom wept. "They should know the hell you're going through. And don't talk to me like that, young lady!"

We drove home in silence and I stormed upstairs. I tried to fall asleep to the afternoon rain pelting the terra-cotta roof. Mom knocked on the door a little while later.

"Chess, honey, I'm so sorry," she apologized. "I thought we agreed we'd tell them what happened, and you weren't saying anything, so I wanted to help you out. There's nothing to be ashamed of."

I couldn't stay mad at Mom for long. She was the protective

netting underneath me, ready to catch me at all times. She never blamed me for what happened; never questioned why I went on the Senior Salute or why I didn't fight back. She was always checking my emotional thermometer—sometimes a little too often—to make sure that I was okay.

In that meeting at CSN, Mom had finally found a group of adults who were willing to listen to her, who looked her in the eyes and acknowledged that we had been wronged by St. Paul's.

Mom had so few people to count on these days. She zealously tried to protect my privacy, so most of her close friends and extended family didn't know about the assault. Even her own mother didn't have the full story. All we had was each other. We had to stay united. I stood up and hugged Mom.

"I just don't want my teachers to treat me differently," I said as I burrowed my head into the crook of her neck. "But I know I'm not going to be able to catch up on my work so easily, and I'll need some help. So thank you for talking to them. Thank you for everything you've done."

Waves of nausea rolled over me as we drove the seventy miles from Logan Airport in Boston to Concord, New Hampshire. We arrived a few days before the trial so I could do some prep work with the prosecution team. Mom and Dad stayed in the waiting room while I met with Catherine and Joe, the attorneys working on my case.

I told them about the private investigator invading my community in Naples and how threatening that felt.

"This isn't going to be easy, Chessy," Catherine said. "And it's important to tell us up front if there's something out there that we need to know about. That way we can do damage control."

They wanted all my dirty laundry? No problem. I ticked off my personal scandals matter-of-factly: drinking with the rector's son at St. Paul's. Trying weed with a few boarding-school friends during a break in New York City. Sipping leftover wine when cleaning up after Mom and Dad's dinner parties.

"And when I was in the fifth grade at Sacred Heart, a group of us used the library computers to chat with strangers," I said emphatically. "I was writing lines from the movie *Zoolander* and we got in trouble."

If I was brutally honest, maybe they'd find a reason not to move forward with the trial. But when I finished my list and glanced over at Catherine, she hardly looked startled.

Catherine was a no-nonsense kind of woman, always wearing her hair neatly pulled back and a string of pearls around her neck. She had worked as a dental hygienist before starting law school at age twenty-nine and had two kids by the time she landed her first job as a lawyer. Catherine seemed unflappable, not the least bit worried about facing off against a big-shot Boston attorney.

"Carney was Whitey Bulger's lawyer, but Whitey Bulger is now in prison, so how did that go for him?" Catherine said of Carney's infamous mobster client.

I liked her tenacity. I jotted down her tips for testifying in my spiral notebook.

Take my time . . . can take a break . . . Correct him (Carney).

At the bottom of the page I wrote in all caps:

TRUTH.

Then Catherine pressed a small figurine of a knight in shining armor into the palm of my hand.

"Chessy, it can get very difficult on the stand. I want you to have this knight in shining armor to hold when you're up there," she said.

"I give this to all victims who testify. It's something to protect you and to hold when you're feeling stressed."

"Thank you," I said, and carefully placed the silver figurine in my pocket.

Catherine wanted to show me what the courtroom looked like and where I would sit for my testimony, so I followed her across the street to the Merrimack County Superior Courthouse, a drab yellowish-gray brick building.

When we exited the elevator on the second floor, we were quickly moved to the side because a man in shackles was being led away by a guard. I'd never seen a real prisoner before. Was that how Owen would leave the courthouse?

A bailiff let us into Courtroom 1. It was empty, with natural light streaming through the windows, casting a warm glow on the wood benches. It almost seemed peaceful. Catherine told me she usually lets victims sit in the witness stand before testifying. I eased into the maroon chair, grasped the cool metal microphone with one hand, and squeezed the knight in my pocket with the other.

You can do this, Chessy. It's time for the truth to come out.

My parents rented a beige two-story colonial home on the outskirts of Concord in a wooded area that abutted St. Paul's. It was large enough to accommodate me, Lucy, Mom, Dad, Grandma Prout, and Uncle Tom, Dad's older brother, who had served as a history teacher and a Jesuit chaplain at Saint Ignatius Loyola School in New York City. Still, this was only a fraction of the entourage of extended family and friends who'd attend the trial.

The house had a charming wood porch, but it was a bachelor's pad at best and devoid of basics like curtains. Mom launched into fix-it mode and took blankets off the beds and tacked them over the windows so we could have privacy. We were worried about people finding us, especially after the Associated Press wrote a story about the upcoming trial, propelling the case into the national spotlight.

I couldn't fall asleep the night before the trial, even after taking two Advil PM. Christianna had stayed at home with a babysitter to start fourth grade, so I didn't have my usual snuggle buddy. My pillow kept falling in the crack between the bed and the wall, so I put my head on my furry pink stuffed bear.

But even Bearsie couldn't soothe me on this soupy August night. As I tossed and turned, I thought about the kids on Cat Island and felt guilty about not visiting them over the summer. If they had managed to escape abusive homes and live joyfully in a house with broken windows and no fresh water, certainly I could survive a two-week trial.

I remembered little Mark saying, "Please bless Chessy," and calling each female leader by my name. His words clung to my conscience: my pursuit of justice was never entirely about me. I could stand up for many women, for Briana and the rest of the girls who Owen had violated. Finally I drifted off to sleep.

I dragged myself out of bed at six a.m. just in time to throw up into the toilet. Everyone could hear me in our house. I sat on the cool bathroom tile and rested my head on the seat. In that moment, coiling up near a pile of my own vomit seemed more appealing than getting on the stand.

I eventually hoisted myself up into the shower. I tossed on a white blouse and an oversize navy cardigan, even though it was over ninety degrees outside. Catherine didn't tell me what to wear, but I wanted to look as bulky and ugly as possible so no one in that courtroom found me attractive. I couldn't stomach anyone looking at me like *that*.

I joined the rest of my bedraggled family at the kitchen table. No one was hungry for breakfast. Uncle Tom had his traveling mass kit and passed out copies of Psalm 62. We held hands and prayed together:

In God alone is my soul at rest;
my help comes from him.
He alone is my rock, my stronghold, my fortress:
I stand firm.

Dad, Grandma Prout, and Uncle Tom headed to court for open-ing statements while I stayed behind with Mom and Lucy. The three of us were identified as potential witnesses and sequestered until we testified. Carney had pulled more of his sick tricks and put Lucy on the defense witness list.

We had heard rumors that Carney was trying to make up a nar-rative that Owen was the victim of a sibling rivalry between me and Lucy, playing into misogynistic tropes that women are temptresses who seduce men and control their sexuality. Under this perverted worldview, Owen was a sympathetic guy who'd been tricked by two women—rather than a rapist who took what he wanted no matter how many times a fifteen-year-old said no.

Lucy pulled me aside in the kitchen and gave me a yellow Post-it Note that she had decorated with a giant *C* in the center and a shaded border like the Superman logo.

You are my superhero, she'd written on one side, and printed lyrics from Rachel Platten's "Fight Song" on the other.

> *And all these things I didn't say Wrecking*
> *balls inside my brain I will scream them loud*
> *tonight Can you hear my voice this time?*

"This is so you'll have a piece of me with you when you testify," Lucy said. "Go fight, Chess. You have it in you, strong girl."

I slipped the note inside the pocket of my khaki skirt, giving the knight figurine a paper blanket. I heard Mom yelling by the door, freaking out that construction workers had dug a trench at the end of the driveway and blocked our car. She marched straight outside to confront the workers, who couldn't comprehend her blistering rage.

"What do you want me to do, lady?" one of them said with a shrug.

Lucy and I followed Mom's orders and got into the car. She lurched into reverse, then drive, and tore straight across the lawn and down an incline, narrowly missing exposed sewer pipes.

Mom pumped up the volume on the rental car and loaded her playlist. Hunched over the wheel, she picked a tune by Flo Rida because she liked the first line of the chorus, *Welcome to my house*. In Mom's mind, the courthouse was *her* house, and where Owen would pay for what he'd done to me.

DAY 1

We parked at the prosecutor's office to meet up with Catherine after opening statements. My heart flew out of my chest when I looked across the street at the courthouse and saw tents set up in the parking lot and rows of white trucks with satellite dishes on top of them.

"Why are there so many of them? Is this normal?" I asked Catherine.

"This is a lot of press coverage," Catherine responded. "But don't worry about them. We're going to do whatever we can to protect your privacy."

Unfortunately, my name had been inadvertently broadcast during opening statements, so Judge Larry Smukler suspended the live streaming before my testimony. But we had to rely on the goodwill of the media to protect my identity once I stepped outside.

I wanted to crawl inside a hole. Instead Catherine led us across the street and into the rear door of the courthouse to avoid the throngs of journalists who swarmed the front entrance.

Catherine brought us into a small room on the first floor, where Dad and Grandma Prout were waiting. I couldn't believe this was finally happening. Nausea seized my body. The only way I could survive was to shut down.

"Listen, Chessy, anytime you need me, I am right here," Dad said. "I am sitting ten feet away from you. You can keep your eyes on me."

Dad was my hero. He had literally dropped everything and risked his career to make sure I was supported and protected each and every day. He had attended various court hearings over the past year so that Owen knew we weren't going away and so the judge didn't forget about me—the victim—and my family.

But there was nothing Dad could do in that moment to make things okay. I disintegrated into uncontrollable pieces: bloodshot teary eyes, trembling lower lip, sunken shoulders, shaking hands. I followed Catherine upstairs, stumbling over my feet with my head down, a blanket of shame on top of me.

Before we walked past the defense table, I shifted my body to Catherine's right side and used her as a shield to hide me. I was at least half a foot taller than Catherine, but I tried to scrunch down to her height.

I walked toward the witness stand and grimaced at Judge Larry Smukler, bowing my head in respect. I had watched a ton of episodes of *Law & Order* over the years. But nothing could have prepared me for that courtroom. Harsh fluorescent ceiling lights had replaced the natural sunlight. Strangers packed the benches. I couldn't tell who was an enemy and who was a friend. I spotted a few former classmates next to Owen's family; it was a dagger in my heart.

After raising my right hand to get sworn in, I surveyed the important people around me: the judge, the lawyers, the constables. I felt so small and frail, like I could be blown away by the breeze of a nearby fan.

Catherine began her direct examination, asking me about my family, growing up in Japan, my relationship with Lucy.

"We are the best of friends," I said, my voice quivering. "She has taught me so much throughout my entire life."

I explained to Catherine how having an older sister at St. Paul's made me a target for attention from senior boys as a way for them to tease Lucy, to get under her skin. When I described the Senior Salute, I refused to look over at Owen. A tunnel formed around my head, blocking out everything except Catherine's understanding eyes. I hoped I could get through my entire testimony without seeing him.

But then Catherine asked me to identify Owen by describing what he was wearing in court that day. I turned my head in his direction, fighting every instinct to keep my gaze on the prosecutor's table and Dad sitting behind. Owen stood up defiantly. His hair was thicker and darker and he wore thick horn-rimmed glasses that made him look like Harry Potter. It was as if he had put on a costume. I panicked again. I shook and gasped for air.

"Your Honor," Catherine pleaded.

"He didn't have to stand up," Judge Smukler said.

"The defendant does not have to stand up," Catherine scolded Owen before turning to me. "Chessy, do you see Owen in the court-room today?"

"Yes, I do," I whimpered as I clenched the knight and sticky note in my pocket. "I'm sorry," I said, apologizing for letting my emotions show.

I locked eyes with Dad. He gave little nods like the ones he'd make during softball games to let me know I was doing okay. I tried to keep my composure for the rest of the afternoon as Catherine questioned how well I knew Owen and asked about the photos of the two of us at Ecofest and the Nash Christmas party.

"Were you closely acquainted with the defendant at the time this picture was taken?"

I felt defiled just looking at the photos.

"No, I wasn't. I was invited by a boy in the dorm, one of my friends. He invited me to the Christmas party," I said. "And, again, these events are used to take a lot of photos for Facebook and stuff. But he just came up to me, jumped in a photo, and left."

Catherine pressed me on why I agreed to go on the Senior Salute after initially rejecting Owen. I explained that a close friend had approached me and caught me off guard, and convinced me to change my mind.

"I'd been persuaded and told I was wrong on many accounts and he tried to make me feel comfortable with the idea," I said. "And eventually I was thinking okay, here's a person who has paid special attention to me, how nice."

Salty tears burned my eyes as I listened to how truly naive I sounded.

DAY 2

The next morning was like Groundhog Day: my arms wrapped around the toilet, prayers at the kitchen table, and another Post-it Note from Lucy.

She drew a stick figure of a girl pumping her fists in the air.

> Today you stand up. For you! For those who don't understand For me, For Christianna For girls everywhere For the unheard For those silenced.

I put the yellow square inside my pocket along with the knight. Back on the witness stand I had trouble getting words out, much less speaking loudly. Court officials had to turn off a fan that was drowning out my testimony.

I clutched the figurine in my sweaty palm while I described pulling up my bra straps and holding on to my underwear in the mechanical room. My voice shook when I recounted Owen biting my breasts.

"Did you say anything to him when he did that?" Catherine asked.

"I didn't say anything," I responded.

"What were you thinking when he did that to you?"

"I was thinking, Ow, I'm in pain, but I couldn't think of anything else," I said. "I was—I felt like I was frozen."

"What did you do when his face was near your vagina?"

"I took his head and I moved it up and said, 'No, no, no, let's keep it up here,'" I explained, gesturing above my waist.

"And what did you mean by that?" Catherine asked.

"I meant no, that I didn't want any of that," I said.

"What didn't you want?"

"I didn't want him to touch me down there," I said.

"'Down there' means what to you?"

"My vagina. I didn't want him down there orally, I didn't want him down there with his hands, I didn't—I wish I kept my pants on."

"What did you think you were communicating to him when you moved his face and said, 'No, no, let's keep it up here'?"

"I thought that was a sure no," I said. "I thought he would respect me. But he laughed and said, 'You're such a tease.'"

Catherine was trying to be gentle, but it felt like I was being stoned to death as I laid out the worst moments of my life in excruciating detail for a roomful of strangers. I broke down again when I talked about showering after the assault.

"I tried to wash every little part of me," I said through tears. "I felt like something had just been taken away from me."

I stared at Carney's bald, egg-shaped head as he stood up. It was his turn now. I imagined I was standing in a boxing ring and silently hummed lyrics from Katy Perry's "Roar," one of the songs Lucy put on a playlist to make me feel brave on the stand: *You hear my voice, you hear that sound, Like thunder gonna shake the ground.*

I refused to return Carney's fake smile and waited for the showdown to begin. He jabbed me with short questions at first, but they were embedded with wrong assumptions about me, about decisions

I'd made, about words I'd used. I knew he was trying to lure me into agreeing with things that weren't true, and it took all of my brain-power to decipher what traps he was setting.

First he insisted that Lucy taught me that I could ignore Senior Salute invitations. Then Carney said that school advisers recommended the best approach was to simply not respond.

"That's not correct, no," I said, looking straight into his beady little eyes. "They knew that they had no power in that situation, that these boys would still keep objectifying us."

"Chessy, you've been using words like 'power,' 'empowerment,' and 'objectify,'" Carney said. "Are these words that you've learned in the last year?"

"No, they are not."

What a cocky, pretentious asshole. He'd fit right in at St. Paul's. Did he not think teenage girls are capable of knowing what it means to be objectified? That they can't understand what empowerment feels like?

Carney tried to pave a golden brick road to my meeting up with Owen, lined with romantic French poetry and flirty song lyrics. But he left out important facts—namely that Owen asked a boy to pressure me into accepting his invitation. I made sure not to let those details slip past the jury, and that pissed off Carney.

"Chessy, I think things would go better if I asked a question and if you can answer it yes or no, you do so. Would you be willing to do that if you can answer a question yes or no?"

I looked over at Catherine. I had zero court experience, but I was pretty certain that I didn't have to answer with just a yes or no.

Catherine approached Judge Smukler: "I object that the witness cannot be restricted to merely yes-or-no questions and that she is allowed to explain herself."

"She can explain," Judge Smukler said, "but if it's a yes-or-no question, she can answer either yes or no, then explain."

Catherine: 1. Carney: 0.

Carney pushed his glasses back onto the bridge of his nose and moved on to my prior sexual experience—as if that had anything to do with whether or not I was assaulted.

"You hadn't engaged in oral sex with a boy? Or you hadn't been digitally penetrated by a boy?"

"No, I had not."

Then Carney turned his attention to my expectations before meeting up with Owen. He showed me a copy of Catie's interview with the police and pointed forcefully at the page. Carney got so close that I could smell his breath, rotten like sour milk.

"Did you tell Catie that your expectations were like I'll probably let him finger me and like at most I'll blow him and that's what you would allow to have happen, right?"

"No, that's not true," I responded, completely blindsided.

"Isn't that what you told Catie when you were talking about what your expectations were of what you were going to do that night when you were with Owen?"

"No, I honestly have no recollection of saying that to her," I said. "And if I had—no, I have no recollection of saying that to her. And it wasn't how I was feeling while he was doing these things to me."

I loved Catie dearly, but I knew she could be spacey and say things off-the-cuff. All that mattered was what happened in the mechanical room. I said no. And if Carney had read out loud the rest of Catie's interview, the people in that courtroom would have learned that I told her I said no. That I pulled up my bra straps and yanked up my underwear twice. And I didn't just confide in Catie—I told several other friends.

But of course Carney didn't do that. Instead he latched onto Catie's words like a cat who wouldn't let go of a dead mouse. He asked me the same question over and over again. He was a manipulative bully, just like his client.

Carney stopped the pummeling around four p.m., just after asking me for the definition of a blow job. He paused dramatically when I answered and then suggested it was time to recess for the day. I had been on the stand for less than an hour, but I felt bloodied and bruised.

As Carney bent down to collect his papers on the table, he turned and stared at Dad, as if daring him to jump over the bench. They locked eyes, and the tension was palpable.

"How can he treat me this way?" I bawled as I climbed onto Lucy's lap in the room downstairs, where she had been holed up with Mom all day.

Back at the rental house, I numbed my brain by binge-watching episodes of *Grey's Anatomy* and *Young & Hungry*. I closed the door for hours and resurfaced only when I smelled food downstairs. I couldn't eat anything all day, so I was usually ravenous by dinner.

Around eleven p.m., Steve Kelly, the lawyer we had met in Washington, DC, came over for some late-night counsel. He wasn't part of Catherine's team prosecuting Owen. Steve was there solely to make sure my rights as a victim were protected in the criminal trial.

"He was a bully," I said of Carney. "I didn't know what to do. I was all jumbled with fear and anxiety."

"You're the star of the show," Steve said. "This is your testimony, not his. So you can control everything about how this goes. You can control the pacing. I always tell witnesses to breathe and count to three before you answer. It gives you time to think. And it prevents him from getting into a rhythm."

I scribbled in my notebook that I was supposed to use for my CSN homework: *Power of the pause.*

"If Carney asks questions about a document, ask him for your own copy of the document," Steve said. "And if he's asking a yes-or-no question and you can't accurately answer it with yes or no, then say this question cannot be answered truthfully with just a yes or no. You're not being evasive; you're trying to be careful and answer the question honestly."

DAY 3

I woke up the next morning to a text from Tabitha, my freshman-year roommate at St. Paul's.

> Tabitha: Hey Chessy! I know we haven't talked in a while, but I wanted to let you know that I think about you all the time, and I'm really proud of you. What you are doing is incredibly brave, and I can't imagine how hard it must be. I also wanted to thank you because in speaking out, you're giving a voice to people like me who felt like they had to remain silent when these things happened to them. I know this probably doesn't mean or help much, but you have my support, and I'm sending virtual hugs your way.

I was grateful for Tabitha's message, but I didn't have time to write back immediately. I needed to get ready for battle. I threw fear in the corner and shoved vulnerability under the bed. Anger was coming with me to the courtroom today.

I knew I had nothing to hide. And I felt confident and empowered enough to ask Carney to rephrase loaded, winding questions and to take my time answering them.

At 9:15 a.m. Carney walked over to the witness stand again so that I could follow along with a police report he was holding. He inched so close that I could see beads of sweat on his bald head. I called him out when he missed several words in the transcript, and I looked up to Catherine for support. Carney needed to physically back up.

He resisted giving me a copy at first and whined to Judge Smuk-ler, "Your Honor, what I'm trying to do is hold it right in front of her and use my finger so she knows exactly where I'm reading."

Catherine found an extra copy in her file and handed it to me.

Catherine: 2. Carney: 0.

While reading another passage from my interview with Detective Curtin, Carney asked if he could skip the "ums" and "ahs." He was asking for permission to misquote me and change the meaning of my words. His efforts to manipulate me were so obvious that I almost laughed.

"I'm sorry," I said. "I would prefer if you read it word for word so they can get an accurate telling."

"Does that change the meaning of the sentence?" Carney asked.

"It does."

"How?"

"Because this is just a transcript and this doesn't tell the whole story," I said.

"Does the word 'um' change the meaning of the sentence?"

"I was unsure of myself," I said. "It's the whole sentence, it's the whole truth. I just want the whole truth to be read."

I wasn't going to let some expensive defense attorney steamroll me into changing my testimony. Then Carney pounced on my use of the word "cloudy."

"Now, you used that word yesterday throughout your explanations to the prosecutor about why you said or did or did not do or did not say things, it was because you were cloudy or confused. Were you already being cloudy and confused the day before you got together with Owen?"

"No."

"Well, why were you cloudy?" Carney asked.

I cocked my head sideways in disbelief. Was he stupid? What the hell was this guy's problem?

"I was raped!" I gasped, sobbing. "I was violated in so many ways. Of course I was traumatized."

Carney tensed up and asked if we should take a recess. No. I didn't need a break. I just needed this nightmare to end. Today would be my last day of testifying. It had to be.

Somehow I found an inexplicable strength within me to go on. I grasped on to the support around me as if it was a knife and cut away my fear, helplessness, and exhaustion. I emerged with a new armor, a steely resolve. I would not let him break me. I would not crumble.

I maintained eye contact with Carney as he tried to shut me down and make me agree to things that were untrue.

He hammered me on the seemingly cordial emails I sent to Owen after the assault, reading them in a singsongy voice and turning my assault into a fucking musical.

He quizzed me on my grooming habits, as if shaving my private parts was an invitation to have sex with me against my will. I wished I could grab his white beard and rip it off his face. It was preposterous to ask me, a teenage girl, about how I took care of my body and imply that it had provoked a sexual assault. I said no multiple times! This wasn't complicated.

I was so naive to think that all the evidence would be presented fairly and objectively to the jury. Important details—including that there were other girls who reported that Owen violated them and that I told my friends I said no—would never see the light of day because of stupid legal rules intended to protect the defendant. No, this was a chance for Carney to twist and spin, shame and blame. Distract the jury with my shaving habits instead of my words. I said no.

I watched Carney's eyes dart back and forth as he grew uncomfortable with my relentless glare. He ramped up his aggression, jabbing his finger at me, almost touching my shoulder. Carney repeatedly accused me of lying and asked absurd questions like whether I twirled my hair or tapped my fingers when I lied. I wanted to stand up and object for relevance. How could this man get away with such revolting behavior? He was the type of person who makes it so hard for victims to come forward.

Finally, by eleven a.m., Carney finished his interrogation. I left the courtroom and bolted down the stairs to find Lucy and Mom. Steve Kelly followed and told me I did great, but fury pricked my skin. I wished I could punch Carney.

Steve, as any civil attorney would do, advised against that and instead suggested that I write down some questions for Carney in my journal. Steve promised he would ask them of Carney when the trial was over, as long as the questions wouldn't get him disbarred.

August 20, 2015: Questions for Mr. Carney/ From C.
Q. What are you wearing? Do you think the defendant could have misread intentions by your clothing?
Q. Mr. Carney, are YOUR balls shaved right now?

I showed Steve and he smiled.

When we got home that afternoon, I holed up in my room and tore through more episodes of *Grey's Anatomy*. I'd finished season four since the trial started. But I hadn't done a lick of homework.

I bounded down the stairs before I smelled dinner.

"Mom, I'm hungry," I announced for the first time in a week.

"Yes, honey, let's make whatever you want!"

Mom was so ecstatic that you would have thought I told her we won the lottery.

"Mrs. Hebra left us bags of groceries. Let's see what we can find," Mom said.

I dug through the pantry and hunted for my comfort food: pasta. It wasn't gluten free but I couldn't have cared less. I slurped down the noodles without taking a breath.

I returned to my show after dinner, leaving the room only for bathroom breaks. During one trip to the toilet, I heard my own voice blasting from the television downstairs where the rest of my family was gathered. It was the moment when I lost my composure with Carney and wailed, "I was raped! I was violated in so many ways. Of course I was traumatized."

My voice was slightly distorted a few pitches lower in an attempt to protect my identity. I started laugh-crying in disbelief and heard Dad yell at Uncle John to lower the volume. I felt helpless. My words were being paraded on CNN, NBC, ABC, MSNBC, BuzzFeed, the *Today* show, and local stations. I had no idea the trial would get this much attention. But I did it. I told the truth. I sat in that courtroom for hours over three days.

I was done, finished being grilled like I was the offender. I was a survivor. My heart was held in God's hands. He had given me strength in so many ways. No matter how weary I was, I would never lose the will to tell the TRUTH. I wouldn't take responsibility for Owen's actions anymore. I had cleared my conscience, emptied my heart and soul and brain for that jury. I hoped they believed me and trusted my truth. I knew I'd only gotten over one hump of this mighty tour, but in my heart, I'd already won.

The rest was out of my control. We had a break for the weekend and then court resumed on Monday.

As I conquered season five of *Grey's Anatomy*, I wrote back to Tabitha. We'd never talked in detail about the night of my assault, so her message of support was especially meaningful.

> Me: Thank you so much for that Tabitha. I was afraid of disappointing you that night, and now i've been using that shame to blame myself ever since. You did not have a chance at justice, and I do, which I think is so unfair, but

I will push myself forwards for the community of young women and men who couldn't and continue to not be able to seek justice, yet. Tabitha, your support and thank you mean the WORLD to me. Thank you so much for continuing to believe in me, through all the cloudy bullshit, I hold that really close to my heart.

FIFTEEN

The Slayers

DAY 4

The seating arrangements in the courtroom were absurd. The media circus had commandeered the section near the door usually reserved for the defendant's family. That meant we had to climb over Owen's relatives in order to sit on the cramped benches behind the prosecutor's table on the farthest side of the room. I didn't know whose knobby knees I knocked and toes I stepped on, but I apologized instinctively.

"I'm sorry, I'm sorry," I muttered.

"Don't apologize to them," Dad snarled. "You have nothing to be sorry about. You owe them nothing."

I was glad my time on the witness stand had ended, but things seemed just as hostile back here. Owen's father cursed at my uncle Pete. One guy planted his middle finger on the cheek facing

Dad. Another idiot refused to get up and allow my eighty-six-year-old grandma to pass by. Michele Finizio, the mother of a former St. Paul's student and a criminal defense attorney who let Owen move in with her after his arrest, called Mom a fucking bitch.

I took deep breaths as we waited for Owen's friends to testify. I wasn't required to be in the courtroom, but this was my life under the microscope. I had to be there to remind people of my humanity, and I wanted to hear what these boys had to say, and make them say it to my face.

Earlier that morning Dad and I had observed the guys huddled in a room together with the St. Paul's witness coordinator. I shook my head in disbelief as betrayal seared my skin. They wore matching prep-school uniforms with navy blazers and button-down shirts. Even Owen had on the same colors. Had they all planned this? And if so, what else had they coordinated?

Back in the courtroom Owen MacIntyre was up first. It had been nearly a year since we had walked around campus together so he could give his forced apology, the one that mutated into regret for violating bro code. I couldn't believe I had considered this kid a friend. He refused to meet my glare.

On the stand he opened a window into the twisted sexual culture at St. Paul's, defining hook-up terms like "slay" as "more aggressive" than "score." O. Mac said there was a competition between Owen Labrie and his roommate, Andrew Thomson, to see who could Senior Salute the most girls. After pressuring me into accepting the invite, O. Mac got a message of appreciation.

> O. Mac: Oh and btw Chessy says yes. You are welcome
> Owen: you're a fucking dawg
>   i will owe you ten thousand bjs
>   /get you fucked up the night of grad

I guess those were the benefits of honoring bro code.

Malcolm Salovaara was up next. This was only the second time I'd ever seen him in person, and he looked as sleazy as I had remembered, wearing an open-neck white shirt as if he was going clubbing. Malcolm was entering his junior year at Dartmouth College and he seemed antsy. His personal lawyer took up a chunk of the morning with concerns that Malcolm's testimony might be self-incriminating and violate his Fifth Amendment rights. Apparently, Malcolm might have been in possession of stolen keys from St. Paul's, like Owen, and the messages the two exchanged about me could be damaging. I didn't know what they said, but I was about to find out.

I took no joy in hearing Malcolm publicly acknowledge his slimy behavior: he and Owen had created a Facebook group known as Slayers Anonymous to send messages to each other, and they used to rub the name of an alumnus, Robert Barrie Slaymaker, etched on the wooden paneling lining the walls of the Upper leading into the dining room. I remembered guys rubbing the name on their way to dinner, but never knew the deep significance to the gesture.

"We thought it was funny that his name had the word 'slay' in it," Malcolm explained.

Catherine didn't find it amusing and peppered Malcolm with questions about the Facebook messages. She projected them onto a large white screen so that the jury could see them. Then she made Malcolm read them out loud.

"So after you ask, 'who do you want to pork more than anyone bro,' what does the defendant respond to you?" Catherine asked.

"'Chessy Prout,'" Malcolm said reluctantly.

I shuddered.

"And then what do you answer?"

"'Hahaha are you kidding me bro?'" Malcolm read.

Rage coursed through my veins and lifted me outside my body. I was frozen again.

"And what does he respond to you?"

"'Total babe,'" Malcolm said.

"And your next message?" Catherine asked.

"'Isn't she a tessa?'"

I knew what that meant. Tessa was the name of a senior boy's younger sister. I frantically scribbled in my notebook and showed Dad.

"And what do you mean by that?"

Malcolm couldn't wipe the smirk off his face. "Isn't she someone who is really young?"

"And your next inquiry, what do you ask him next?" Catherine pressed.

"'Does she even have nips yet?'" Malcolm said.

"And what did you mean by that?"

"I don't recall what I meant by that," Malcolm said, his thin lips disappearing into his long chin.

Those grimy pieces of shit.

"What does that mean to you today?" Catherine asked.

"Is she mature physically," Malcolm said.

"Were you aware of Chessy Prout's age?"

"Yes," Malcolm said.

I gnashed my teeth.

"And is that why you were asking about her maturity?"

"Yes," Malcolm said.

"I'd ask you to testify to the date of these exchanges."

"January 29, 2014."

I gasped audibly. That was a whole five months before I was assaulted. I felt like I was going to throw up. They had been targeting me for months. And they'd been making crude comments all that time about my body, and my age.

Catherine had Malcolm read another message he sent Owen a few weeks later. "'Have you slain Chessy already?'"

I wanted to bust out of my seat and clobber him. Both Malcolm and Owen. They needed to feel the pain they had inflicted on me. They talked about me like I was a wild animal to be hunted violently, or "slain" as they so crassly put it.

And minutes before Owen took me to the top of the mechanical room on May 30, 2014, he had messaged Malcolm in all capital letters.

Owen: I'M SLAYIN CHESSY

Dad put his arm around me as I started weeping. It made so much sense now, the smirks Malcolm gave me during graduation weekend. But why the hell did it have to be me?

I looked in horror to my right at Laura Dunn, the survivor and lawyer I had met in the spring. Every victim who fights in criminal court needs a Laura Dunn by their side. She had rushed up to deal with the media onslaught after my identity was broadcast on the live video feed during the first day of the trial and then several news outlets used my name.

To prevent me from doing anything rash, Laura told me to funnel my feelings into the notebook while the boys were testifying. So I let loose on Malcolm.

> *He is a COWARD . . . I don't know how he lives with himself every day. He is a weak excuse for a human being. Both of them are.*

Malcolm was such a fucking hypocrite. I later found out that he was quoted in the Dartmouth student newspaper after attending a protest in February 2014 against sexual violence. "Sexual assault was a problem at his high school," the story said, and Salovaara "takes the issue very seriously."

So seriously that he encouraged Owen at the same time to "slay" me, a fifteen-year-old minor?

Catherine switched her focus to Malcolm's interview with the Concord Police Department.

"And isn't it true that you said Labrie told you that he had sex with Chessy Prout?"

"That's not true," Malcolm said.

"So what's in the police report is not accurate?" Catherine said incredulously.

"That's correct."

I knifed the notebook on my lap with a pen, cutting through several inches:

> *I hope Malcolm gets arrested for lying ON THE FUCKING STAND SO MANY FUCKING TIMES!*

Carney didn't even bother asking questions. He must have known that the slimeball now had zero credibility.

Andrew Thomson made his way to the stand next as Joe, the other county attorney, prepared for his questioning. Anger gnarled my face as I thought of the single red rose Andrew had bought me for Valentine's Day and the secret snuggle email he sent, too. Was this all part of one big conspiracy against me? What more had they done that I had no idea about?

Andrew started off by claiming that the Senior Salute could mean taking a walk around campus. What a freaking joke. When he was done with that set of lies, he denied ever being in a competition with Owen to score the most girls. Andrew's mother, Lucy Hodder, was on the board of trustees at St. Paul's, so he had a lot at stake. I could only imagine what his mommy's advice was. Sadness wedged in my throat as I thought about Andrew's younger sister, who had been one of my best friends freshman year. I now realized that meant nothing to these people when their reputations and social standing were on the line. They'd rather protect a criminal than help someone in need, just to save their own skin.

Andrew said he had talked with Owen before we met up at the Lindsay building and warned him that it "probably wasn't a great idea" because I was a lot younger than them. That disclosure tortured Lucy and my cousin Tony, both of whom used to count Andrew as their friend. After Owen returned later that night, Andrew said he'd pried for details.

"He wasn't giving me much information," Andrew said. "I kept asking, and he eventually told me that, in his words, that he had boned her."

"And in that context, what did that mean?" Joe asked.

"I took it to mean that they had had sex," Andrew said.

How could Owen's defense be that we'd never had sex when that was what he told so many of his friends? I didn't think he was that stupid.

Next, Tucker Marchese waltzed into the courtroom as if this was the social event of the year, grinning at Owen and waving hello to people like a pageant queen. Tucker was now a student at Holy Cross in Massachusetts—the college both Mom and Carney had attended. It was a connection that made Mom sick.

Before Tucker took the stand, he turned around and smiled smugly at me and my family. I almost lunged at him, my hand in a fist.

"Chessy, you can't do that. They can call a mistrial," Laura whispered sternly, holding me back. "If you feel like you're going to attack someone, maybe consider not sitting in the courtroom."

"Okay, fine. I can handle it," I said, settling back in my seat.

More messages from Owen appeared on the big screen. Owen had sent them to Tucker from his St. Paul's email address in March, on the cusp of the Senior Salute season—apparently known as "Slaypril" and "Slay" for April and May.

> Owen: welcome to an eight-week exercise in debauchery,
> a probing exploration of the innermost meaning of the
> word sleaze-bag, we'll be exploring the several essential
> questions. is life on earth heaven? are there any gazelles
> left in this desolate savannah? can sisters be slain in the
> same evening??

Sexual conquest was just a simple game to these guys. Girls had zero value, no human dignity. The messages eviscerated all hope that one of these boys would come to his senses and apologize.

Tucker said that he and Owen had gathered at the library one night and assembled a list of girls for the "eight-week exercise in debauchery." The list was presented to the jury, and my name was the *only one* in all capital letters. Lucy was also on the list. Sisters slain.

I almost passed out. I tapped my feet on the floor like Buzz taught me and found my bearings. I scowled at Tucker. He stared right back, shamelessly. I didn't want to do anything stupid, so I looked down and wrote in my notebook:

> *Wasn't afraid of meeting my stare. Ballsy for a boy with no balls . . . They really are a bunch of losers.*

Tucker said Owen was upset after I rejected his Senior Salute invite, and Tucker was surprised later when Owen told him that we'd met up and had sex. He wanted details and messaged Owen later that night.

> Tucker: How did it go from no to bone.
> Owen: just pulled every trick in the book
> Tucker: Be straight with me
> Which one worked

Owen: had to munch
Tucker: It was crystal clean so whatever
   How'd you even get to that point bro
Owen: she replied to my first email
Tucker: ight man the story has too many holes, i
   appreciate the end result and your resolve
   and congrats i hope it was everything you imagined

Congrats? Congrats on raping a fifteen-year-old virgin?

The next night, after Lucy punched Owen on the chapel lawn in front of their friends, Owen messaged Tucker.

Owen: the chessy thing will blow over
denied until i died tonight
her friends forgave me
KIND OF

Each new bit of evidence was a punch to the gut. I didn't know how to react to the vulgar messages anymore because I had seen too many of them. Learning for the first time how these boys plotted against me for months made me feel like I was being assaulted again, but this time in a roomful of strangers. "Deny until you die" was the motto of these Slayers. And I was just an object to them—something to be traded, degraded, and manipulated.

When court let out for the afternoon, I felt so defeated and worthless. As I skulked down the stairs to the first floor, I spotted a group of St. Paul's students who had been sitting with Owen's family all day: Ian, a friend who was in Lucy's class and also took Japanese with me; Jennifer, my volleyball teammate; and Mac, who I met for the first time during St. Paul's Revisit Weekend.

I looked down at them in the high-ceilinged lobby and wondered how they could still stand by him after everything that had been revealed.

I moved swiftly in their direction, and when I was just a few feet away, my eyes blazed right through them.

"Are you proud of yourselves? Are you proud of who you're supporting?" I barked. "Are you happy that he did this to me?"

They fell silent and their mouths hung open. Dad quickly moved me away from the group and into the room reserved for our family, where I collapsed in a chair. Would this ever be over? I didn't know yet that the pain that made me want to disappear forever would eventually be replaced by a slow-burning anger that simmers within me to this day.

Grandma Prout pulled me aside later that evening while we were sitting on the porch. Grandma was elegant, with her perfectly coiffed white hair and red lipstick. She always chose her words carefully.

"Don't stay angry at these boys. They're not worth it," she said in her Japanese accent. "And don't hold resentment."

"Yeah, yeah," I grumbled. "But I don't think I'm ever gonna be ready for forgiveness, Grandma."

"Someday. But for now, just pity them. Pity that they don't have morals. Pity that they aren't worth anything," Grandma Prout said as she tapped ashes from her cigarette. "Imagine how they feel inside because of how horrible they are."

I could not care less how they felt. I was raw from seeing and hearing them all day. Later I talked to Dad—my usual anger outlet—and told him what Grandma had said. He chuckled.

"You know, Chess, that's the kiss of death from Grandma," he said. "If you ever hear she pities you, that means you're dead to her."

Fine, I could handle that. Those guys were dead to me, too.

DAY 5

Detective Curtin looked exhausted on the witness stand, bags under her eyes. She and her team, including Detective Chris

DeAngelis, had worked relentlessly on the case for more than a year. They had interviewed close to thirty people and combed through tens of thousands of messages, including 119 exchanges that Owen had deleted after meeting with police. I thought there couldn't possibly be any more surprises, but there it was. Owen's mother had advised him to delete incriminating Facebook messages. I didn't understand why they both weren't charged with obstruction of justice.

During his police interview, Owen explained how the school kept painting over a sexual scoreboard that students put up in Sharpie on the wall behind the laundry machines—something Chad Green, St. Paul's dean of students, euphemistically described in court as a "map of relationships." Owen also told Detective Curtin that he'd had a moment of "divine inspiration" and stopped us from having sex. I laughed at that one.

Carney tried to depict Detective Curtin as an overzealous woman who was empowering a liar on a witch hunt for Harry Potter. His strategy backfired. Detective Curtin came across as careful, methodical, and persistent—the kind of employee any police department would be lucky to have.

I knew Detective Curtin had interviewed other girls that Owen had violated, but New Hampshire's rules of evidence prevented his prior bad acts from being introduced during the trial. It seemed so unfair. And Judge Smukler refused to let our expert witness testify and explain that people who are sexually assaulted often freeze like I did. It's not simply a matter of punching back or running away. It's fight, flight, or freeze. Now I knew why so many girls were reluctant to report their attackers and pursue charges. The court system seemed designed to trample us into lifelong silence.

I worried that Judge Smukler was biased toward Carney and captivated by the superstar and the media attention that followed. Each day Carney held press conferences outside, the reporters salivating at every word to feed the public's appetite for boarding-school scandals.

DAY 6

On the stand, Owen spewed lie after lie—saying that we'd danced together, that we'd hugged, that he'd never had sex with me. It would almost be laughable if it weren't so sickening. When he read the messages we'd exchanged before we met up on May 30, bile shot up from my stomach and scorched my throat.

I looked down at the floor and knew I was going to be sick. I pushed my way out of the courtroom and into a side room to throw myself over a garbage can. Steve and Barbara, the victim advocate, followed me. Reporters who were live-tweeting said I ran out of the room in tears. I want to make it clear that I was about to hurl chunks.

Eventually, Steve and I headed to the overflow room where there were televisions and workstations for the media.

"Don't say anything to the journalists," Steve advised before entering. "They will use it."

One of the female reporters watched Carney question Owen as if he were the victim and then turned to me.

"I'm sorry," she said. "He's a sociopath."

I just nodded. *Finally, someone else sees it.*

I returned to the courtroom for Owen's cross-examination after the lunch break. I was strong enough to handle this. For the first time, I looked Owen in the eyes, through his stupid glasses. I stared him down and watched him wriggle uncomfortably in his seat.

That's right, you fucking loser. You can't even look me in the face. Weak coward.

It was showtime.

There was an instant change in Owen's demeanor when Joe stepped forward. Joe was tall, a dairy farmer's son, and relatively new to sexual assault cases. He usually had a gentle disposition, but when Joe got up to the podium, he was a fire-breathing dragon.

"You wanted to have sex with Chessy Prout, correct?" Joe asked Owen.

"When?" Owen said.

"During your senior year."

"Not necessarily, no," Owen responded.

"You wanted to slay Chessy Prout, correct?" Joe asked.

"I mentioned that to my friends, but sure, okay," Owen said.

"You wanted to score Chessy Prout, correct?"

"Maybe, I don't know," Owen stuttered. "Not during the year."

"You wanted to pork Chessy Prout, correct?"

"I don't know what that—what do you mean by that?" Owen asked with a faux look of innocence.

"You don't know what the word 'pork' means?" Joe said skeptically.

Joe's gonna bring him down. He's finally gonna get what he deserves. This is what justice looks like.

Joe focused on the January 2014 messages with Malcolm Salovaara.

"We can be sure that on January 29, 2014, you wanted to slay Chessy Prout, correct?"

"Once again, these are joking messages and my affection for her. I don't think that's accurate to say that I was thinking about slaying her on January 29."

"Forgot it was funny," Joe retorted. "We can agree that on January 29, 2014, you wanted to score Chessy Prout, correct?"

"I mean all these words are used synonymously, so, you know, had I thought about it? Yeah," Owen said. "But, you know, was this a serious conversation? No, it wasn't."

"All of these words are used synonymously and they all can mean sex, correct?" Joe pressed.

"They all can, yes."

"So on January 29th, 2014, you wanted to have sex with Chessy Prout, correct?"

"No. That's not what that means here."

"You just wanted to pork her?"

This dodging and weaving made my head spin. I couldn't keep track. Joe moved on to Owen's messages in late March.

"In your words, Slaypril was 'a probing exploration of the inner-most meanings of the word sleazebag,' correct?"

"Those are my words, yes," Owen said.

"You would agree with me that it would take a sleazebag to take advantage of a fifteen-year-old girl, correct?" Joe asked.

"Yes," Owen said.

"It would take a sleazebag to have sex with a fifteen-year-old girl, correct?"

"Yes."

"It would take a sleazebag to slay a fifteen-year-old girl, correct?"

"That word is different," Owen said.

"That's right," Joe said sarcastically. "That word means going for walks in the park, right?"

"Not exclusively," Owen responded.

"Because it could mean sex?"

"It could, yes," Owen admitted.

"And only a sleazebag would sleep with sisters in the same night, correct?"

"Yes," Owen said.

"Only a sleazebag would slay sisters in the same night, correct?"

"Yes."

I was speechless, frozen in my seat. I didn't understand how he could agree to all of this and insist that he was innocent. Maybe he wasn't as smart as everyone thought.

Joe presented Owen with a new email from May 8, 2014, with the words "still at large" at the top. Once again my name was the only one in all capital letters. Owen continued to deny ever wanting to have sex with me—until he put on a condom. Then, he claimed, he had a moment of "divine inspiration" and stopped himself. Did anyone else realize how absurd this sounded?

He tried to sidestep the damning DNA evidence by saying he pre-ejaculated—a revelation he never told police. And that he deceived his best friends by saying we had sex because that was easier than telling the truth.

I was crushed by the lies, from my body being one big joke to these boys. And I wasn't the only name on those lists, wasn't the only girl who'd been violated. How many others had to sit in my place to get the point across? Would it take thirty-five—the number of women who had recently appeared on the cover of *New York* magazine and said Bill Cosby assaulted them?

We had the right to say no. Our consent mattered. I took out my pen one last time and dug into my journal.

He's gonna rot in hell.

DAY 7

Closing arguments started late. Everyone was present but something— or someone—was holding things up. Joe told us we were waiting for Carney's wife to arrive so she could watch him. I hoped Carney choked on his own hubris.

I scowled at the back of his shiny bald head and seethed at his every word, the victim-blaming, victim-shaming tale he wove using my pain and misery to try and free his guilty client.

He twisted my words and likened me to an armed robber at a bank. Carney downplayed the red abrasion on my vagina that was present three days after the attack as simply "a quarter-centimeter superficial red mark."

I wrote furiously in my journal:

*If I cut 1/4 of a centimeter off your DICK would that
be a sustainable injury?*

I looked over at Lucy, who was finally sitting next to me. Carney never called her as a witness, so she sat sequestered in that room for the entire trial. But now Carney was yammering about what an important role Lucy played in this case. He rambled on about how younger brothers and sisters often look up to their older siblings— and then mentioned his own family: "I have three younger brothers and a younger sister."

Carney then suggested my admiration for Lucy was what caused me to falsely accuse Owen of rape.

I saw Steve Kelly tense up.

"That's so unprofessional," Steve hissed.

I blocked out the rest of Carney's closing argument, imaginary cotton balls in my ears. My brain capacity for bullshit was full for the day.

After court ended, Steve approached Carney in the parking lot. Laura Dunn watched at a distance. We were back at the rental house at the time, but Steve had accidentally pocket-dialed Dad so we listened in on the confrontation.

Steve was a stocky Irish Catholic from Baltimore, the youngest of nine children. Mary, his sister who had been raped and murdered, was like a surrogate parent to him. After her death, Steve and his family were treated terribly by law enforcement and he had fought tirelessly for victims' rights ever since—in the courtroom, in the classroom, in the legislature, and now, apparently, in parking lots.

"This is not going to be a pleasant conversation," Steve said to Carney. "What you did during this trial violated professional ethics by physically intimidating a child and mentioning your family in closing arguments while your wife was there and sitting in the courtroom. You crossed a line."

Carney growled, "You self-righteous prick."

Those were fighting words. We were huddled around the kitchen table, listening to Dad's phone on speaker, wondering what would happen next.

"You're a fucking sleazeball," Steve shot back. "Why don't you slither your way back to Boston?"

I loved Steve for being my foulmouthed defender. The case was in the jury's hands now. But at least we seemed to win the parking lot skirmish.

Lucy tried to comfort me before the first day of the trial with hugs (above) and positive messages written on a sticky note.

When my cross-examination was over, I wrote some questions for the defense attorney in my journal (left). Q. Mr. Carney, are YOUR balls shaved right now?

Later that afternoon, I collapsed at the rental house, exhausted after three days on the stand (below).

Dad tried to keep me calm before Owen's friends testified in court (left).

Grandma Prout (above) dispensed wise advice: "Pity them."

We had a birthday dinner (below) for Laura Dunn, a lawyer and survivor who helped me during the trial (bottom row, left). Our civil lawyer, Steve Kelly (top row, left), and Uncle Tom (top row, second from left) came to the celebration.

SIXTEEN

Verdict

DAY 8

I couldn't stop thinking about what Carney said during yesterday's closing arguments—that I had taken the "easier choice."

Since when was being a victim of rape the easy way out? Who would subject her body to an invasive genital exam for kicks and willingly take harsh drugs to kill gonorrhea and other STDs? Answer phone calls from detectives before softball practice asking questions like how often do you share your underwear? Spend the first weeks of junior year getting grilled by a mobster attorney? Expose yourself and your family to high-profile scrutiny? No one would choose this.

What many people didn't understand was that the second my counselor Buzz called the police, my assault became the *State of New Hampshire v. Owen Labrie*. It was not up to me whether charges were pressed. I was the primary witness in the state's sexual assault case.

My body was evidence. I agreed to make a statement and cooperate because it was the right thing to do. I wanted to stop the cycle of abuse like I wished someone at St. Paul's had done for me.

While the jury deliberated, I huddled with all the people I loved so much. We gathered in a conference room at the prosecutor's office, surrounded by law books, coffee mugs, and boxes of Munchkins from Dunkin' Donuts. I couldn't eat a thing. I folded my arms on the table and put my head down.

I was indebted to the people around that long wooden table—Mom, Dad, Lucy, Uncle Tom, Grandma Prout, Uncle Pete, Aunt Carol, Uncle Bernie, Aunt Blair, Aunt Judy, Uncle John, my other Aunt Carol, my cousins, the lawyers, the advocates, the knight in shining armor (though I had to give him back so he could protect Catherine's next witness).

I was also thankful for the supporters who showed up during the last two weeks, including old friends from Tokyo, the Raymonds and Heintzelmans, and Mom's crew from college: Annie, Joanie, and Nancy.

I especially appreciated my brave allies from St. Paul's, like Buzz; my friends Catie and Lilly; Lucy's adviser, Ms. Carter; and Dylan and his mom, Mrs. Hirschfeld. I knew my case was a nightmare for Buzz—the school had intimidated her and refused to let her speak to police without a lawyer from St. Paul's present. It helped speed up Buzz's retirement; she left the school a few weeks before my trial.

One day after court, I sat on a stone bench in front of the prosecutor's office with Mandi, an older girl who had driven Lilly to my trial and had been on my softball team at St. Paul's. Mandi had faced her own challenges at school as one of the few openly gay students.

"I know how hard it could be at that school. I'm so sorry that this happened to you," Mandi said. "It makes me so angry."

She looked down at her arm and took a Lokai bracelet off her wrist and handed it to me. It had one white bead infused with water from Mount Everest and a single black bead that contained mud from the Dead Sea—the highest and lowest points on earth—as a reminder to find balance during life's peaks and lows.

I gripped the bracelet on my wrist, trying to let strength seep into my fingertips.

"Thank you, Mandi," I said. "This means so much to me."

The rest of the St. Paul's community hunkered down into perfection-protection mode. Students and alumni lashed out at the negative media attention with the hashtag #SPSfam and suggested that people were just jealous. One alum supposedly posted a photo of himself and buddies from the baseball team with the hashtag #theyhateuscuztheyaintus. We were incredulous at the mob mentality.

I tried to avoid social media during the trial, but Dad and Lucy monitored everything. On my first day of testimony, Sally, the girl who'd bullied me and whose brother was arrested for assaulting Allie, posted a photo on Facebook with my former friends. She tagged Ivy and Faith in the picture.

Sally: Love these people and love my #spsfam.

That hashtag was like a big middle finger sticking up at me. But I didn't have the energy to get offended. It just made me feel demoralized and depleted. Those *were* my friends—Ivy and Faith were the girls who'd comforted me in the minutes after my assault. And they didn't care about me anymore. Didn't care about how devastating this was. Sometimes it made me wonder, was I a horrible person? If they couldn't stand by me, what was wrong with me?

Eventually, I realized there were many others rooting for me from a distance. While the jury deliberated, I read a stack of messages that people had sent Catherine and Laura over the last two weeks.

There were letters from a former Miss America who was an incest survivor, a former assistant district attorney, and other survivors, including Adrienne Bak, who was sexually assaulted by the infamous "preppy rapist," Alex Kelly. I couldn't believe that complete strangers who didn't know my name offered more encouragement than my former classmates and teachers.

A male philosophy professor from Massachusetts emailed:

> High profile cases such as yours, which expose the
> ugly reality of male sexual violence, do enormous work
> in exposing this system and encouraging other girls
> and women to stand up for their rights. So merely
> by speaking, in taking a stand not only on your own
> behalf but on behalf of public justice—justice for all girls
> and women, everywhere—you are not only protecting
> future girls or women from Mr. Labrie's violence, but
> are helping to undermine rape culture in the US and
> globally. Don't doubt yourself! Literally millions of people
> are rooting for you. . . .

I smiled and thought of Uncle Ron. Millions of people? No way. All that mattered right now were the twelve individuals on that jury. Nine men and three women.

At the time, I was nervous about all those men. I later learned that female jurors are more likely to acquit defendants accused of rape, according to some studies. I wondered if that's because it's easier for women to blame the victim than face the harsh reality that we don't have the power to prevent rape. Either way, I really wanted to see Owen be taken away in handcuffs and locked up for the rest of his life.

Of course, Catherine had explained the possible outcomes: guilty on all counts, not guilty on all counts, or a split decision. Owen was facing four felony charges, which are more serious crimes that can be punished by more than twelve months in jail. Three of these were for rape and one was for using a computer to solicit a minor. The state also charged him with three counts of misdemeanor sexual assault for penetrating me with his penis, mouth, and fingers; one misdemeanor for endangering the welfare of a minor; and another for biting me on the chest.

Catherine tried to temper expectations of a complete victory because rape cases have very low conviction rates. A fraction of rape cases are reported to police, and even fewer get prosecuted. One study on the justice gap for sexual assault cases estimated that of every one hundred rapes committed, less than 5 result in a conviction. And less than 3 percent of rapists ever see a day in jail. It was hard to keep the faith in such a broken justice system, but I still held out hope.

Minutes churned into hours as we waited for the jury. I whipsawed between second-guessing myself—if all those boys thought it was no big deal, maybe I was being too dramatic—to fuming over the thought of Owen walking free. Anxiety kicked my ribs.

Whenever people walked by the conference room, we all jumped up from the table, hoping they had an answer. Finally Catherine got word that the jury was back. They had a verdict after deliberating for about eight hours over two days.

We walked across the street to the courthouse. Cameramen waiting by the rear door put down their equipment and nodded sympathetically. I trembled with fear as I entered the courtroom and tried clenching my fists to keep my body still. It only got worse when I looked up and saw Owen staring me and Lucy down. That piece of shit. Did he think he could intimidate us now? Lucy and I linked arms in silent solidarity.

My family built a fort around me in the front row: Mom's arm on my shoulder, Dad's hand on my head, and Lucy's fingers intertwined with mine. Everyone in the courtroom stood as we waited for the verdict to be read. I fidgeted with the white beads on my bracelet and prayed for a peak.

"Madam Foreperson, has the jury reached a verdict?"

"Yes, we have."

"How say you, Madam Foreperson? How do you find the defendant Owen Labrie on indictment number 973494c, accusing the defendant of prohibited uses of computer equipment in that he knowingly utilized a computer online service and/or Internet service to seduce, lure, or entice a female child under the age of sixteen . . . to commit an offense of sexual assault and/or related offenses by utilizing St. Paul's school email and/or Facebook? Guilty or not guilty?"

"Guilty."

My knees buckled and I nearly collapsed.

"Do you say, Madam Foreperson, that the defendant Owen Labrie is guilty?"

"Yes."

"So say you all members of the jury?"

"Yes," they said in unison.

Finally. I cried and pressed my forehead against Dad's shoulder. They believed me! They saw through Owen's lies. I looked gratefully at the jurors; some met my gaze, others cast their eyes downward.

I soon learned why. The jury found Owen not guilty of the felony rape charges. I was a cauldron of confusion and anger: How could they believe me but not convict him of raping me? Was it because I didn't kick or scream? I said no!

But there was more: the jury then convicted Owen of three counts of misdemeanor sexual assault for penetrating a minor with his penis, finger, and mouth and another count of endangering the welfare of a child. They cleared him of the misdemeanor assault charge for biting my chest.

It was a split verdict.

I glanced at Owen, hunched over the defense table, crying

dramatically. I rolled my eyes. He wouldn't have been in this position had he just treated me like a human being and respected my words. This was all his fault.

Mom and Dad formed a protection pod around me as we left the courtroom. Catherine and Laura focused on what we had accomplished—not what we'd lost. Owen was found guilty on five of the nine counts.

They reminded me that each of the misdemeanor sexual assault charges could carry a one-year sentence. And the felony computer charge would require him to register as a sex offender in a public database and could restrict him from working in places such as schools or churches where he could prey on other children.

My mind was a dark forest as I tried to make sense of the verdict. We ducked out the rear entrance while Steve, Laura, Joe, and Catherine walked out front to address the horde of journalists.

I had made plans to get ice cream with Dylan after court, but Dad hightailed it out of Concord that afternoon, zooming down the highway at Indy 500 speeds. I texted Dylan in the car as we drove to the airport in Boston.

> Me: I hope you know that the things my family and I hold against the school though is definitely not personal at all. You have been such an amazing friend through this, and your mother has been amazing showing her support every day at the courthouse . . . and hope you can always consider me to be a friend.
>
> Dylan: I pray every day that the school can resolve the massive problems that it clearly holds. It makes me very sad sometimes that I grew up my whole life here without knowing that such a place could be very poisonous. Throughout this year I have contemplated leaving myself however one of the many things you have

taught me is that standing up is the right thing to do.
I want you to know that I think of you very often and I
won't leave school without giving it my every effort to
make sure that such a sick person will never walk these
paths again.

I had barely stepped out of the taxi in Naples when Christianna
sprinted down the driveway and catapulted into my arms. The babysitter had promised to keep Christianna away from trial coverage on
TV, but I wondered if my little sister had any idea what I'd been
through.

I was completely wiped out, my eyelids heavy with exhaustion.
And I felt bad that our whole family had abandoned Christianna
on my account, so I let her dress me up in a ridiculous outfit—a red
polka-dot clown costume and a knit ski cap with #SELFIE embroidered
on the front, topped off with a straw hat. We did silly dance moves
and took photos frolicking around the house. All I wished for was to
be a kid again and forget the trial ever happened.

But my efforts to resume a normal teenage existence were short-
lived. Days after the verdict, Detective Curtin called Dad, her voice
taut and serious: anonymous hate sites were popping up all over the
Internet. I typed my name into Google.

Online trolls had published photos of thirteen-year-old me in a
bikini with a friend from Naples and listed my full name and home
address, along with pictures of my house, Lucy, and Christianna. They
stole photos from my Facebook account and my private Instagram page
and called me "an attention whore at St. Paul's School who tried to
slime an innocent bro with a fake-rape charge." They made racial slurs
about our Japanese heritage and hurled threats like "i know my ivy frat
bros are putting a target on her. she is gonna get used and abused."

Without telling me, Dad called the father of one of Christianna's
friends, who enlisted his company's IT guy to investigate the online

attacks. After working all night and Dad dishing out thousands of dollars, the IT guy found no substantive leads. Everything was cloaked in anonymity.

Another company wanted almost $250,000 to help clean up this mess. $250,000? Dad had been out of work for nearly a year, and our savings reflected that. Lucy had two jobs to help cover her expenses at Georgetown. We didn't have that kind of money. When Dad balked, they offered a cheaper option that was still way out of reach. Dad spared me the details at the time—he just promised to do whatever he could to exterminate the trolls.

Detective Curtin was trying her best and emailed updates.

> Susan and Alex,
> Please know that I am working hard on this end to find
> out what we can do about the websites. . . .
> Sincerely,
> Julie Curtin

She had contacted the National Center for Missing & Exploited Children, the New Hampshire Coalition Against Domestic and Sexual Violence, and the US Attorney's Office. She was launching a criminal defamation and witness-tampering investigation. Our lawyer, Steve, sent takedown requests to websites registered in the United States, accusing them of violating laws around child endangerment, copyright, cyberbullying, and, potentially, child pornography.

I didn't understand what any of that meant. All I knew was that nothing was working. The sites were still there. Panic creased my face. I was brittle with fear, worried that people would climb over the fence and storm our house. I locked all the doors and pulled down the shades. I was scared to go into my room at night and stand in front of the glass doors to close the curtains.

In the middle of all this, Dad had to leave for a business trip to

New York—just like old times. He'd received a job offer right before the trial and scheduled a meeting in early September with his new employees at Morgan Stanley. The position was based in Manhattan, so Dad planned to live in his childhood bedroom at Grandma Prout's during the week and fly home to Naples on the weekend. I was relieved Dad finally had a job, but it seemed like terrible timing. I wanted all of us to stay together. Mom needed her husband, and Christianna and I needed Dad.

The plane was delayed at the gate, and while waiting in his seat, Dad called a friend who used to work for the FBI. Dad tucked his head into the window and fought back tears: "There are these websites going up and I don't know what to do. They are posting these horrible things about my daughter and using violent, pornographic language. Susan and I are completely distraught and there is nothing we can do. Do you know anyone who can help?"

When he hung up, a woman with short blond hair in the row ahead turned around.

"I'm so sorry, but I overheard your conversation," she said apologetically. "Do you mind stepping into the galley with me?"

Dad warily followed her to the cramped area where the flight attendants prepared food and drinks.

"There is a reason the good Lord had me sit in front of you," she said, and handed him a business card. "My name is Cinny Murray and I'm the president of Chico's."

"Okay," he said, looking at the card for the women's clothing chain.

"I don't know what your story is, but all I know is that you're in trouble," Cinny said. "One of my friends is super connected to Google and Apple and has tremendous knowledge and I would love to see if he could help you."

"What?" Dad asked incredulously. "Oh my God, yes."

He hesitated for a moment before explaining exactly what was going on. He had worked so hard to protect my privacy for more than a year and now that was obliterated.

"My daughter is the victim in the St. Paul's case," he whispered. "You may have heard about the trial the other week where she testified."

"Of course, everyone has seen that story," Cinny said. "I've done a lot of work for women in shelters and I'm an advocate for these kinds of issues. My good friend Eric Singleton will change your life. He used to be the company's chief information officer. He has extensive experience in cybersecurity."

"I'd love to talk to him," Dad said.

Cinny pulled out her cell phone and called Eric and summarized the situation. She was calm but spoke with urgency, as if this crisis threatened the multibillion-dollar retail empire that she oversaw.

"I'm standing in front of the father now. Okay, we'll call you when we land," she said, and then turned to Dad. "Eric is happy to help. He won't be able to fix everything, but he said we can make progress."

Eric immediately jumped in and began navigating the shadowy world of Internet trolls. It's nearly impossible to take down rogue international sites, so the next best thing was to remove them from appearing in search engine results. Eric called his high-powered friends at Google, Bing, and Apple and sent them screenshots of the sites so they had the evidence they needed to delete them from search engines.

Eric reached out to contacts at the Secret Service, other cyber-security friends, anyone and everyone he thought could help. But it was like whack-a-mole: as soon as one site was removed, another popped up, taunting us. I deactivated my Facebook and Instagram accounts and expunged my Snapchat of any St. Paul's people I didn't trust. Mom and Dad deactivated their accounts and Lucy removed family photos, trying to wipe clean our digital footprint.

I didn't appreciate at the time how lucky I was that Cinny had overheard Dad's anguish on the airplane and stepped up to help.

Most victims of cyberbullying have no clue where to turn when online haters destroy their lives and reputations. Eric cut through red tape that most victims of cyberbullying wouldn't know exists—much less know how to navigate.

I had people at the highest levels fighting for me and the majority of the sites eventually vanished. But in those weeks after the trial, I felt so unsafe, like no one could protect me. Not my parents, not the police, not the courts. No one.

When I returned to start my junior year at CSN, I struggled with how to resume my place at school. I felt like I was in limbo in my classes, my church, my community. I wondered how many people knew about the trial. And if they knew, did they support me?

My best friend Arielle told my friends not to talk about the trial unless I brought it up first. I tried to keep up a faux-normal demeanor during the day. But without warning, pitch black would suddenly seize me. Triggers were everywhere, from people who looked like Owen to stories on the Internet about sexual assault.

Dad attempted to buoy my spirits. He put together a pink scrapbook with messages of support I'd received, the psalms we read together in the morning before trial, and other inspirational quotes: "I never knew a real hero until my daughter became one."

In mid-September, Dad shared a letter with me that appeared in the *Hartford Courant*. A man named Charlie Pillsbury, a 1965 graduate of St. Paul's, was thanking me for helping to expose the school's culture of male hierarchy and domination: "St. Paul's has always had its dark *Lord of the Flies* side."

Finally. A St. Paul's graduate willing to stand publicly by my side and call out the school. And a *man* in his late *sixties*! Cracks were starting to appear in the wall of silence that had surrounded me since my assault.

A few weeks later Mr. Pillsbury wrote an opinion piece for

the *Courant* titled, "The Courage to Confront My Boarding School Burden." He explained in more detail why my case hit him so hard: one night during his freshman year at St. Paul's, two schoolmates entered his dorm room. While one boy pinned him to the bed, the other sexually abused him.

"You can't believe it's actually happening to you, and then you can't admit that it did, even to yourself. I didn't tell anyone," Mr. Pillsbury wrote. "It took my reading about this young woman's remarkable moral courage and strength to report her assault at St. Paul's to break the seal for me."

I couldn't believe he was crediting me, a sixteen-year-old high school junior. Maybe all the pain I'd endured wasn't pointless after all. Mr. Pillsbury said he'd paid a high emotional price for his world-class education, and it angered him that students were still paying that price. He demanded that St. Paul's confront the school's culture of male entitlement and the power dynamic that undergirds sexual abuse.

"St. Paul's must do better by its students," he wrote.

My heart hurt for Mr. Pillsbury. I couldn't imagine keeping my sexual assault a secret from my family and friends for half a century. I think I would have crumbled under the immensity—succumbing to bad coping mechanisms, reckless attempts to reclaim my sexuality, and who knows what else.

Mr. Pillsbury's article got me thinking: If he was able to come forward after reading about an anonymous sixteen-year-old girl, what would happen if I put a name and face to my story? Could I help more people? Would the good outweigh the bad? Maybe, just maybe, I could find the strength to do even more.

I heard rumblings that Owen's lawyers were trying to protest the felony computer charge, saying it was overreaching. He'd plotted online for months to "pork" me, put my name in all capital letters on two separate score lists, and lured me with emails and Facebook messages to a locked mechanical room to "slay" me. Wasn't it obvious?

I generally shunned media coverage of my case because it instantly took me back to the dark room and the cold concrete floor. I never wanted to hear or see or think about Owen Labrie ever again. I refused to say his name. He wasn't a person to me. He was an it, a thing. And hopefully it would rot in jail.

But before I could dead-bolt him out of my brain, I needed to write a victim impact statement for his sentencing scheduled at the end of October. I had attempted this torturous task a year ago before he backed away from a plea deal that would have kept him off the sex offender registry.

I loathed acknowledging—in public—how the crime had changed me, the things I tried to hide each day. The ways I anxiously picked the skin off my fingers until they bled. How I bruised my legs when I punched myself to stop the panic attacks. I still dissociated, feeling evicted from my own body. Nausea greeted me each morning. Showering scared me. I hated being alone and having to touch my naked body.

If anything, the trial gave me new wounds to nurse. Learning how Owen and the Slayers had plotted against me for months made me paranoid that others were doing the same. But as raw as I felt, the trial was a necessary part of my healing process. There was no alternative to justice.

Lucy wrote her own impact statement while she was at Georgetown, and Uncle Bernie read it at the hearing. I was proud of Lucy for showing vulnerability and standing up with me against Owen. I was thankful that she decided to call out the nefarious culture at St. Paul's rather than deny it like everyone else seemed to do.

"It was not the easy way out for anybody in my family," Lucy wrote. "My sister knew coming forward would not be a popular choice. In fact, it would have been easier to have the public perception that she had lost it to a senior boy. At St. Paul's where scoring is constantly talked about, she would have seemed older and had a cool story to tell. Instead, she did the hard thing; she told the truth."

The collateral damage was enormous. Everyone in our family paid the price. Dad lost his job. Christianna had to move countries and schools again. Mom lost friends. Lucy lost the remains of the community she thought she had at St. Paul's. Rape is a crime that affects more than just the victims; it hurts everyone who loves them.

I decided to videotape my statement. I had a life and a new school year to worry about. I couldn't bear breathing the same air as Owen in that wretched courtroom for one second longer. But I still wanted the judge to hear my voice, to see my face, to look into my swollen eyes.

My parents rented video equipment and we set it up in my headmaster's conference room at CSN. I spoke from my reservoir of pain: "What he did to me made me feel like I didn't belong on this planet and that I would be better off dead."

I sniffled through tears for twenty-three minutes and stressed that my pursuit of justice was not just for myself: "It came to my attention only after I was assaulted and taken advantage of and violated by this young man to realize that and to be told that he's done this to so many other young women. And I am so, so frightful that he's going to do this again."

My friend Lilly texted before the sentencing and asked if she should attend with Catie. I was annoyed with her and Catie after seeing some of the people who'd bullied and ostracized me appear recently in their Snapchat stories. Lilly and I were always really honest with each other, so I decided to vent.

Me: I mean like it sucks (for me at least) to have to see
    you and sally together, and harry and catie all over

> eachother, even though they have made my life and
> others' hell.
> Lilly: I see what you mean
> Are you upset with us?
> Me: I get you guys are moving on and stuff but it still
> hurts. I also don't want you guys to be manipulated by
> them.

I knew I was being a bit sensitive and paranoid, but I had lost the
ability to trust people. I had been stabbed in the back too many times.
Lilly tried to ease my mind.

> Lilly: Let us help you get through it chess
> Me: Thank you lilly. I'm sorry for being confusing and
> calling you out on minor things
> Lilly: Of course I love you so much chess
> Please never forget that

Shortly before the sentencing hearing, Catherine submitted a memo
to the judge and attached a new trove of vile Facebook messages
between Owen and Malcolm Salovaara. They were meant to show
Owen's callous attitude toward young women and sexual intimacy,
and his complete disregard for the age of consent. Dad stayed up all
night revising his statement to include Owen's grotesque words.

In one message Malcolm aptly described Owen's seduction techniques in all caps as "THE LEBREAZY SLEAZY METHOD."

> Owen: feign intimacy
> then stab them in the back
> THROW EM IN THE DUMPSTER
> i lie in bed with them
> and pretend like i'm in love

After egging Owen on to "break the slaying records," Malcolm turned his attention to me and Lucy in March 2014—two months before my assault.

> Malcolm: You slayin both Prouts in one night?
> Owen: that's the plan
>   now that i'm in to schools
>   imma do absolutely whatever

When a girl turned down Owen's advances in late April, he complained to Malcolm.

> Owen: fucking hate forbidden fruit
> Malcolm: Why'd she deny bro?
> Owen: dunno
> Malcolm: Other girls tell her too
> Owen: probably
>   fuckin hate girls so much
> Malcolm: bro
> Owen: another dumb cum-bucket struck from my nut
>   sucking, suck it slut, slut fucking bucket list.

Owen described the last line as "poetry," apparently quoting the comedian Bo Burnham.

> Malcolm: this is amazing

On April 29, 2014—one month before my attack—Owen and Malcolm talked about girls as young as twelve and fifteen and made references to junior boarding school.

> Malcolm: HER PREPUBESCENT BUM

Owen: LOVE IT

Malcolm: MCCARTHY AND I ARE GONNA BE BAILIN YOU
   OUT OF JAIL

We'd learned Patrick McCarthy was another member of Slayers Anonymous. He'd been one of Lucy's friends, someone who'd stayed in an apartment our family had rented in Tokyo. According to Catherine, Owen and his buddies had relished their traditions, including passing around stolen keys, a papier-mâché slaying mask, and templates for Senior Salute invites.

It was beyond hideous. Owen was actually joking about stabbing girls in the back and throwing them in dumpsters. He was laughing about murder! I wished all this information had made it into the trial. I still couldn't believe that Owen had pulled the wool over the jury's eyes and gotten off so easy. He deserved to be put away forever if he wasn't going to get help or acknowledge what he'd done.

Uncle John, Dad's eldest brother, stayed with Christianna and me while Mom and Dad traveled to Concord for the sentencing. I came home from school early because I feared having a panic attack in front of my classmates.

Uncle John sat on the living room couch with his iPad and plugged in his earbuds.

"Your parents told me not to let you watch this today," he said protectively. "So I'll watch it and give you highlights, okay?"

I rolled my eyes and observed Uncle John's reactions: cringing at the victim impact statements, laughing at Owen's stupidity, nodding in agreement with Judge Smukler. Lilly texted some updates from the courtroom as she sat with Dylan and Catie.

Eventually I found the strength to watch Judge Smukler on YouTube when my parents came back from the sentencing.

"This was not consensual. You did not take the time to get to know the victim to know whether what you were doing was something that she wanted or didn't want," Judge Smukler said, his arms folded across his chest. "It may have been a consensual date in the sense that the victim went with you willingly, that's clear. I'm not saying that she didn't, but she never—I don't think you can infer that she consented to the sexual penetration."

Judge Smukler believed me. He understood what had happened in that mechanical room. To hear those words, that a man of the law knew that Owen was a lying rapist, helped restore some of my faith in the justice system. But unfortunately, Judge Smukler could not punish Owen for the more serious crimes.

This outcome devastated me. Everyone tried to explain that juries often compromise by "splitting the baby." They convict defendants of some crimes, like a misdemeanor, and not more serious felony charges that could put them behind bars for years. But if the jury didn't believe Owen's underlying defense—that he didn't have sex with me—then how could they believe anything else he said? If it was clear enough to the judge, why didn't the jury have the guts to uphold the law? It seemed like the system was rigged.

"So you did and are denying till you die," Judge Smukler told Owen. "And in some ways, I mean you've been successful, and in some ways you're a very good liar."

Then he sentenced Owen to a year in jail and several years of probation. He would have to register as a sex offender, but he'd get to remain free on bail while his lawyers appealed the verdict. I'd waited thirteen months for a trial, and two months for the sentencing, and now, who knew how many more years I'd have to wait for the appeals process to play out? When I started this journey, I never envisioned the case dragging on through my college career. At every junction, the rights of the perpetrators trumped the rights of victims. When would this nightmare ever end?

On the morning of Owen's sentencing, Mr. Hirschfeld read a prayer in chapel at St. Paul's. The prayer was submitted by a girl named Mac—a known supporter of Owen's who I'd snapped at in the lobby of the courthouse during the trial.

On this day, let us remember those who may have fallen into darkness. Let us recognize their pain, and let us remember the strength of each individual heart. Let us, with these hearts full and swinging, gift unto those weary ones, that light which we can see so far above us. Let us help them home. Let justice reign.

Justice my ass.

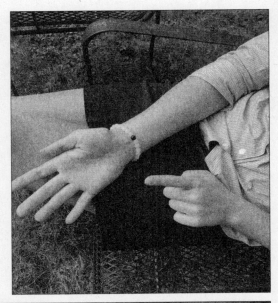

While we waited for the verdict, I read letters from supporters as Catherine, the prosecutor (below left), Aunt Blair, Uncle Bernie, and Mom gathered around the table. Encouraging words from strangers and small acts of kindness, like this Lokai bracelet from my friend Mandi, helped give me strength during the trial.

When we got home to Naples, Christianna gave me one of her signature koala hugs (left).

I wanted to resume a normal life, but days later, Internet trolls posted hate sites. They included my name, address, and pictures stolen from my social media accounts, including this photo of me and Lucy taken in Japan (above).

SEVENTEEN

New Normal

I had counted on volleyball being my major stress release after the trial, spiking the ball with teammates that I'd been play-ing with since middle school. But after missing the first two weeks of practices and games, I sat on the bench for the rest of the season.

I needed another outlet, so I threw myself into singing for our annual Christmas show. My friend Elsa and I convinced our the-ater director to let us arrange and perform "Winter Song" by Sara Bareilles and Ingrid Michaelson.

We wore burgundy-colored dresses and perched on two tall stools in the center of the stage with a pianist and a violinist behind us. The bright lights turned the audience into a sea of blackness. Sitting up there in my long dress, hair pulled to the side, I felt beautiful. Sing-ing a beautiful song, in a beautiful place, I didn't care what people thought of me. I wasn't an anonymous "victim" or "accuser" onstage. I sang as if I would never have the chance to again.

The lights went down at the end of the performance, and Elsa and I squeezed hands before carrying our stools off the stage. She understood.

The day after Christmas, my family flew up north to visit Grandma Prusaczyk and Aunt Blair. Aunt Blair had been diagnosed with breast cancer, and Grandma's health had deteriorated after a long battle with Parkinson's.

We visited Grandma at a hospital and talked for a bit, catching her up on our lives. The last time I'd seen her, she was still able to boss Mom around, but now she was confusing Mom with her roommate in college and was asking for Grandpa, who had died eight years earlier.

"Chessy was in a show last month and she sang this beautiful song," Mom said as she wiped tears off her face.

Lucy and Mom prodded me to give Grandma a rendition. So there, under the hospital's harsh lights, I softly sang.

We all cried. We tucked Grandma into her bed before we left, Lucy and I knowing that this might be the last time we'd see her. How do you say good-bye forever?

Mom made another trip in mid-January when Grandma was transferred to hospice. I didn't like thinking about all this sickness. I tried to bury myself in studying for the SATs that weekend. I'd always been a good test taker but my grades had slipped after the trial. There was so much work to catch up on, and I was in over my head.

I walked out of the SATs bleary-eyed, my brain drained.

I pulled my silver VW bug into the garage, flung off my flip-flops, and walked barefoot across the slippery white floor. I saw Dad sequestered behind the glass doors in our family office with the phone to his ear and his forehead pressed against his palm. Something was wrong.

I found Christianna upstairs, cleaning her room.

"What's going on?" I asked. "Why is Dad in the office? Is Grandma okay?"

"I don't know," Christianna said. "He was talking about Uncle Ron."

I bounded down the stairs and knocked on the door, heart racing.

Dad lifted his head and waved me in. He was fighting back tears, his eyes rimmed red.

"Sweetie, Uncle Ron died," Dad said.

I sat down on the small couch next to Dad and hugged him. I wasn't used to seeing him cry. He was always the rock in our family. But this was too much. Uncle Ron was one of his best friends.

Christianna snuck in from the hallway and curled up with us on the couch. Dad had more calls to make, so Christianna and I moved to the living room and lit the fireplace. I stared at the dancing orange flames and thought about everything Uncle Ron had told me. About looking for a bigger meaning, pushing out of my frequency, changing lives.

He didn't deserve this. I'd wanted to get to know him better, ask his advice, work on cool media projects together. Most of all, I wanted to honor Uncle Ron by doing what he said I could do and doing it well. No more feeling sorry for myself. Uncle Ron had overcome so much—he had been homeless at one point and had to fight for his survival. I could do the same, thrive just like him. I could help people.

Five days later I came home from school to find Mom weeping on the couch with the phone in her lap. Christianna and I cuddled up to her as she shared the news that Grandma had died.

It felt surreal to be surrounded by so much death at once. Mom was a wreck when we got up to South Windsor, Connecticut. Lots of family and friends, including people Mom hadn't seen in years, planned to attend the funeral. But then a blustery snowstorm blanketed New England, canceling flights and snarling traffic across the region.

Mom was devastated as we sat in a hollow church, with high ceilings and two little windows covered in snow. Slowly people trickled in—Mom's first-grade teacher, friends from Grandma's Bible study group. Christianna, Lucy, and I tried to smother Mom with love to make up for the missing guests. I could never imagine life without Mom.

Lucy accompanied Christianna to the front of the church to read a poem called "My Grandmother." Christianna recited a few lines but then started quivering and handed her notes to Lucy.

I went up to sing "Surely the Presence of the Lord Is in This Place," one of Grandma's favorite songs.

> *"In the midst of His children the Lord said He would be.*
> *It doesn't take very many, it can be just two or three."*

I looked out in the pews at our small group of mourners. The people who showed up for Grandma were the same ones who had attended my trial just five months earlier, smushed together on another uncomfortable wooden bench.

The song reminded me that it can be just two or three people to carry you through difficult times. My eyes connected with Mom's and my heart swelled as I sang for Grandma, a strong, caring woman who had raised the most incredible daughter.

Mom and Grandma shared a deep love, but sometimes they couldn't talk about difficult topics—like my assault. Grandma brought it up to me once, saying these things happened when she was young. Mom thought she was being dismissive and took offense.

After that, we never discussed it again. When we emptied the drawers of Grandma's wooden dresser, Mom found a stack of newspaper clippings about my trial.

"Wow, I had no idea she knew all this," Mom said, breaking down in tears. "She loved you so much, Chess."

You'd think the last place on earth I'd choose to be was back in court. But there I was, trying out for my school's mock trial team. I wanted to own the courtroom this time.

I prepared as if my life depended on it, poring over documents, developing questions, practicing my approach. It was a powerhouse team run by the senior class president, the class valedictorian, and the son of the board's president.

The seniors brought me on, making me the youngest member and one of only two girls on the six-person team. They were all nice, smart, and determined to win. But I still had my suspicions that they let me on as a big joke, knowing what I'd gone through, and were plotting to humiliate me at some point. Thank God I was wrong.

Mock trial teams from around Collier County prepared for months and then faced off in a competition. Each team had to know all sides of the case and be ready to serve as the prosecution or the defense.

Once I got more comfortable around my teammates, I disclosed my one caveat: "I'm not going to do anything for the defense. If you put me on the defense, I just can't . . ."

My classmates tilted their heads to the side but didn't ask questions, so I nervously chattered.

"But I'll do everything for the prosecution," I vowed. "It's just beyond me to defend someone."

Maybe they knew my story. Maybe they didn't. Maybe it didn't matter. I wasn't Chessy the rape victim anymore. Now I was Chessy the prosecutor. I hoped Catherine would be proud.

The case at hand: cyberbullying. More specifically, cyber-photo harassment and cyberstalking by a student against his ex-best friend. Go figure.

The team leaders encouraged my enthusiasm and assigned me the prosecution's opening statement. It seemed like a big deal, and I was up for the challenge. I combed through the case files, studying every bit of testimony and evidence to pull together a compelling narrative. We worked constantly, sometimes meeting three times a week for several hours to debate and dig deeper into the case.

On the morning of the trial, I woke up early and made some last-minute tweaks to my opening statement. Then I put on my black pantsuit and nude-colored heels and pulled my hair back like Catherine. For the first time, I didn't vomit before heading into a courtroom.

I strode confidently up to the prosecutor's table and put down my papers. It was so cool to sit in front of the bar, not silently behind it.

My team had very specific courtroom protocol: no notes, keep the table organized, have enough laminated copies of evidence for members of the jury, the judge, and the witness.

I also used the lessons I'd learned from watching Catherine: be personable with the witnesses, treat them with respect, and be assertive. I'm proud to say I took nothing from Carney.

At the end of the first mock trial, a county judge running the courtroom gave us feedback. He complimented my opening statement for being poised and pointed, especially without any notes.

"Have you done this before?" the judge asked.

"This is my first year, Your Honor," I said, laughing inside. *If he only knew.*

I found Mom and Dad toward the back of the courtroom, shell-shocked. Dad said he had flashbacks to Courtroom 1. Mom looked at me in disbelief, as if she was seeing me for the first time.

"I can't believe you voluntarily stepped into a courtroom again," Dad said, his eyebrows arched so high they nearly jumped off his forehead. "I'm just so proud of you, kiddo."

"You've got guts," Mom said with a smile.

I was exhausted but ecstatic. At the end of the day, I put the top down on my VW bug and called Lucy on the drive home.

"Lulu, it was amazing. I want to do this for the rest of my life," I yelled over the wind. "I want to be able to fight for other people."

I slammed my laptop shut and threw it across the bed. I had just watched part of a *Law & Order: SVU* episode called "A Misunderstanding." It was obviously ripped from the headlines. My headlines. And they got it all wrong.

The show's sloppy interpretation made a farce of my assault. It minimized my pain; it justified what he did. If they were to depict something so close to the trial, they should have at least gotten some of the most important facts right. Like this wasn't a fucking misunderstanding. Mom reached out to her old college classmate Peter Jankowski, who served as an executive producer for the show. He didn't respond.

I wanted to confront all the people who felt they could speak for or about me. I needed them to see who they were speaking for. I was a real human being! I wasn't going to take this shit. This was not justice.

In December, Mom and Dad told me about a horrendous story in *Newsweek* that featured a photo spread of Owen and his father building a chapel in the woods in Vermont. The writer, Matthew Cooper, sympathetically portrayed my attacker as an aspiring minister whose world imploded after breaking "Romeo and Juliet" laws, crimes that are rarely prosecuted.

It made me gag. And Owen was complaining about people recognizing him and sending hate mail? Seemed like a great solution then to plaster pictures of his house in a magazine.

I was desperate for the media to lose interest in my case. Didn't they have better things to focus on? Couldn't they sink their teeth into something far more important—like the surging popularity of

Donald Trump in the Republican presidential primaries?

I worried about Dad's lengthy conversations with a *Vanity Fair* writer named Todd S. Purdum. He was a St. Paul's alum married to Dee Dee Myers, a former White House press secretary under President Bill Clinton. Mr. Purdum was working on a story about my case and had been speaking with Dad for months. Dad trusted him and hoped Mr. Purdum would shed light on the ugly underbelly at St. Paul's. But I didn't trust anyone, especially a male graduate.

Lucy and I both agreed it was a bad idea and tried to tag-team Mom and Dad one night while we were watching the news in the family room. Lucy and I were sprawled out on two side couches, and Mom and Dad sat together on the middle one.

"I really think you shouldn't give him your time. You can't trust him," I said. "He's from St. Paul's. He's of the St. Paul's breed. He's gonna use your words against you. They all have their own agendas."

"You don't have any control over what reporters do with your words," said Lucy, who'd recently started working for her college paper.

I had read a little bit of *Vanity Fair* before—it was one of the magazines Mom subscribed to when we were in Japan.

Dad was visibly upset that we were second-guessing his openness. "This story is taking a broader look at the school," he said, "and there are things people need to know."

Dad hated anything resembling a fight, so he switched topics: "Let's watch a movie."

I refused to speak with Mr. Purdum, and Mom and Dad supported that. But I got nervous as publication neared.

Mom and I had a trip to Los Angeles scheduled at the end of February 2016 to visit some colleges in California, as far away from the New England boarding-school bubble as possible.

"Do you want to meet him?" Dad asked. "Mr. Purdum lives out in Los Angeles. I think the story is already done, but maybe you could just sit and talk to him?"

"That sounds like a good idea, actually," I said. "I'm tired of being an anonymous victim while my attacker is this superstar scholar athlete. I want Mr. Purdum and all the people who write about me to have to look me in the eyes and see I'm a person. I want them to know who the faceless, nameless victim they write about is."

Mr. Purdum invited us to his home and brought me and Mom into his study, where books and photos of important people lined the shelves. The windows were shrouded with Harvard-esque ivy. Mom and I sat close together on a brown couch while Mr. Purdum's big, fluffy dog sat at my feet.

Mr. Purdum seemed a bit reserved, doughy, with glasses and a slight gap between his two front teeth. We talked for a while about the broader issues at St. Paul's, and at the end of the conversation, he finally asked, "Really, how has all of this been for you?"

I looked him straight in the eyes, ready to tell my truth: "Honestly, absolutely terrible. Some days it's made me lose my will to live. And the school completely turned its back on me. They have treated us like dirt."

Mr. Purdum turned white. "Oh, well, I'm so sorry."

I excused myself to use the bathroom. When I returned, I saw Mom and Mr. Purdum speaking quietly and seriously. They stopped talking as I approached.

He signed a copy of a book he'd authored and gave it to me before we left. I handed it to Mom and walked out of his house, feeling relieved. Mr. Purdum had seen my face and heard my pain. Now, he'd have to live with whatever he'd written.

While we were out in Los Angeles, Mom tried to get us a meeting with Mr. Jankowski at *SVU* so we could revisit "A Misunderstanding," but once again, he didn't respond.

A few days later, the *Vanity Fair* story hit the stands. Mr. Purdum emailed Dad a copy.

> Alex,
> I realize all too well that the story only scratched the
> surface and I hope in that sense that it wasn't too much
> of a disappointment. By the time the lawyers got done
> with it, some damning material fell away . . . .
> All best,
> Todd

The headline said all I needed to know about how I'd be treated: "18-year-old scholar-athlete Owen Labrie and a 15-year-old freshman girl."

Of course. Once again, I was a blank nothing and he was a golden boy. It got worse when Mr. Purdum finally found words to describe me in the second sentence: privileged, preppy, naive, impressionable, flummoxed.

It was as if Mr. Purdum picked up where Carney left off. He mentioned my daily medication for anxiety and depression and my shaving habits and anonymously quoted the father of one of my "contemporaries" saying I struggled at times with my identity "in competition" with my sister. Again, playing into the idea that women are evil temptresses, constantly fighting each other for the attention of men.

What pompous, arrogant ass who knew nothing of me or my sister felt he had the authority to comment on our relationship? Things with Lucy were hard enough after pain and guilt had taken up permanent residence in each of our hearts. But we weren't competitive. And now we had some strange, apparently all-knowing, anonymous source spreading lies in a national publication. Perfect.

Owen, meanwhile, was depicted as captain of the varsity soccer team, handsome, suntanned, a winner of the headmaster's award for selfless devotion to school activities who had won full-ride admission to five Ivy League schools and fell asleep on the floor of his house comforting rescue dogs that his mom took in. Oh, and his life was "in shambles."

I was hurt and disappointed, but at the same time, I had expected nothing more from a guy like Mr. Purdum. The feminist website Jezebel trashed the *Vanity Fair* story, saying it "echoes tropes from so many male-authored deep dives into rape investigations: he was the star, she was the confused child who ruined his life."

I called Lucy at Georgetown, and we tried to figure out who could have spoken with Mr. Purdum. The only father who both of us had met was Ivy and Georgina's dad. We had a good laugh over how he must have gotten confused and really was describing the bizarre, competitive relationship between his own two daughters.

I wanted to smash a wall. I stormed downstairs, clutching my laptop over my head.

"See, Dad, aren't you mad you spent all this time with this guy and he's just spewing this?" I hollered. "It's a glossy sleaze piece that people read when they get tired of their boring lives. This is terrible. This is my life that they're exploiting!"

Dad was speechless. Not knowing what else to do, he called up Mr. Purdum to tell him that I was spitting anger. Mr. Purdum apologized in an email to Dad, saying he regretted that his words "unintentionally hurt" me.

What a cop-out. When would these men stop the shameless victim blaming? If we talk or write about sexual violence, the "complications" people seem most willing to discuss are based on victim blaming: Why did she put herself in that situation? What was she wearing? Isn't she unstable?

I slammed my door and lobbed myself onto the bed. I was pissed at Dad, but I couldn't stay mad for long. He was trying to do right by me, right by our family. He thought he had found an ally in Mr. Purdum, someone who was invested in fixing the school as a fellow alum and could help by exposing the problems at St. Paul's. But this wasn't helping anyone, especially not me.

I eventually resurfaced from my room and found Dad downstairs. I turned to him and as kindly as possible offered my advice: "I think you should stop talking to reporters and start talking to a therapist."

Hey, it was working for me.

Mom called me in the middle of the school day on March 18.

"His bail was revoked," Mom said softly. "He's going to jail, honey. He's finally going to jail."

I broke down crying in the outdoor hallway lined with lockers. I'd never thought this day would come. Arielle was sitting with me on the green benches, and gave me a bear hug and let me vent.

I had read a story a few weeks earlier by Susan Zalkind, a reporter for *Vice*, who had covered my trial and ran into Owen on a subway in Cambridge, Massachusetts. Owen said he'd gone out to brunch with his girlfriend, a student at Harvard University, the college he was supposed to attend. Then he lamented having his life "torn apart" in the media. Poor Owen. At least he'd made it through high school.

The story caught the attention of Detective Curtin in Concord, who wondered whether Owen was violating his curfew restrictions, which were part of the agreement keeping him out of jail while he appealed the verdict.

The meticulous Detective Curtin went to work: she interviewed bus drivers and a ticket salesman and examined surveillance video. Her investigation revealed that Owen was regularly violating his curfew. At least eight times already! The news terrified me.

"See, I'm not paranoid! They're not watching him. He could come here and hurt all of us. He could go to DC and hurt Lucy,"

I wailed to Dad. "He honestly doesn't care about anybody besides himself and has no regard for the authorities or the legal system."

Catherine filed a motion to revoke Owen's bail, but I had no confidence that he'd be punished because he seemed to weasel his way out of everything.

"Have some faith in the system," Mom said. "This is significant."

Judge Smukler agreed it was a big deal. He revoked Owen's bail at a hearing and sent him to jail.

The next day Dad handed me his iPad.

"Look at this," he said.

It was a photo of Owen being handcuffed by a sheriff. His local New Hampshire lawyer tried to block the photographer from capturing the metal cuffs.

"Why would you show that to me?" I hissed. "You know I don't want to see that."

It made me queasy to see Owen's face, like I was being violated all over again. I thought I'd feel triumphant knowing that my attacker was sitting in jail. Instead I was dejected that it had come to this.

I grabbed Dad's iPad and scrolled down past Owen's head so all I could see was the sheriff's badge.

"Okay, that looks pretty cool," I admitted. "He can wear those handcuffs forever, for all I care. He's finally getting what he deserves."

But of course, we couldn't find a moment of peace even while the jerk was locked up for several weeks in solitary confinement (for his own protection, apparently). We learned that Owen had recently asked for permission to meet with new lawyers in Washington, DC, where Lucy attended college.

In April, while Owen was still in jail, his lawyers filed a motion seeking a new trial based on ineffective counsel. They were claiming that Carney—the six-figure lawyer paid for by the precious St. Paul's community—was ineffective. You had to be kidding me.

I didn't understand what that meant. Would I need to testify again? Would this interfere with another year of high school? I didn't have time to focus on the case. I had lines to memorize. I was the lead, Gabriella Montez, in our spring musical, *High School Musical*. Just as my life was becoming more normal every day, this other crap kept bringing me down.

Catherine told me not to think about it. There would be a hearing at some point, but I wouldn't have to testify. Did Owen think I'd back down now? After everything I'd been through? Bring it on. I was more ready than I'd ever been. This was a totally arrogant move—one I hoped he'd come to regret.

EIGHTEEN

A Girls' Bill of Rights

It was a lazy Sunday afternoon in early May, just a few days before my AP US History exam. I turned on a Netflix series about America in the 1960s to help prepare for the test and invited Mom and Christianna to watch with me in the family room. I draped myself over the couch while Mom snagged her favorite over-size striped chair and Christianna spread out next to me.

We snacked on cubes of watermelon and made it through five episodes, ending on "A Long March to Freedom," an in-depth look at Martin Luther King Jr. and his efforts to lead the civil rights movement.

Halfway through the episode, Mom paused the show with Martin Luther King's face frozen on the screen.

"So, girls, what do you think?" she asked. "What other rights do we need to fight for?"

It was a classic Mom move—trying to find a teachable moment in everyday life. But for once, I was on board and not rolling my eyes at her cheesy timing.

"Sounds like it's time for a girls' bill of rights," Christianna declared matter-of-factly.

Mom and I looked at each other and grinned. Christianna was one strong, smart nine-year-old!

"Yes, Christianna, that's a great idea," Mom said, pivoting seamlessly to teacher mode. "What else? What kind of rights?"

"I dunno," Christianna said, self-consciously receding into the crevices of the couch. She'd had her moment, and now she was done.

"That's such a great idea," I said, vigorously nodding my head. "Girls need a bill of rights." I turned and faced Mom. "I didn't even know that what happened to me was against the law. I didn't know I had the right to be respected—the right to my body, something as fundamental as that!"

Christianna sat there wide-eyed, her head swinging back and forth between me and Mom. I'd never talked like this in front of her before.

"Let's get this down on paper!" Mom exclaimed. "We can make this into a children's book for kids Christianna's age, so they know their rights. We should all make a list!"

Mom loved any reason to make a list.

"That sounds like an awesome idea," I said, quickly feeling the pressure of this imaginary project land on my shoulders. "But can I just focus on my AP exams for now?"

I now knew my limits, especially after struggling through the first semester of junior year. I had forcefully told my teachers not to give me special treatment after the trial, and I ended up having to drop AP Chemistry and got a D in my first quarter of honors precalculus.

One of my teachers, Mr. Phimister, went out of his way to make sure I wasn't overwhelmed, allowing extensions for weekly essays if any legal surprises came up. When I recently had a panic attack in his class, he ushered the other kids out of the room and handed me a box of tissues.

"It's okay," he said. "You can stay here as long as you need."

Mr. Phimister became a huge ally, the kind of adult every survivor needs at school. Back at home, I wanted fewer demands on me, not more. But Mom wouldn't let go of the girls' bill of rights. Every other day it seemed like she was nagging me about the list.

"Chessy, you should start writing that down—making your list."

"Uh-huh," I said dismissively. "I'm keeping some notes on my phone."

I wasn't. I just needed to stay afloat.

Also, it was still difficult for me to acknowledge that I hadn't known my rights as a fifteen-year-old girl. I had considered myself to be a pretty smart teenager, an independent kind of girl who had traveled the world and could take care of herself.

But during my assault and the days that followed, I thought I was being too sensitive, too much of a baby for being so distraught. I had no idea at the time that what happened to me was wrong, no clue that it was a crime. How could I have been so ignorant? Every time I thought about it, a little piece of my heart charred black.

I later realized that Mom's semi-obsession with my list was as much about her as it was about me. Her own mother had a full-time job, and Mom was part of the generation who fought to secure women's reproductive rights and to ban sex discrimination in the workplace and schools.

She assumed that her daughters would be treated equally at St. Paul's, that our bodies and voices would be respected. She'd never imagined the most dangerous thing she could ever do was send us to boarding school. Mom felt complicit and she wanted us to claim the rights she'd thought we always had.

I walked into the kitchen one morning to make coffee and avoided Mom's gaze so she wouldn't pester me again about the darn list. I examined the Nespresso machine as if it was the most fascinating contraption in the universe.

Mom came over and kissed me on the forehead. "Take your time, honey. Whenever you're ready. You don't need to do the list right now."

Of course, as soon as Mom said I *didn't* have to do something, I *wanted* to do it.

Later that day Lucy and I splashed around in the swimming pool, trying to cool down from our volleyball game in the backyard. I looked over at Mom and Christianna, sitting in the shade, playing Bananagrams and eating Popsicles.

The ice pop dripped down Christianna's chin and left blue streaks at the corners of her smiling mouth. That innocent little girl had always been the bright light in our family, helping me find my sense of purpose after the earthquake, giving me reasons to live when I locked myself in my closet and felt like I didn't belong on this planet. She showed me that as long as we have each other and stick to what we believe in, things will be okay.

Finally I was ready to write my list. I stepped out of the pool, draped a towel around my waist, and dashed into the house. I grabbed a pink marker and a white piece of paper from my desk and folded the paper in half.

My hand was like a jet on a runway, tearing across the page and leaving a trail of empowering words:

> *I have the right to . . .*
> *Dress the way I want.*
> *Be alone with a boy without anything being assumed.*
> *My privacy, keeping my well being first.*
> *Say no, and be listened to.*

Be respected.
Be upset, or sad.
Be happy and live my life.
Be respected when I bravely testify in a trial.
Be called a survivor, not an "alleged victim" or accuser.
A system that prioritizes healing.

I took a deep breath. That was good enough for now. I slinked back downstairs and joined Mom, Lucy, and Christianna at the table outside. I slid the list in front of them and said, "Momma, I did it."

Mom teared up on cue. I passed out pens and scraps of paper to Christianna and Lucy so they could claim their own rights. While they worked, I stared out at the pool and watched tiny ripples move from the edges toward the center, joining together into one long line. This was the beginning of something big; I could feel it.

After the trial had ended, Mom and Dad turned their full attention to St. Paul's. The disturbing things we learned in that courtroom— revelations that will haunt me for the rest of my life—exposed how St. Paul's fostered a toxic culture that put me and other students at risk for sexual violence.

Mom and Dad couldn't bring criminal charges against St. Paul's, of course, but they could use the civil courts to try and hold the school accountable for what had happened to me and make sure more kids didn't get hurt.

It was undeniable that school leaders were aware of the sexual conquest games and did nothing to stop them. Months before my trial, Mr. Hirschfeld acknowledged in a chapel speech that he had heard students using the word "slay" and "slayer" a couple of years earlier: "While these words made me uneasy, I did nothing as the head of the school to address their use nor, to my knowledge, did anyone else."

It was a stunning admission. Just a year before my assault, a male student brazenly sent a Senior Salute to Mrs. Hirschfeld—the wife of the head of school! It was the one useful tidbit that *Vanity Fair* dredged up on its own.

We'd also learned that Mr. Hirschfeld served as an adviser on a student project called "The Little Red Book," where an entire page was devoted to scoring.

A few weeks after Owen's sentencing, Mike Delaney, an attorney for St. Paul's, reached out to our lawyer, Steve Kelly, to start negotiations. If talks were successful, St. Paul's would avoid a lawsuit and prevent damaging information from becoming public.

Dad gathered me and Lucy in our office. He wanted us to come up with ideas for how to improve the school so Steve could present them in an upcoming meeting. Dad saw this as our chance to restore dignity to the school he still loved, to the place he'd once called home.

"Let's try to make St. Paul's a shining example of policies and procedures and training," Dad said. "It would be a wonderful legacy."

"Yeah right," I grunted. Membership to the exclusive world of St. Paul's required a blind and unwavering loyalty. Didn't they see that?

"You guys are fooling yourselves if you think you can change things there," I fumed. "The privileged boys run the school and the administration looks the other way. If they haven't done anything to change it already, why would they do it now?"

Dad and Lucy bristled.

"You have no idea what you're talking about," Lucy barked back, proving my theory that St. Paul's could force anyone into being blindly loyal.

I balled my fists in anger thinking about all the times Lucy came to me her senior year to complain about the blatant sexism she confronted, the bullying she faced from the guys after she broke up with her longtime boyfriend because of his controlling and manipulative tendencies. I was there for it all. But I knew I couldn't win this fight right now.

I sulked in the corner while Dad and Lucy duked it out. They wrote down more than twenty suggestions that focused on education, accountability, and transparency. Some of the ideas included publicly taking action against anyone involved in the Senior Salute; adding training to prevent sexual assault and support victims; empowering girls through gender studies courses; and having an outside agency survey the school community about sexual violence, bullying, and substance abuse and make the findings publicly available.

Dad even floated the idea of starting a foundation to set standards for preventing sexual violence and supporting survivors at private schools. Perhaps St. Paul's could help fund the organization.

"Chess, do you have anything you want to add?" Dad asked.

"Fine," I huffed. "Here's my suggestion. If St. Paul's refuses to implement our ideas, then return the school to an all-boys institution so no more girls get hurt. Right? If they won't do what it takes to protect girls, then they shouldn't enroll them in the first place."

Months of conversations between the attorneys led nowhere. St. Paul's trumpeted changes it had made, such as revisions to the school handbook, new locks on doors, and bystander training, as if they were more than just window dressing. I was furious when I learned that St. Paul's invited a former college football player to give a talk about sexual violence. Why not give a young woman the platform to talk to the students?

Mom and Dad knew the problems at St. Paul's ran deep. They'd been digging into the school's past, exhuming appalling stories of abuse, of victims who had suffered in silence, shame, and isolation for decades.

Alexis Johnson, a St. Paul's graduate from 1976, cold-called our house one night and talked to Mom for hours. Alexis worked as an attorney and was part of an alumni task force that launched after several people revealed at a reunion in 2000 that they were victims of faculty sexual misconduct. The group had gathered allegations against more than twenty adults.

Alexis told Mom about the first case of abuse they documented from 1949, when a boy named Samuel Collier hung himself in his dorm after being molested by a teacher and then hazed by students who knew of the abuse. Mom gasped. Samuel was related to the friend who had first tried to track down the Internet trolls behind the hate sites. Everything was so connected.

Mom and Dad discovered that school leaders back in 2000 refused to investigate many abuse allegations, including cases of rape, because the employees no longer worked there. St. Paul's discouraged further reporting, ostracized survivors, and tried to hide the school's history of abuse, according to alumni. The message was clear: St. Paul's cared more about preserving its reputation than protecting students.

While researching for the civil case, Mom and Dad unearthed various student-on-student hazing incidents involving boys and girls. In one recent case that actually made headlines in 2004, senior girls forced freshmen—i.e., newbs—in their dorm to simulate blow jobs with bananas and answer sexually explicit questions as a way to introduce them to St. Paul's. During Lucy's first year, she heard that seniors in her dorm got a freshman so "drunk" on cough syrup that she later threw up.

Mom and Dad saw a direct link between the victims of faculty abuse, perpetual hazing problems, and my assault. St. Paul's seemed like a noxious breeding ground for the abuse of power. The entrenched male entitlement—along with the school's "deny until you die" mantra that Owen had adopted—had allowed this abuse of power to thrive among faculty and students.

Mom and Dad were drowning in the St. Paul's cesspool. Sometimes I heard yelling coming from the office. Things were tough enough with Dad working in New York. And then he'd come home and spend most of his free time on this.

I barged into the office one evening. "This is toxic. Just stop it. Don't let them waste another second of our lives. You shouldn't have to fix everything for them."

I was worried about the toll this battle would take on our lives. It was all we talked about sometimes. But I knew deep down that if it wasn't our family dragged through the mud, then it would be somebody else's. I had talked to other girls who'd been assaulted since I left St. Paul's and had read letters during the trial written by past survivors from the school. I learned that a boy attempted to rape an employee's child at the school—and the rector and board president would eventually find out. It made me sick to think that our secret society of St. Paul's abuse victims would grow larger in the future. We had to do something to stop it.

The day after we filed our civil lawsuit in early June, another rape trial dominated headlines. A judge in California sentenced Brock Turner, a former Stanford University student, to a mere six months in jail for assaulting a young woman known as Emily Doe as she lay half-naked and unconscious next to a dumpster.

I was outraged by the judge's sympathy for the twenty-year-old criminal: "A prison sentence would have a severe impact on him. I think he will not be a danger to others." Did he even take into consideration the severe impact that this man's actions had on the victim?

I felt guilty that Brock Turner got half the sentence Owen did. At least I didn't end up unconscious next to a dumpster. My attacker only wrote about stabbing girls and throwing them in dumpsters. I'd heard that Emily Doe had written a lengthy victim impact statement that went viral on BuzzFeed, but it took me a few days to muster the courage to read it. I was scared about how my body would react. I closed the door to the office and curled up on the couch with my laptop resting on my knees.

My stomach churned as I recognized my own story in her words. I only made it through the first paragraph before I started sobbing uncontrollably. My leg muscles lit on fire, my hands clenched into fists. I pulled my legs into my chest, trying to make myself as small as possible, hiding my vulnerable body parts.

It seemed like we were going backward. How much pain would young women have to go through before people realized that what these men were doing was not okay?

As I finished reading Emily Doe's statement, I remembered all the letters I'd received during my trial, how complete strangers had lifted me up. I never had a chance to respond to everyone individually. But I felt a responsibility to let Emily Doe know that she was not alone. I wanted to offer suggestions to help her heal, even if I was only a high school junior.

> *Dear: Warrior, hero, <u>superwoman</u>, amazing sister,*
> *survivor, pioneer, faraway friend . . .*
> *I could go on forever in awe of you, but instead I want*
> *to share some things that have made me feel better*
> *over the last couple months:*
> 1. *let the panic attacks wash over you and squeeze*
>   *yourself tight: no one can hurt you anymore, I like*
>   *to believe that lightning doesn't strike in the same*
>   *place twice not only because the world is big, but*
>   *because the earth is smart and learns from pain.*
> 2. *The fear will lessen over time.*
> 3. *Don't get lost in Netflix like I did . . .*
> 4. *Write (You seem to have that part mastered!) and*
>   *draw.*
> 5. *Follow Rachel Brathen on social media (Instagram*
>   *and snapchat), her words brighten up my day and*
>   *I hope they brighten up yours too.*

6. *Yoga. AND BOXING. I've been wanting to take*
   self-defense classes forever but realized I like
   self-offense much better as a good anger outlet. (I
   never get tired of boxing . . . I also feel sooo much
   stronger)
   My friends used to make fun of my appreciation of
   nature, but honestly, thats my favorite thing about ME.
   Always breathe in your surroundings and know that
   there is still good in the world, (it also helps with episodes
   of dissociation)

I enclosed a small black-and-orange pin that I got during a courage retreat that I helped lead at my school earlier in the year. I also gave Emily Doe my phone number.

> *. . . if you ever want to talk to somebody who may have*
> *a tiny sliver of understanding (and a penchant for*
> *social justice) . . . I want to eventually build a web of*
> *survivors so strong that can be there for every young*
> *woman enduring a trial in the US, and maybe even*
> *try to stretch it overseas. (I know it's a little grand,*
> *and there are plenty of victim advocates, but I'm a 17*
> *year old with millions of dreams!)*

I never heard back from her, but sometimes I liked to imagine Emily Doe boxing somewhere, getting stronger just like me.

I have the right to...

Dress the way I want, ~~with~~
~~any~~

Be alone with a boy without anything ~~it~~
being assumed.

My privacy, keeping my well
being first.

Say no, and be listened to.
Be respected.

Be upset, "sad, ~~or be happy~~
Be happy and live my life.
Be Respected when I bravely testify
in a trial.

Be called a survivor, not an
"alleged victim" or accuser.

a system that prioritizes healing

I wrote this list in May 2016. I'd later name my advocacy
campaign after the first line.

NINETEEN

Jane Doe

When I sent my letter to Emily Doe, I gave her my phone number but not my name. It seems silly now. I obviously would have told her if she called. But at the time it seemed impossible to write down my name, Chessy Prout, in the same sentence as "St. Paul's assault victim"—even to another survivor.

That's why when Mom and Dad filed our lawsuit against St. Paul's in early June, we did so anonymously under the name Jane Doe. It's a common practice among survivors of sex crimes as a way to protect their privacy and avoid revictimization. Though there had been leaks, my name was not widely known—not even among some of my relatives—and I wanted to keep it that way. I could not weather more hate mongering.

The lawsuit triggered a new wave of stories from national news outlets, including the *New York Times*, the *Wall Street Journal*, NBC,

CBS, and others. Many of them called up our lawyer, Steve Kelly, and asked if I was ready to talk.

A heavy anchor sank in my stomach. Coverage of my case wasn't going away. When we'd refused to comment to *Newsweek* last year, we ended up with a hatchet job. Meeting with Mr. Purdum after he finished the *Vanity Fair* piece didn't help either.

If I wanted my truth fairly and accurately represented, it seemed like the only option was to speak out. I knew I was my own best advocate, but I loathed the limelight. I worried that people would judge me and assume that I craved this attention. And I was nervous about the long-term ramifications. I peppered Steve with questions.

"Do I really want to be known for the rest of my life as the St. Paul's rape victim?" I asked. "Are people going to Google this forever? When I have children, will they see this?"

"Let me tell you something," Steve said. "I was an activist from the age of fourteen, when my sister was raped and murdered. My name was all over the media. But when I graduated from law school and went to work at a big firm, I didn't want anyone to know anything about my past. I didn't tell anyone anything."

"Why?" I asked.

"I wanted to make it on my own. I wanted it to be on my merits," Steve explained. "I didn't want to use my sister's murder as an excuse or anything about my family's background as a way to get ahead."

"I understand. I don't want to be seen as profiting because of this—like getting famous because I was assaulted," I said. "So how'd it go for you not saying anything?"

"I was miserable. It was the most miserable time of my life, because it's such a huge part of me that I was hiding," Steve said. "You don't have to go around telling everybody. But when you go through something like this—a centrally defining event—it feels dishonest if you don't acknowledge it."

I understood what Steve was saying. It seemed impossible to compartmentalize this part of my life. My experience seeped into classroom discussions and casual conversations with friends about fairness and women's rights. It shaped my worldview.

"So you think I should speak out publicly?" I asked.

"For me, it was the right thing," Steve said. "But it's not the right choice for everyone. For some people, they do better by not speaking out. I have people in my family who are like that. It's okay to stay private. It's a personal decision."

I sighed deeply. I didn't know what to do.

Dad suggested that while we were in New York for more college visits, we could have exploratory meetings with some of the producers who were calling. It would be a chance for us to learn about the process and how they would like to present my story. At a minimum, Dad explained, we would show them that we were real people and perhaps educate them on the impact of these crimes so they could be more sensitive in their coverage.

"We're not committing to anything, right?" I asked.

"Absolutely no commitments whatsoever," Dad reassured me. "This is your call all the way."

That sounded fine by me. First we met a team that had impressive credentials making documentaries for HBO.

I anxiously inhaled french fries as I listened to their pitch: they wanted to be flies on the wall and film me at home, in school, on my upcoming trip to Cat Island. They wanted everything: my name, my face, my friends, my life. I'd be completely, totally exposed.

On the one hand, being able to show people what my life was really like was something I'd thought a lot about since I was a kid and read the book *The English Roses*, where a group of mean, popular girls got to see the difficult home life of a girl they bullied at school. Afterward, they felt bad and took her into their circle and learned not to make assumptions about others. I was tired of people judging me immediately as a pretty blond girl, popular and ditzy and shallow. That wasn't me.

But a documentary like the one they were proposing felt too intrusive. I explained my hesitation and smiled politely while I polished off my fries.

The next day we met with a producer from a network who promised that I'd have control over any questions if I decided to do an interview. I told the producer of my dream for victims to be called survivors instead of accusers by the media and the need for reporters to pay more attention to the difference between jail and prison and misdemeanors and felonies. She listened and we agreed to stay in touch.

Our last stop was NBC at 30 Rockefeller Plaza. This was one of my all-time favorite spots in New York City. It's a Prout tradition to visit every holiday season to watch the ice skaters and admire the towering Christmas tree.

It was June, so the skating rink was closed and an outdoor summer concert stage was built up in an alleyway by 30 Rock's side entrance. Dad and I met Savannah Guthrie, one of the cohosts of the *Today* show, in between her filming schedule. Savannah told me about her background: first as a lawyer, then as a legal correspondent for Court TV. Issues like sexual assault mattered to her.

She listened attentively and nodded while I explained what I hoped to achieve if I went public. Suddenly someone knocked on the door to give her a three-minute warning that she was needed back on air.

Dad and I watched Savannah attend to her news duties, and then she resumed our conversation several minutes later. Her professionalism and compassion impressed me.

Later that morning it was time to get down to business. We met with the *Today* show producers and talked about the importance of bringing more awareness to high school sexual assault.

"If I *do* do a TV interview, I don't want to show up empty-handed,"

I said. "I want to create a concrete place where people can get help or be empowered."

I was assertively dipping my toes in the water. I liked having important people listen to me and care about what I had to say.

"We could do something like this," one producer said, and pulled up NBC's #DreamDay website, which featured celebrities and politicians sharing their dreams in honor of the fiftieth anniversary of Martin Luther King Jr.'s "I Have a Dream" speech.

NBC was willing to do whatever it took to make me comfortable. I could use my initials instead of my full name. I could be filmed in profile or in shadows to protect my identity. I nodded my head but again made no promises.

As the meeting ended, Dad and I thanked everyone for their time. I walked out bowled over by their enthusiasm and their interest in helping survivors.

But still, I wasn't ready. I wasn't sure if I'd ever be.

"You're coming with me!" I declared to Mom. "You're coming to Cat Island. You're going to love it."

After we boarded the tiny aircraft in late June, I tried to find my place. The prop plane had two people per row, seats A and B. My ticket read C. Chance—or rather Bahamasair—put me in a rear-facing jump seat, and I had no choice but to buckle in.

Just like my visit two summers ago, the kids mobbed our van as we pulled up to Old Bight Mission Home. I was shocked that they all remembered me. This year I was one of the oldest youth leaders, so the kids decided to pair me with the most "eligible bachelor" in our group and said they would marry us in the nearby church.

Luckily, Mom was there to stop them from getting carried away. I was wary of introducing Mom as "my mom" because these kids had been abandoned or removed from their families. Instead, I introduced her as Ms. Susan.

Mom and I handled different activities for the children during the day and came together at night for Bible study with the youth leaders and other adults.

We went around the circle, talking about the prayers and how they related to our personal struggles. For the first time in front of Mom, I confided that I was questioning my faith. It seemed hard to believe that a loving God would put someone through so much pain: an assault, a trial, hate sites, panic attacks that just wouldn't go away. I didn't reveal every detail in that circle, but Mom understood.

We'd talk more when we were alone at night. Mom and I shared a "private room," except that it had a bathroom connected, so everyone walked in to use it.

We couldn't flush the toilet until morning because of water restrictions. So the stench of urine (and other things) competed with the smell of decaying crab carcasses wafting from the compost pile outside the one window above our bed.

Still, I treasured these late-night moments. I curled up next to Mom like when I was little. We'd pray together in bed, Mom whispering in my ear, "You're not alone, sweetie. God is definitely walking with you. Keep asking questions and searching. You're going to find answers."

On our second-to-last day, we got up at five a.m. to trek to the top of the Hermitage. I climbed out on the ledge of the stone monastery and squinted at the turquoise-blue blanket rolling endlessly to the horizon.

Waves crashed against the rocky cliffs as the sun crawled up the sky. I stood by myself and closed my eyes. A breeze swept over me while I listened to an orchestra of chirping crickets.

I slipped into a nature coma. I felt peaceful. Confident. I felt brave. When I'd last stood on the Hermitage weeks after my assault, sweaty and swollen from a wasp bite, I was reminded that I was seeking justice for more than myself. Now I thought about Mr. Pillsbury and how he had suffered in silence for half a century. Was I ready to speak out for more than just me? Could I sacrifice my name and my comfort to help other survivors? God, are you out there?

It felt like déjà vu back in Naples. Instead of fighting over my return to St. Paul's, my family was now divided on whether I should publicly tell my story.

Mom and Dad embraced the idea of me finding my voice and speaking out. I had nothing to be ashamed of, they said, and I could help other victims.

Lucy, protective as always, disagreed. She didn't trust the media for one second, even after then NBC News president Deborah Turness met with our family in July and talked about the network's commitment to raising awareness around sexual assault.

"Everyone just wants a sound bite," Lucy said to me afterward. "They're not going to give you time to tell your whole story."

She worried that I wasn't thinking through how this would affect the rest of my life. I'd always be branded the St. Paul's sexual assault victim. Didn't I want to be more than that?

Lucy was also nervous about the fallout for her own life if we went on television together as a family and bashed St. Paul's. She didn't want to lose her remaining friends from boarding school and feared a new surge of online bullying would hurt her job prospects.

I understood Lucy's concerns. My assault had already exiled all of us from the St. Paul's community. It had decimated Lucy's happy high school memories. The Internet trolls had taken aim at her once before, hurling lewd comments that still popped up on Google.

But what she didn't understand at the time was that no matter what I did in life, I would always be a survivor of sexual assault, and it was up to me to own my trauma and support others with the resources I had.

Steve sensed that I was being pulled in different directions, so he set up a meeting in Washington, DC, with Angela Rose, a survivor who went public as a teenager.

Mom gave me some background articles to read on the flight, and my eyes nearly fell out of my head: Angela was seventeen when she was abducted in 2001 outside a shopping mall near Chicago and assaulted by a repeat sex offender on parole for murder. Angela had spent the last fifteen years funneling her anger into activism by starting an organization, PAVE—Promoting Awareness/Victim Empowerment—to help shatter the silence around sexual assault and to provide support for survivors across the country.

Months earlier Angela had sent me a copy of her book *Hope, Healing & Happiness* and wrote me a note.

> *Brave Survivor—*
> *Please know you are not alone in wanting to be strong*
> *for your family. I had to as well. But I also needed to*
> *embark on my healing journey too. You are not alone—*
> *I'm here if you need me!*
> *Love,*
> *Angela Rose*

I guess I was finally cashing in on that offer. Mom, Dad, and I were settling into our hotel room in Washington when a very tiny, very pregnant lady came barreling through the door with outstretched arms and an enormous smile. This was Angela. She had on a gorgeous red dress with a thin satin ribbon above her belly and a sparkly necklace. I hoped I could look as glamorous as that if I was pregnant one day!

Steve observed as Angela gave us an overview of PAVE's work organizing chapters at high schools and college campuses to engage young men and women in conversations about sexual assault and healthy relationships.

As an example, Angela handed out white wristbands with the

words CONSENT IS _____ printed in blue on the front. That campaign encouraged students to fill in the blank and express why consent was important to them and to post about it on social media. Some PAVE chapters successfully targeted boys' soccer teams and other athletes to help spread the word and make the bracelets cool. That was definitely needed at St. Paul's. Especially for the soccer team. PAVE was all about proactive, positive messages.

I silently digested the information, while Mom and Dad asked questions. Steve looked over at me and then announced, "I think everybody should leave except Angela and Chessy. They're the ones who need to talk."

After the room cleared out, Angela and I moved over to a brown sofa and chatted as if we were old friends. I told her the assault reminded me of the earthquake I'd experienced in Japan, and how my world was turned upside down yet again. I wanted to get my life back.

"I'm not sure what I should do about telling my story publicly," I said. "Everyone in my family feels differently."

"Chessy, this needs to be your own decision," Angela said. "Sexual assault is a crime of power and control. You need to have one hundred percent control over what you want to do next. You can't be pushed one way or another."

"I'm worried about how it's going to change my life. I've started to feel some sense of normalcy back in Naples," I said. "There's part of me that just wants to be a kid again."

"That's completely understandable," Angela said. "There's time to do whatever you want. You can speak out now or later or never. And even if you speak out, it doesn't mean you have to be an advocate forever."

I told Angela that I was most scared of the backlash, scared of the negativity, scared the fragile protective shell around me would crack. I worried that I'd open myself up to more harassment when people knew my face and name.

I asked Angela how her friends reacted when she came out as a survivor at seventeen.

"Most of them supported me," she said. "When someone comes out as a survivor, the response is usually very positive."

"Really?" I asked skeptically.

"You know what, I need to connect you with Delaney Henderson," Angela said. "She'll tell you what it's like. You're going to adore her."

Delaney was a high school survivor who went through three criminal trials, Angela explained, and had recently become a PAVE ambassador, speaking out against sexual violence in high schools. That was something I felt passionate about.

"Yes, I'd love to talk with her!" I said. "I've never met someone my own age who's been through this."

Angela had Delaney on speakerphone before I finished my sentence. Delaney said she'd been following my case for years, one of the many strangers in my cheerleading squad.

Delaney lived a few hours away in Florida and wanted to visit me in Naples. I couldn't wait—it had taken me two years to find a survivor my age who'd gone to trial and was trying to make a positive change. We exchanged phone numbers and made plans to FaceTime the following week. When we hung up, I was struck by how young Delaney sounded but also how fierce and strong she seemed.

"I really do want to make a difference," I said to Angela. "I want justice for me and for other people. I want to remove the shame and blame that's so pervasive around sexual assault. I don't want people to feel that way anymore."

"Those are incredible messages, Chessy. You have a voice and important things to share," Angela said. "What does a win look like to you? What would you like to see happen?"

"I want the people at St. Paul's to care. I want this victim blaming to stop. I want every person, boy or girl, who has been victimized to feel empowered. I want them to know that they have the right to be heard, to be respected, and to seek justice."

I'd never met anyone like Angela. She was a pint-size fireball of passion and endless optimism. She made me feel powerful, really powerful, for the first time since my assault.

We talked about putting together a social media campaign and website based on Christianna's fantastic idea for a girls' bill of rights. I didn't want to ignore male victims of sexual violence, so we kept it gender neutral.

I decided to call my campaign #IHaveTheRightTo—after the list I'd made with my sisters that day—to let other girls and boys know that they have the right to their bodies, respect, and a safe place to learn.

I had a voice. I had a message. I was almost ready.

Delaney and I began texting and FaceTiming almost every other day. I didn't know how to share my story, so she told me hers first.

It was the last day of school in June 2011, and some friends came over to her house to celebrate. Her parents were away, and several boys brought pot and pressured Delaney to try it. The weed made her feel dizzy and sick, so she headed upstairs to sleep. Later, Delaney said, two classmates entered her bedroom, locked the door, and raped her.

For three months Delaney hid her assault from everyone except a few close friends. But then her parents found out and told administrators at her private Catholic school. The boys and their friends—older, wealthier, and more popular—began tormenting Delaney.

"They cornered me in the halls and followed me to class. They yelled 'slut' across the quad when they saw me and threatened me on social media," Delaney said. "I had night terrors and panic attacks and I began sleeping in my parents' room with the lights on. I never slept in my own bedroom again."

Delaney's parents never wavered in their support and tried to get the school to intervene. When rumors spread that one of the boys,

Shane Villalpando, had sex with a freshman, Delaney approached the fourteen-year-old girl, and together they decided to report their assaults to the police.

Things at school took a turn for the worse. Kids shoved Delaney in the hallway, threw garbage at her during a football game, and made T-shirts that read #FREESHANE. Like me, Delaney had a community of people protecting the criminal rather than supporting the victim.

"And some of them were people I had considered friends," Delaney said.

I examined Delaney's heart-shaped face, her mouth contorting, her hazel eyes welling up with tears. No one deserved this.

"Oh my God, I'm so sorry. I'm so, so sorry," I said, wishing I could reach through the phone and hug her. "My friends turned their backs on me, too. It's disgusting how communities blame us, the victims, for the crimes these boys committed."

One month after reporting her assault, Delaney hit rock bottom. She got dozens of text messages in one day from people calling her a liar. Delaney locked herself in the bathroom at home and sobbed as she wrote on the mirror, *I am so sorry.*

Then she took a bottle of pills.

Delaney's mom heard her crying and broke down the door.

"I remember waking up in the hospital and wondering how my life had gone from normal to nightmare in such a short time," Delaney said.

Both boys eventually took plea deals for her assault, but the harassment got so bad that Delaney left her school and moved to another town.

Several weeks after she started college, a friend of her attackers wrote a rap song that threatened to kill her, using her full name, and published it online. It was downloaded more than one thousand times.

In the middle of the chaos, Angela reached out to offer her support.

"Angela changed my perspective on my attack," Delaney explained.

"I was no longer Jane Doe, the high school rape victim. I was Delaney the survivor. I had a reason to fight and take back control of my life."

Angela invited Delaney to speak at a fund-raiser for PAVE in California. Their first meeting was featured in the fall of 2014 on an episode of *48 Hours*. Since then, Delaney had traveled the country, speaking out about her experience.

"My work for PAVE helped give me something I'd lost a long time ago"—Delaney paused—"hope and a purpose to live."

A lump was growing in the back of my throat. I began to cry as I told her my story.

I was hanging out in my pajamas and surfing the web when I came across a story in the *Boston Globe* about St. Paul's demanding the identity of Owen Labrie's victim be made public.

I'd told Mom and Dad not to bother me with every legal development, but this seemed insane. I found the school's response to our civil suit online and started reading. It was ridiculous.

St. Paul's was in full denial—they literally used the words "denies" or "denied" 124 times in their response (Dad counted). The school was unwilling to even admit that Owen had assaulted me, despite the fact that he'd been convicted by a jury.

I thought about the email that St. Paul's head of school, Mr. Hirschfeld, sent me on the day of the verdict.

> Dear Chessy,
> You will forever be an inspiration to me as a person of remarkable moral strength and as a truth teller. Your courage has inspired many others and it has prevented Owen Labrie from ever doing to another person what he did to you. As many others have also said, you are a hero.
> Sincerely,
> Mr. Hirschfeld

Tell me now, Mr. Hirschfeld, what did you mean?

And on top of denying everything, St. Paul's sought to strip me of my anonymity and put a gag order on our attorney, Steve. If I was doing my math right, the school wanted to humiliate and silence me at the same time.

Archibald Cox Jr., president of the St. Paul's board of trustees and son of the famous Watergate prosecutor who'd been fired for defying President Nixon, decried our family's "coordinated media attacks."

Mom and Dad looked warily at me as I stomped down the stairs and into the office, carrying my laptop like a weapon.

"So basically, St. Paul's thinks they can shut me up by threatening to reveal my identity?"

"Yes," Dad said tentatively. "But we'll fight it. Don't worry about it."

He said this was straight out of the playbook for institutions trying to bully victims into silence. St. George's School, a prep school in Rhode Island, had been in the news recently for covering up decades of sexual abuse.

In one instance, St. George's tried to out the identity of a victim after the former student filed a lawsuit in 1989. The judge excoriated the school at the time, but the tactic worked: the survivor kept quiet for another twenty-five years. She spoke out publicly for the first time in 2015.

"So St. Paul's still thinks that they're going to keep me quiet? They think that's going to push me down?" I laughed, my cheeks red with anger. "Well then, they've completely underestimated me."

I dashed to my room and FaceTimed Delaney.

"That's total bullshit," Delaney declared after I gave her the update.

"I'm not going to let the school bully me into silence. I want to tell my side of the story. I want to reveal my identity," I heaved into the phone.

Delaney paused. The silence felt thick.

"You need to trust your gut on this."

"I'm worried about the negative responses," I said.

"I first started talking to the media anonymously, and then I went public with my name. Both ways, the feedback was almost universally positive," Delaney said. "You already know how the school community is going to respond. They won't be nice, but you know that. You've experienced it already. It's the rest of the world that matters."

"Do you think this could help other people?" I prodded.

"Yes. But this is your decision to make," Delaney said gently.

Ugh. I really just wanted someone to tell me what to do.

"We met some really nice people at NBC who've asked many times for me to come on the *Today* show," I said. "They're willing to help raise awareness for other survivors. What do you think?"

"I think it's awesome that they want to help survivors," Delaney said. "But I can't tell you what to do here."

"How am I going to figure this out?"

"If you close your eyes and breathe in, you'll feel your gut instinct and you'll know what to do."

I shut my eyes, and my lashes gently brushed against my cheeks. I inhaled deeply.

As the breath escaped my mouth, I felt the ground shifting and the earth pushing up beneath me, a force so strong that it nearly lifted me off my feet.

Before my eyes fluttered open, I whispered to Delaney, "I'm gonna do it."

I met with Savannah Guthrie, cohost of the *Today* show, in June 2016 (left).

Mom and I watched the sunrise from the top of the hermitage in Cat Island in July 2016 (below).

TWENTY

Jane Doe, Revealed

Savannah and the NBC team graciously agreed to schedule the interview on Saturday, August 27, so I didn't have to miss any school. I was just a few days into my senior year, and homework was already piling up.

On my first day back, I told two friends about the prospect of a TV interview as we chatted about our summers. I linked arms with Nicole and Hope while we walked to the library to have our yearbook photos taken.

"I met with the producers of the *Today* show because I'm thinking of telling my story publicly," I said cautiously.

"That's so awesome," Nicole said. "I'm so proud of you."

It meant a lot coming from Nicole. She was one of my friends at CSN who'd confided in me that she had been assaulted a few years earlier by a student at her old public school. I wanted other survivors to tell me I was doing the right thing.

After we took our yearbook photos, Hope joined me on the floor of the library while we waited for the first day's assembly to begin.

When she plopped down next to me, she said, "Chessy, when I was on Cape Cod this summer, my friends who go to boarding school mentioned how their schools just started talking about sexual assault and consent because of your case at St. Paul's. Isn't that incredible?" she said. "You're already making a difference."

"Wow." I teared up. "I had no idea."

I grabbed her hand and smiled. I loved that my friends were comfortable talking about this with me and supported my efforts to speak out.

But as the weekend drew closer, my courage was a roller coaster. In the morning I'd be brave, around noon I'd fade, and by night I'd want to howl at the moon.

I FaceTimed Delaney whenever I needed to rebuild my backbone.

"I'm so nervous," I said, my voice trembling, limbs shaking.

"Everything is going to fall into place," Delaney promised.

I slumped down on the couch in my bedroom and hunched over my computer.

"You're going to change lives," Delaney insisted.

"I don't know if I can do this," I whimpered.

"I know you can. This is a lot bigger than you and me," Delaney said. "You're not just speaking out for yourself; it's for survivors everywhere."

The opportunity to give others a voice weighed heavily on me, but it also lifted me up. I understood that I was getting a platform to speak in part because I was a white, privileged girl who somehow became an object of fascination. I wouldn't necessarily have this chance if I was poor or a young woman of color or I attended a public school.

And I knew that my privilege had followed me throughout the justice system. My background and supportive parents established credibility with law enforcement that others might not have. I wondered what it would have been like for someone with a single parent. For a family who couldn't afford to attend every court hearing. For someone with no family at all.

The trial was epically brutal, but at least I had a shot. Most rape cases never get prosecuted. Sexual violence is notoriously difficult to measure, but the Rape, Abuse, and Incest National Network has estimated that out of every one thousand rapes, only 310 are reported to police, and of those, just eleven cases get referred to prosecutors.

It wasn't fair that some survivors didn't have the chance to have a voice and to hold their attackers accountable. I knew I was in a unique position, and it seemed selfish to squander the opportunity to talk to those who didn't get justice, who felt ashamed, isolated, silenced. I had a responsibility to help right these wrongs. I needed to tell them I believed them and that they were not alone. I wanted parents to see my family up there with me during the interview so that if their children were ever sexually assaulted, they knew to stand by their side.

"Okay," I said to Delaney. "I'm really gonna do this."

I'd only known Delaney for three weeks—and we hadn't even met in person—yet she understood me completely. I was about to embark on a journey she'd already made and I needed her to steady my ship. NBC offered to fly my whole family, Angela, and Steve up for the interview. But I had one more ask: Delaney. When a producer at NBC said she would happily bring Delaney and her mom to New York City and put them up at a hotel, I burst into tears.

I woke up on the dark side of the morning feeling helpless and confused. It was Friday and I wasn't sure I could get on that plane to New York. I rummaged around for my prayer book.

It contained daily devotionals, or spiritual readings for each calendar day—one in the morning, one at night. I'd been reading them since I was a child. Mom gave me and my sisters these books as gifts every year, hoping to share with us the faith that she held so close to her heart.

I opened the brown hardcover book and turned to August 26:

> *TRUST ME in the midst of a messy day. Your inner calm—your Peace in My Presence—need not be shaken by what is going on around you. Though you live in this temporal world, your innermost being is rooted and grounded in eternity. When you start to feel stressed, detach yourself from the disturbances around you. Instead of desperately striving to maintain order and control in your little world, relax and remember that circumstances cannot touch My Peace.*
>
> *Seek My Face, and I will share My mind with you, opening your eyes to see things from My perspective. Do not let your heart be troubled, and do not be afraid. The Peace I give is sufficient for you.*

I took a deep breath. Wow. Okay, maybe God had a plan for me after all. I realized I needed to untangle myself from other people's opinions and know that God was taking care of me. I tucked the prayer book in my luggage and got ready for the flight.

When we arrived in New York, Angela was all smiles and literally bursting at the seams, half joking that her water could break at any moment. Nothing seemed to bother her—not the oppressive heat or her swelling feet.

I waited anxiously for Delaney and her mom in a conference room at the hotel where we were staying. Their plane was delayed and they were hours late. I paced back and forth. "I hope Delaney's going to make it."

Finally my petite blond soulmate arrived. We were in the middle of a meeting with Angela and our lawyers when Delaney ran over and bear-hugged me. We held each other and wept for several minutes.

After the exciting introductions, Angela focused us on prepping me for the interview: "Chessy, I just want you to remember that you can still change your mind. The choice is absolutely yours."

"Okay," I said. "This is really overwhelming, but I want to do this. And I'm so thankful that you're all here with me."

"I couldn't be more proud," Angela said. "I'll be proud of you either way. But if you're going to do this, let's talk about ways for you to feel in control of the interview."

She launched into a number of tips for how to redirect an uncomfortable question and how to speak concisely.

"And don't be afraid to tap into your emotions. It's not all rainbows and butterflies," Angela said. "It's okay to be angry up there. It's okay to be sad. You're a survivor and that's not easy."

"And whatever you do," she advised, "trust your gut."

It was August 27, 2016, the day to reclaim my identity. I wanted my voice back. I wanted my life back. And I also wanted my wardrobe back.

I put on the loose blue shirt that I'd worn the day after my assault, when I was trying to cover up my body. It had been one of my favorites, bright and flowy and full of life. But after the attack, it hung in my closet, fossilizing in the plastic dry-cleaning wrapper. Each time I saw the shirt, I thought of standing at the flagpole and Malcolm's smirk. I shoved it farther back until it was completely hidden. Now I was finally ready to reclaim that shirt.

I picked out my jewelry: dangling dragonfly earrings that Aunt Cathy had given me. In Japan, dragonflies are symbols of courage and strength. I slid on the black-and-white beaded Lokai bracelet from Mandi so it nestled between woven friendship bracelets made by one of the little girls on Cat Island. A silver cross and an Italian glass pendant that Lucy had bought me hung around my neck. I wanted support clinging to every part of my body.

I asked for space that morning, staving off Christianna's hugs and kisses. I needed to collect myself.

Dad dropped off Christianna at Grandma Prout's apartment while the rest of us headed to 30 Rock. We got ready in the dressing room usually used by Jimmy Fallon's guests. The woman doing my hair said the last person she'd styled was Zac Efron during the Olympics in Brazil. It was a nice distraction from the nerves snaking through my body.

Lucy sat quietly as makeup artists tried to get us camera-ready. They glammed me up a bit too much, so I asked them to remove some of the makeup.

"I'm sorry, I just want to look as natural as possible," I said. "I just want this interview to be real. The real me."

Delaney flashed me a thumbs-up. We headed over to the room where the interview would be taped. There were half a dozen people scurrying about, questions coming from all directions while the camera crew set up their equipment.

A woman with a clipboard approached me. "How do you want to be referred to in the interview?"

We still hadn't decided whether I would use Chessy Prout, Francesca Prout, or just my initials.

Mom and Dad favored my initials so I could retain some privacy. Others said I needed to own my name and come out as Francesca Prout to be more accessible. Everyone chimed in with an opinion, and I kept agreeing with whoever spoke last. I was completely overwhelmed.

Then Delaney piped up: "Uh, if you don't want to use any name, that's fine too."

The lady with the clipboard frowned in Delaney's direction. "Uh, no, that's not actually true. She has to use a name."

"Chessy, you are the captain of this boat. This is your decision, not theirs," Delaney said loudly. "Whatever you want, goes. End of story."

I didn't know what to say. In my head, I questioned whether I should be doing this interview at all. I looked down at my feet.

Suddenly Delaney grabbed my hand. "Can we talk for a minute?"

I nodded and followed her into a tiny side room with no chairs and no light switch that we could find. We sat down on the floor facing each other. Delaney put her hands on my shaking fingers and told me everything was going to be okay.

She took a silver bangle off her wrist that was engraved with the words EVERYTHING HAPPENS FOR A REASON.

"I bought you another bracelet that said 'Unbreakable,' but it didn't arrive at your house on time and I'm really pissed. So I want you to wear this instead. I wore it during my first interview. I want you to hold it when you feel like you're going to break down and remember all the love and support you have behind you," Delaney said. "You are a hero. We're here for a reason."

My eyes brimmed with tears as I ran my fingers along the words on the bracelet.

"Don't mess up your makeup!" Delaney scolded.

I giggled, breaking up the storm raging inside my brain. We made a quick pit stop at the bathroom, and as we walked out, Delaney pulled me aside again.

"Chess, this is your moment to take back your voice. But if at any point you want to leave, we're leaving. No one is going to stop us."

"Okay." I breathed out. But I knew that wasn't going to happen. I had to do this.

"No matter what, your entire life is going to change after this day. All the pain you've been feeling for so many years is now transforming into fuel to light the fire of positivity in your world," Delaney said, pulling me in for a hug. "I'm so proud of you for being the voice of survivors all over the world who are unable to share their stories."

We walked out hand in hand through the double doors. I found the woman with the clipboard.

"I want people to know me as Chessy Prout."

I felt a fire in my belly. The confidence I'd been waiting for finally arrived. I was ready for my one-on-one interview. Savannah and I sat alone on two chairs facing each other near a window. There were cameras behind me, in front of me, and to the right. A cold sweat moistened my skin even as the hot lights broiled above me.

Savannah sat close enough that I could touch her arm. She smiled warmly, her blue-gray eyes fixed on me.

"This is the first time you've come out and said publicly what happened."

"Yes. Yeah," I said.

"Why did you want to do that?"

This should have been the easiest question. I'd spent weeks convincing so many people, including myself, that it was the right thing to do.

"Well, uhh," I sighed deeply.

I looked down at the floor, up at the ceiling, then at Savannah, and back down again. I spent nine whole seconds on national television rolling my eyes around, fumbling for words.

"It's been two years now since the whole ordeal, and I feel ready to stand up and own what happened to me. And I'm going to make sure that other people, other girls, other boys, know that they can own it too and they don't have to be ashamed either," I said, shaking my head defiantly.

I saw Angela standing behind Savannah, pumping her fists in the air. Delaney was standing next to her, cheerleading for me with imaginary pom-poms.

I wasn't broken or fragile. I was fierce. When Savannah asked questions about the trial, I redirected the conversation and told her

I'd been answering questions about my past for two years now and I was done. I wanted to talk about the future instead.

So Savannah turned to my advocacy campaign: "You have an idea of how you can take something terrible that happened to you and turn it into something good for others. What are you hoping to accomplish?"

"We have been talking a lot about a woman's bill of rights. And I decided I want other people's input," I said. "I want other people to feel empowered and just strong enough to be able to say I have the right to my body. I have the right to say no. And I wanted to bring this initiative that would be #IHaveTheRightTo and to have people contribute to it."

I could have talked for hours about the campaign, but it was time for the family interview. I fidgeted with my bracelets as Lucy sat to my right and Mom settled in on my left. Dad was on the end and grasped Mom's hand. The cameras started to roll.

Savannah began with the news—our civil lawsuit against St. Paul's.

"Some will say, oh, a lawsuit. Is the family trying to get money? What's the real motive here? Why not just let it go?"

The money question.

"Well, we're talking about children and we feel an obligation that this not happen to any future kids at the school," Dad said calmly.

Lucy sat silently, her hair hanging down the side of her face like a protective shield. She thought the interview was focusing on my experience, so she was surprised when Savannah began probing her on the Senior Salute and the hook-up culture at St. Paul's. Lucy got defensive and talked in half sentences, refusing to give them a usable sound bite.

I loved my Lulu. She was under no obligation to answer anyone's questions. She was there to support me and that's all I wanted. I reached out and grabbed Lucy's hand.

"Your family has been right there with you all along," Savannah said.

"Yes." I smiled and bowed my head in appreciation.

"And a lot of people don't have that. I can only imagine how helpful that's been," Savannah said.

"Somebody's got my back and somebody's going to believe me, somebody's going to help me," I said, raising my hand with Lucy's. "And even when I get my panic attacks and I lock myself in my closet because I don't want my little sister to see-ee-ee me like that," I said, my voice shaking, my vowels stretching for miles. Mom grabbed my left hand as my chin trembled and I blinked back tears.

"And she comes into my room sometimes and she'll—she'll come into my closet when I'm rocking on the floor and punching my legs, trying to get myself to calm down, and she'll try to give me the biggest hug and she'll say, 'Chessy, you're okay, Chessy, you're okay.'" I sniffled loudly. "And it just, I just can't imagine how scary it is for other people to have to do this alone and I don't want anybody else to be alone anymore. I don't."

I really didn't want to cry on national television. Now the whole world would know how damaged I was, that I punched myself in a closet.

I looked across the room and saw Delaney collapsed in Angela's lap, muffling her sobs so nobody could hear. Delaney and I had commiserated over our struggles with panic attacks and placed as much blame on our attackers as the school communities that supported the predators.

It made me angry to see Delaney so upset. But it also made me feel better about blubbering on TV—people should see the true impact of these crimes. I could be fierce and vulnerable. That was the real me.

"You nailed it!" Angela shouted as she waddled over.

Delaney pounced on me like a panther. "I'm so proud of you! You're going to change the world!"

Mom, Dad, and Lucy converged on me for a family hug. The tear ducts opened again and this time I didn't care about streaking my makeup. I was fried. I needed a bed. I needed food. And I needed my sweet Christianna.

○○○○○

Our large group migrated to Soba Nippon, my favorite Japanese restaurant just a few blocks from Rockefeller Center. On our way back to the hotel, we stopped at a Momofuku Milk Bar to satiate our collective soft-serve craving and to pick up some chocolate truffles to bring back to Christianna. It was time to splurge.

I fell into a serious food coma and flopped on the bed in Mom and Dad's hotel room and tried to take a nap while Christianna jumped up and down on the mattress.

I wished Christianna could have been with us during the interview, but it didn't seem right to expose her in that way. Every time something new popped up with the case, we gave Christianna the abridged version of events.

"Chessy's going to be on TV this week to talk about her experiences," or "We have to leave you with Uncle Pete and Aunt Carol this weekend because we need to meet with lawyers in New Hampshire."

Lucy hung around for a while after the interview but then snuck out of our hotel room, fighting back tears. Dad ran after her and for the next three hours, Lucy opened up about how difficult her own experience had been at St. Paul's. My public confession had ruptured the inner peace she had struggled to maintain. Even Dad dredged up painful memories he had buried for decades: how the legacy kids teased him and called him a boofer—a derogatory term for a black person—because he was friends with other minority students.

Later that evening, we all reconvened in Angela's hotel room and began working on the #IHaveTheRightTo website. Dad ordered five plates of french fries and nachos for everyone to nosh on as we labored late into the night.

Angela put out a call to her network of survivors, asking them to submit selfies as they claimed their rights with #IHaveTheRightTo signs. We picked out the graphics and I got my first look at the creation of a professional website. Helping to build something made me feel like I was finally on my way to truly becoming a thriving survivor.

Delaney and I focused on putting together our own video to post to the website. We had lost the fancy NBC camera crew, so Angela's video camera would have to suffice. Christianna took on the role of holding the lights and Delaney's mom, Kym, gave us a big grin.

Delaney and I sketched out a short script where we would finish each other's sentences and show our strength together as survivors. We sat on a long brown couch, and Delaney interlaced her fingers with mine and we lifted our fused arms. This was girl power.

I looked at the camera as Delaney started, "I have the right to . . ."

"Seek out survivors whenever I feel ready," I finished.

I turned to Delaney: "I have the right to . . ."

"Follow the road to justice no matter how long it takes," Delaney finished.

After a couple of tries, and a long string of bloopers, we settled on the last one.

I smiled at Delaney and she rested her head on my shoulder. Angela beamed from the other side of the room. I felt so lucky that these amazing women had landed in my life and taken me under their wings.

Girl power with survivors Delaney Henderson (center) and Angela Rose (right) after taping the *Today* show interview in August 2016.

We began making a website for #IHaveTheRightTo with the help of Delaney's mom, Kym (above).

TWENTY-ONE

Doubt

An avalanche of doubt and regret tumbled down on me once I got back home. Nothing, not even Delaney's soothing voice, could free me.

"Did I just make the worst decision of my life? Who even wants to hear me speak?" I squeaked into the phone. "What if I made everything worse?"

"How could it get worse?" Delaney said. "You've already dealt with the worst."

That was hardly reassuring. Each time I thought I hit rock bottom, the earth ripped open beneath me again and swallowed me whole. After the assault came the school backlash, rejected plea deals, a mobster attorney, hate sites, media distortions, curfew violations, appeals, and attempts by St. Paul's to bully me into silence. What was next?

I was ensnared in a web of self-loathing for the next two days. I had nightmares as soon as my head hit the pillow. When I woke up, I grabbed my journal and contemplated what life would be like "if I were gone."

> *If I were gone Christianna could have my room. She could have all my clothes and wouldn't have to worry about me getting angry or sad anymore. Lucy wouldn't feel like she had to dedicate her life to social justice, she could find happiness without me dragging behind her. She could finally have mom and dad's actual attention. She needs their help. Mom wouldn't have to worry anymore, about my well-being, about my gluten-free diets, about knowing when to talk to me and how. . . .*

When I read it later, I realized how harmful those thoughts were. I just wanted my family to live happily and carefree. And I felt like I was a giant pit of quicksand trapping everyone in misery.

During my free period on Monday, I searched NBC's website and found a promo video teasing my interview with Savannah. I flipped out and called Dad when I saw it featured pictures of Owen in court.

I had agreed to go on the *Today* show for other survivors, not to give any further attention to this criminal. I intentionally did not say his name once during the interview.

This was my turn to speak. Finally the school community who turned their backs on me, the adults who did nothing and sat quietly, and the strangers who judged me harshly would have to listen and confront the uncontaminated, uncomfortable truth.

Dad promised to talk to NBC and then sent one of his trademark pep talks.

Dad: Chessy—from tomorrow the story will no longer
be about the perp. It will be about survivors and the
impact. . . . Tomorrow, the narcissist will lose. Keep your
chin up and remember why you spoke up.

I was still shaking on the couch ten minutes after the interview aired.
Mom and Dad had made a Chessy sandwich: Dad nestled on my left
and Mom cuddled on the right. I was wearing a white cotton bath-
robe over my pajamas and clutching a mug of Yogi green tea. The
hot Florida sun streamed through the windows in our family room,
but I couldn't feel a thing.

When Owen's face flashed on the television screen, I squeezed
my eyes shut and wondered whether I had made the right decision.
I cringed when I heard Savannah describe our encounter as a date.
But then I saw my own face. Yikes. That's not something you could
ever prepare yourself for. I sank deeper into our beige couch after listening to myself describe my panic attacks. I felt so exposed. Would
people judge me for speaking out? Would they call me an opportun-
ist? Could this actually help someone?

Finally the segment ended. No one said a word. Mom eventually
broke the silence that covered us like a heavy blanket.

"There is a reason this is all happening. We don't understand
why," she said. "But we are trusting that good is going to come from
this. God has this, Chess."

I nodded but couldn't get words out. I tugged at the UNBREAKABLE
bracelet that Delaney bought me. It had arrived in the mail the day
before.

Dad's phone started ringing. We thought it was Grandma Prout.
We hadn't heard from her in twenty-four hours, and Dad had asked
the doorman in her building to go up and check on her.

Dad looked at his phone and saw that Mr. Hirschfeld was calling.
"I'm not picking this up," he said.

"Don't pick it up," Mom advised.

I looked at them, my heart racing. My limp body jolted into action. "I am."

With adrenaline coursing through my veins, I grabbed the phone from Dad's hand and put it on speaker. Boy oh boy, I was ready to unload.

"Hello," I said.

"Chessy, I wasn't expecting to hear from you! I thought I called your dad. Maybe it's the wrong number."

Mr. Hirschfeld had a lilt in his voice, a remarkably different tone from when he spoke through the St. Paul's megaphone.

"No, it's the right number," I answered.

"It was so wonderful to see you on TV," he stammered.

I stopped biting my tongue and cut him off.

"Mr. Hirschfeld, when I was having a really hard time, Dylan let me into your home and we had all those dinners. He took care of me a lot. And I will always be grateful for your son. But I really don't understand what you're doing to our family. You know the truth. How can you do this?"

Wow. I wasn't sure I was gonna get all that out—and I kept my cool, too! I had volcanoes of anger ready to erupt for nearly two years, but by the grace of God I was able to stay calm.

Mom and Dad held their breath.

"Uhh, frankly, I don't know sometimes," he said.

I stared at the phone, mouth gaping. He was the head of the school! An adult, for God's sake!

After a long pause, Mr. Hirschfeld sighed, "It's the lawyers. I don't understand it all."

He was a coward. I saw Grandma Prout was calling and told Mr. Hirschfeld I had to go. I hung up before he had the chance to say good-bye.

I fell back onto the couch, retreating into myself. Our phones were blowing up with text messages from friends and family. My stomach was in knots. What did the rest of the world think?

I needed to talk to Delaney. Needed to hear her voice, her support, her guidance.

"The interview was fantastic," Delaney said. "You killed it. You should feel so proud and good."

I didn't. I saw a jerk on Twitter who called me "nothing but a whore who ruined a mans life." The rest of the message had terrible spelling and punctuation, but I expected nothing less from a troll. I wanted to respond and set this ignorant commenter straight.

Delaney told me not to worry and promised she'd take care of it. She spent the rest of the day hunting down bullies on Facebook and Twitter, flagging their comments and trying to get their accounts blocked. I had my own virtual bodyguard.

Lucy called and said she was hearing from old friends she'd lost touch with from Japan, former teachers, and acquaintances. Even her old head of house at St. Paul's reached out.

"They're all saying how incredible the interview was and are sending their best wishes," Lucy said. "I'm so proud of you, Chess. You're doing the right thing."

I realized Lucy had been attempting to protect me, still trying to make up for the ways she thought she'd failed to safeguard me from the boys at school. It meant so much to have Lucy by my side and hold my hand during the interview. We didn't always see eye to eye on everything (what sisters do?), but Lucy had put herself out there to support me time and time again. She carries my heart.

The reason I'm still standing here today is because of those four words Lucy uttered when I told her what happened in the mechanical room: *It's not your fault.* Her immediate support saved me.

I learned from Angela that the first person survivors disclose to can have a tremendous impact on their healing process. Oftentimes, when we hear that someone we love and care about has been hurt, the initial reaction can be to deny or rationalize what happened. But that can come across as minimizing and disbelieving and can shame victims into silence.

I hoped to get that message across in the statement I put together for the rest of the media.

> #IHaveTheRightTo find my voice and to use it when I am ready. #IHaveTheRightTo be called a survivor, not an "alleged victim" or "accuser." #IHaveTheRightTo spend time with someone and be safe. #IHaveTheRightTo say NO and be HEARD. #IHaveTheRightTo not be shamed and bullied into silence. #IHaveTheRightTo not be isolated by the crime against me or by people who want to shame me. #IHaveTheRightTo name what happened to me because being sexually assaulted is never excusable or "complicated." There is no perfect victim. #IHaveTheRightTo be happy, sad, upset, angry, and inspired anytime during the process of my healing without being judged. But most importantly, #IHaveTheRightTo stand with you.

Angela called, her voice jumping with enthusiasm.

"Chessy, #IHaveTheRightTo is trending on Twitter," she said. "The response is phenomenal. And New Hampshire senator Jeanne Shaheen just gave you a shout-out!"

I clicked on the link she sent.

> @SenatorShaheen: Chessy Prout is a remarkable, brave young woman. Thank you for sharing your story to change stigma of sexual assault. #IHaveTheRightTo

My interview was everywhere. BuzzFeed—the place where I usually go to distract myself from reality—featured it as one of the top stories.

#IHaveTheRightTo was taking off on Twitter, Instagram, Facebook, and Snapchat. Hundreds of people sent videos and photos of themselves holding up signs and declaring their rights. Old friends, even strangers were taking part. But no one from St. Paul's.

Instagram was filled with photos of smiling women holding up handmade signs:

> #IHAVETHERIGHTTO DEFEND MYSELF AND MY BODY AND
>   TO BE RESPECTED
> #IHAVETHERIGHTTO STAND UP TAKE ACTION & BE A
>   CHANGEMAKER
> #IHAVETHERIGHTTO LIVE WITHOUT THE FEAR OF SEXUAL
>   VIOLENCE
> #IHAVETHERIGHTTO TELL MY STORY, TO HELP + INSPIRE
>   OTHERS, AND TO DEMAND JUSTICE
> #IHAVETHERIGHTTO HAVE A VOICE!

A girl from the volleyball team my freshman year at St. Paul's commented on a photo of the interview that I posted on my Instagram page thanking the people who had stood by me. She had left the school, too.

> I, obviously, witnessed the toxic culture that fed into the
> horrible events that hurt you. Know that I support and
> adore you from afar and that I am so so proud of you for
> speaking out about both your situation and the school.
> You are an inspiration for young girls everywhere.

I couldn't believe she was saying this publicly. Inspiration? Me? I couldn't associate those words with myself. I was just telling the truth. I hoped somebody would find comfort in this. And I hoped people would let me lean on them.

Throughout the day, Delaney sent me screenshots of people responding to the story.

> Delaney: Just thought I'd share a few comments so you
> know how loved you are by the world ❤
> Me: Slowly seeing the human connection that is
> happening here, and becoming a little bit more
> comfortable. I am so inspired by the other people
> speaking out.

Delaney was right. The feedback was overwhelmingly positive. Our phones didn't stop ringing, our inboxes were clogged with messages. Charles, one of the older guys who'd brought me onto the mock trial team, sent me a message on Snapchat.

> Charles: I just saw the interview. You're incredibly brave,
> and I'm so glad to know a person as strong as you. You'll
> make an excellent attorney one day, and I know you'll do
> an amazing job at mock trial this year. Make us proud.

The outpouring of support was like an infusion of oxygen. My family could breathe again; we felt hopeful. I wasn't afraid to leave the house for lunch, so Mom and I grabbed burgers at Five Guys and then got manicures to unwind.

I glanced around at the other customers in the nail salon, wondering if they'd seen the *Today* show that morning. I felt proud to be sitting there in public after coming forward with my story. All the shame and blame I had carried around for the past two years fell away.

I was excited to tell Christianna how the campaign—the one

she'd planted the seeds for—was being recognized around the world. The Prout girls were making a difference!

Christianna had wanted to stay home from school with me to watch the interview together as a family, but we needed to see it first and make sure it wasn't too graphic or too upsetting for a fifth grader. As much as I trusted the team at NBC, media coverage of sexual assault can be done insensitively, even with the best intentions in mind.

When Christianna finally returned from a long day at school, she curled up next to me in the family room, back where Mom, Dad, and I had huddled in the morning.

I could feel Christianna's heart beating. Two years of closed doors, whispered secrets, and hushed conversations were coming to an end. Now it was out there in the open for everyone to see.

I had been numb with fear when I watched it live in the morning. The second time, with Christianna clinging to me like a koala, I let the emotions wash over me. Tears made wavy tracks down my smooth cheeks as I watched myself recount the panic attacks.

"I lock myself in my closet because I don't want my little sister to see-ee-ee me like that. And she comes into my room sometimes and she'll—she'll come into my closet when I'm rocking on the floor and punching my legs, trying to get myself to calm down, and she'll try to give me the biggest hug and she'll say, 'Chessy, you're okay, Chessy, you're okay.'"

Christianna's arms were already squeezing me tight when that part came on, and then she hugged me tighter. I started laughing and gestured to her cobra grip. "See!"

Christianna giggled and smiled. Then she nuzzled up to me and whispered in my ear, "I love you, Chessy."

Dad and Christianna comforted me after we watched the *Today* show interview together.

TWENTY-TWO

Advocate

Here goes nothing, I thought as I pulled up to the CSN parking lot. I took a couple of deep breaths and wandered from the safety of my car into the jungle that is high school. I wondered whether anyone had seen the interview yesterday and if they'd even say anything to me.

I walked through the breezeway toward the senior lockers and thought about a party a few weeks earlier at the beginning of senior year. I had been sitting outside, squished between my friend Jeremy and the edge of the couch, eating a vegan pizza and snacking on chips.

I fiddled with the white CONSENT IS _____ bracelet that Angela had given me when we first met. I hadn't filled in the blank yet—I wasn't sure what to write—but I still liked wearing it. Jeremy noticed the bracelet and grabbed my hand.

"What's this?" he asked.

I jerked my hand back and narrowed my eyes. I was afraid of Jeremy's response and considered creating a distraction to end the conversation. But then I realized this was why I wore the bracelet in the first place. We needed to talk about these things, no matter how uncomfortable they may be.

"Oh, it's this bracelet that this woman Angela gave me. She founded this organization called PAVE. I think I'm gonna start working with them. . . . It's supposed to promote awareness of what consent means," I rambled on.

"That's really cool," Jeremy replied earnestly. "I mean, I'd wear one if you had more."

I stopped sinking into the couch and straightened my spine. I lifted my gaze from the floor to meet Jeremy's eyes. He really meant it.

"Okay, I'll get some to bring into school," I said.

This could be the start of something big. It made me hopeful as I headed to class the day after the interview. In first-period math, Arielle hugged me and my ex-boyfriend Dean told me he was proud. One of my other guy friends acted a little awkward when he joined our cluster, but then we joked around like usual for the rest of class.

After first period, I grabbed some books from my locker. I hoisted my math textbook, which weighed about two hundred pounds, onto a shelf as Cory, a big goofy football player, approached me with a solemn smile.

He stopped short right in front of my locker. I'd been friends with Cory since middle school, and I knew he was a good kid. But I still wasn't sure what to expect. Boys and girls who I thought were my close friends at St. Paul's had deserted me after they found out about my assault.

I braced myself and imagined the silver knight figurine that Catherine gave me to hold on the witness stand. I turned to Cory with a smile.

"I don't really know how to say something like this . . . but I just want you to know that I'm behind you one hundred percent," Cory said. "I think it was really brave of you to go on TV. And if there's anything I can do, you know, with the football team to help spread your message, just let me know. I want to do whatever I can to support your cause."

Cory was the epitome of a scholar athlete—he was one of only two students in the world to get a perfect score on the AP Stats exam in the spring of 2015. He was the kind of star student who at St. Paul's would have been too cocky, too self-important to care about anyone but himself.

But here, smack in the middle of conservative Florida, he was taking the time to talk to me, to listen to my words, and to enlist other athletes in this movement. I couldn't believe it. He was nothing like the guys at St. Paul's.

"You don't know how much that means to me," I said. "I'd love for you to get involved. I'm actually working with an organization called PAVE."

And I realized: This is the way it's supposed to go.

Later that day during theater class, a sophomore girl sidled up to me. I was talking to the theater teacher, who was also an ally at school, someone who was as pissed off about rape culture and victim shaming as me.

"I saw your interview," the sophomore girl said to me. "That was so cool what you did, standing up for women's rights. I'd like to help out in any way."

Little by little that day, teachers and administrators came up and congratulated me, saying they'd love to join the initiative. Two graduates from CSN confided their own stories of assault at their new colleges. Text messages from old friends poured in. It was overwhelming and I know I missed responding to a few.

One weekend, a large box light as air arrived from Tokyo on our doorstep. I gently cut through the cardboard and lifted out giant

white paper origami cranes signed by my old friends and teachers at
Sacred Heart and Tokyo Union Church. I sobbed as I read the notes
tucked inside the folds. I hadn't talked to some of these people since
the earthquake five years ago.

Mom, Dad, and I huddled around the low black lacquer table I
used to dance on in Tokyo. Christianna held me as I tried to keep my
tears of joy from dripping onto the delicate cranes. This community,
the one I treasured most, the one who knew me best, was standing
by my side after all these years. I could feel my heart glow.

I wondered whether coming forward would help my classmates at
St. Paul's to stand up to the sick culture there. I received messages
from several old friends, including Dylan, Lilly, and Catie.

> Catie: so so proud of you and im sure girls and women all
> over the world are thankful for someone like you chess 🖤

After months of silence, I even heard from Violet, my friend from
Madhatters who had visited me in Naples. I'd learned since then that
her mother supposedly called me a slut at a cocktail party and Mom
took her to task. Violet, of course, didn't mention that in her text.

> Violet: Hey Chessy it's Violet! I just wanted to let you
> know that even though I haven't showed it, I have been
> thinking about you and I didn't know how to express that
> since we had grown apart, but I've decided that it doesn't
> matter because I really want you to hear what I have to
> say. I cannot believe how strong you've been these past
> two years and I am even more amazed at how you are
> now inspiring other girls and giving them hope. When I
> post things with the #spsfam I am doing it to let people
> know that anyone who went to sps is family and that
> family sticks up for each other no matter what. . . .

SPS family sticks up for each other no matter what? I wrote down some choice words, then deleted them. She didn't deserve a second more of my time.

Mom and Dad were constantly on their phones, fielding messages from friends and loved ones and monitoring social media and news websites. Two days after my interview, the *Concord Monitor* wrote an editorial titled "A Brave Young Woman Stands Up."

A few days later I was eating dinner in the kitchen when Mom showed me a page on Everipedia.com, a crowd-sourced encyclopedia, that featured a photo of me and listed my age and my occupation: activist, student.

I laid my fork on the table. I had been so consumed by the threats and slut narratives posted on shame sites that I'd never imagined a scenario in which supporters buried the trolls. Now I was labeled an activist and a survivor instead of a slut and a liar. Things really could change!

I was overcome with a new sense of freedom. It felt empowering to shatter my silence and try to make people more thoughtful about sexual assault survivors. I agreed to do an exclusive interview with the *Boston Globe*—it seemed like a good way to ensure that my message reached the cloistered New England prep school community.

After school one day, I sat down in the office at our house and talked to a reporter by phone, explaining what life had been like since coming forward. It was scary to be so publicly vulnerable, but I agreed to let a photographer come to Naples to shoot some pictures for the piece. I rushed home and drew up my own #IHAVETHERIGHTTO sign for the first time. As I put purple Sharpie to paper, I reflected on the past couple of months. I never thought I could get to this point.

Angela checked in daily to see how I was doing and to update us on the campaign. The feedback was exhilarating: in just ten days,

#IHaveTheRightTo had nearly five million social media impressions. The numbers dazzled us even if we weren't totally sure what they meant.

The outpouring of support was gratifying, but sometimes I felt tapped out. I still wanted to be a normal high school senior and spend as much time with my friends as I could. It was our last year together, and things were finally going really well. I was also chin-deep in schoolwork, with AP Econ tests, AP French, AP Lit exams—and, oh, that thing called getting into college. I was scrambling to finish my early decision application for Barnard. The pressure was intense.

One night in mid-September, I was hunched over my econ books, trying to memorize price elasticity formulas, when Mom came over to my study station in the dining room.

"Sweetie, Annie Kuster, a congresswoman from New Hampshire, talked about your case today on the floor of the House of Representatives. You've got to see this," she said, placing her phone on top of my books so I could watch the video.

I shoved the phone away. I didn't have the bandwidth to process it. I needed to focus on my schoolwork. If I ever was going to make more of a difference in the world, I'd at least have to graduate high school. Plus, I wasn't ready in that moment for the enormity of what Mom was saying.

Late that night when I was alone in bed, I searched online for Representative Kuster's speech. I learned that she was a survivor of multiple sexual assaults who had stayed silent for decades. Representative Kuster had spoken publicly for the first time in June, inspired by Emily Doe's letter to the judge in the Brock Turner case.

I pressed play on the C-SPAN clip I found on YouTube and watched the New Hampshire woman with short dark hair and glasses stand at a podium in the well of the House of Representatives.

"Speaking out against this painful ordeal Chessy went through took a huge amount of strength and courage," Representative Kuster stated forcefully. "Like so many people, I am inspired by her actions, and I hope that they empower other survivors to come forward."

It was hard for those words to sink in. I was just a kid trying to do the right thing. Representative Kuster was a rock star fighting for actual change, in my eyes. And now she was calling me her inspiration. This was a lot to process. I shut my laptop and passed out as soon as my head hit the pillow.

The next morning I knew an apology was in order.

"I'm sorry I snapped yesterday," I said to Mom as we made breakfast together. "I watched the video last night and it was pretty amazing. Is there any way we can thank her?"

"Of course, Chess," Mom said. "I know I need to share things with you in small doses. I realize you have a lot you're dealing with."

"I do want to hear about these things," I said. "But I'm not always ready at the same time as you."

"Can I share something from a St. Paul's survivor who reached out and said the school's lawyers bullied and shamed her into silence?" Mom asked. "She had some words of encouragement."

"Sure," I said with exasperation. I didn't like going to school with a heavy heart.

"She wanted you to know that there is life after this," Mom said. "Now she is married to a wonderful man, has three small boys, a career, and a life in which she goes weeks at a time without thinking about high school. Can I read you this one part?"

"Okay," I sighed, and closed my eyes.

"'It has shaped me, but it no longer shapes my days. Please tell her that she will have a rich, full, beautiful life in which she does not need to explain this or anticipate its presence in every room she walks into. She may choose to make of herself an advocate, but she can also choose to return to privacy, and it will be okay.'"

I was glad that this woman had found happiness, but marriage and kids seemed so far away. I didn't know how I'd ever get to that point and make new relationships when I felt like I couldn't trust people anymore.

"Thanks, Mom," I said softly, slipping my school bag onto my shoulder. "I've got to get to class now. I love you."

I'd been invited to appear on a panel in Washington, DC, organized by Together for Girls, a global organization dedicated to ending sexual violence against girls. This was my first opportunity to speak to a live crowd, and it was being held on October 11, known as International Day of the Girl.

I was jittery sitting next to incredibly accomplished leaders who'd spent their careers fighting for women's rights. My stomach had been turning since I woke up that morning. I hadn't even finished high school yet and here I was about to address a crowd of activists and human rights leaders. I didn't think I really deserved to be up there with them.

I wore a blue blazer and gray skirt and sat near the end of the stage, gripping my white notepad and pen. There was so much to learn. I looked down at the program and saw my name listed as Chessy Prout, PAVE ambassador. I knew Delaney would be proud.

I spoke last, haltingly at times, and shifted my gaze between the panelists and the audience. I wasn't sure where to look because I'd never shared my experience with so many people at once. Out of the corner of my eye, I saw Lucy nodding in approval.

"In a situation where I had lost complete control, I wanted to take it back and I want to help other young women realize that they can take it back too," I explained.

My voice steadied, and I let go of my notebook and began talking with my hands. I gestured toward the side room, where Christianna was listening to an e-book, and gave my little sister credit for the #IHaveTheRightTo campaign.

"With her generation growing up, and my generation growing up, I want this to be a sort of baseline idea that we have the right to our bodies and that we have the right to say no and to have our bodies be respected and have our words be respected as well."

I shakily stood up from my chair and wobbled off the platform, my joints slowly regaining strength. But I walked away feeling invigorated. It was electrifying to sit onstage as an advocate and share my experience. People *wanted* to listen to me. It made me feel more confident about speaking out. This was where I belonged.

Later that afternoon Lucy and I ventured out to the roof deck of our Airbnb apartment one block from the White House. Lucy was in a good mood, enthusiastically sharing how the panel resonated with the justice and peace studies courses she was taking at Georgetown. We talked about the impressive people we had met at the event. Lucy mentioned she was thinking about doing a study abroad program in the spring that focused on human rights.

Together we imagined a White House under the first female president sparking new opportunities to empower women across the nation. I was hugely inspired by It's On Us, the campaign to end campus sexual assault launched by President Obama and Vice President Biden. Lucy and I discussed expanding it to high schools. I fell asleep on the roof-deck couch, marveling at the view of the White House, the Washington Monument, and an American flag waving in the wind. Instead of dwelling on the past, Lucy and I were planning a better future for ourselves and girls everywhere.

I cherished the title of advocate. But in the beginning, I didn't fully grasp how challenging this work would be. I cried whenever I described my assault or the bullying I'd endured. I nearly had a panic attack in October at Yale Law School, where Mr. Pillsbury, the St. Paul's survivor who graduated in 1965, and a Yale colleague had invited me and my family to speak.

I had flashbacks to Concord while we walked through Yale's campus, passing Gothic buildings and redbrick paths as snowflakes stuck in my hair. I knew Yale was teeming with prep-school graduates, and I worried that my talk would be a battleground. Maybe these kids admired defense attorneys like Carney. Maybe they were just coming to see me weep.

Listening to other survivors share their stories also took a toll. One survivor, Ally Heyman, a teenager from Ohio, sat next to me at a PAVE event organized by Angela in the fall of my senior year.

Ally was a figure skater who had been abused for months by her personal trainer. She reported him to the police, and on the day of his sentencing, the trainer never showed up. Hours later the police issued a warrant for his arrest and found her abuser dead from a self-inflicted gunshot wound to his chest. He killed himself on August 30, 2016.

Chills ran down my spine. That was the day my interview aired on the *Today* show. Ally's parents had seen a clip of my interview on the news later that night and a friend got in touch with the *Today* show the next day.

"I think it was meant to be," Ally's mom said, looking over at me.

I grabbed some tissues before passing them to Ally, who was also in tears.

"The reason I came to speak out is because I never had the chance to have a voice, to feel in control," Ally said.

This was the first time Ally and I were both speaking to high school students our own age. The entire girls' basketball team at Wakefield High School in Arlington, Virginia, stopped by and shook our hands. I was relieved that Mom and Dad were sitting with me up at the front of the room, but I was drooping by the time I finished sharing my story.

I should have scheduled some time to decompress. But I made a rookie advocacy mistake and agreed to back-to-back events. I had committed to participate the next day in a summit on sexual assault and consent at Georgetown Day School.

I tried to keep it together for the opening panel. I broke down at one point and took thirteen seconds and a lot of deep breaths to regain my composure. I was so spent, and the setup was intimidating. Students and adults were staring down at me from ascending rows that curved around. I felt like I was surrounded on all sides.

I thought the most important advice I could give to these teenagers was how not to act like students at St. Paul's. Georgetown Day School was light-years ahead by the mere fact that dozens of private-school students turned out for a sexual assault summit on a Saturday. But I wanted to make sure these kids understood how to be there for a survivor.

"When somebody does come forward in your community, as hard as this is, know how to stand by each other, how to talk about it, make people more comfortable to come out and say, 'This happened to me,'" I said.

I looked out at the vacant stares and wondered whether these people believed what I was saying and if I was truly making a difference. When the opening panel ended, I stepped backward away from the crowd and into the comfort of Mom and Dad. I thought I'd done a terrible job, unable to formulate real sentences or say anything meaningful.

I watched as Ally, another survivor named Julia Dixon, and Angela hugged and listened to the kids who approached them. I was too awkward and felt like I could barely take care of myself, much less help other people.

I told Mom and Dad to let Angela know that I'd meet up with the rest of them later. Lucy followed me upstairs to the room reserved for speakers. I walked quickly to the corner of the glass-walled room to hide the despair inching across my face. My stockings had torn before the day even started, I'd done a crappy job speaking, and I couldn't even be there for the kids who needed it. Why had I even volunteered to show up if I couldn't be useful?

I felt so selfish minding my trail of fat tears when I was supposed to be there as an inspiration. I didn't want Ally to see me like this either. I was supposed to offer her hope for the future—that things got better. But of course, that's not how trauma works. There are good days and bad days, and unfortunately, you never know until you wake up.

An administrator entered the room as Lucy was swaddling me, trying to calm me down, like she did during the trial. The administrator let us sit in her office, which was a little more private, and I cried with my head in Lucy's lap for the next hour. We missed the morning workshops on gender politics, Title IX, and campus sexual assault. Lucy had been really excited for one on criminology, but she stayed with me, stroking my hair and telling me that everything was going to be okay.

I knew I had to resurface. I dried my eyes and drifted over to the room where Angela, Ally, and her mom were sitting. Angela, sensing my Zen was off, led our small group in a quick meditation. She told us all to close our eyes and put our feet flat on the floor. We held hands and took deep breaths together. Angela was a huge proponent of self-care, always reminding me to exercise, take a soothing bath, walk outside, or meditate.

"This work is difficult," Angela said. "You need to be good to yourself every single day."

I realized then that going public didn't mean my healing journey was over. It was just the beginning. Each day I was learning how to be a survivor and an advocate for change. My energy rebounded steadily as I listened to Bobby Asher, dean of students at Georgetown Day School, who led a session on the neuroscience of trauma and its impact on the brain. He talked about the body's three biological responses to frightening or scary encounters: fight, flight, or freeze.

In the afternoon, Ally and I helped run a breakout session and then fielded questions from students.

"What do you think about rape jokes?" one boy asked.

My blood curdled. I pursed my lips and looked him straight in the eyes.

"It hurts." I grimaced. "It's very, very offensive."

I wanted to scream out loud that there is nothing funny about rape. There is no joke, no one-liner, no wisecrack, no prank, no trick, no nothing about rape that is anything but repulsive. These types of jokes are awful for everyone, but especially for those who have experienced sexual trauma. And because you can't see the scars on our skin, you don't know who we are. We could be your daughter or son, your cousin, your friend, your mother or father, your classmate.

I wanted to say more but knew we had to move on. We outlined concrete steps students could take in their own lives to support victims, such as starting PAVE chapters at their schools, launching CONSENT IS _____ bracelet campaigns, and sending survivor care packages.

Before the session ended, we handed out paper so students could make their own #IHAVETHERIGHTTO signs. A hush came over the room. All I could hear was the sound of markers squeaking on paper. I thought about that day in my backyard months earlier, when we'd sat at the wood table outside, eating Popsicles and watching the ripples in the pool join together.

I looked over at Mom in the back of the room. She was all in—and at age fifty-two, busy writing down her rights. One by one, the kids got up and showed us their signs. After the session ended, I noticed students in other rooms filling out their own #IHAVETHERIGHTTO signs.

I was so touched that they were using the hashtag my sisters and I made to claim their own rights. By the time they were done, CONSENT IS _____ and #IHAVETHERIGHTTO covered the walls by the area I had spoken in that morning. Finally my lips curled into my first real smile of the day.

After listening to the closing speech by Soraya Chemaly, director of the Women's Media Center Speech Project, I had the chance to actually speak one-on-one with students from Georgetown Day School. It turned out, they were just as nervous to talk to me as I was to them. I got to be myself around them, and left that day with new friends who believed in the same things I do.

As I navigated this new role of advocate, I needed to find a balance between fighting for what I believed in and living my life to the fullest, which included allowing myself to be a teenager, a sister, a daughter, a friend. At the end of the day, I knew I was doing the right thing by speaking out. I just wondered if doing the right thing would ever get easier.

The 2016 presidential election was stressing me out big-time. Everywhere I drove in Naples, I saw Trump bumper stickers plastered on the back of pickup trucks and yard signs sticking out of perfectly manicured lawns. These weren't just strangers: these were my neighbors, my classmates, my friends, their parents.

Long before the video leaked where Donald Trump bragged of grabbing women by the pussy, I had read that Trump's ex-wife, Ivana, had, in a sworn divorce deposition, stated that he had raped her in a fit of rage. I equated Donald Trump with Owen Labrie. They were entitled, arrogant sexual predators who believed the rules didn't apply to them. It was "deny until you die" all the way. What would it mean if Trump became our president—that men could get away with anything?

Politics was a polarizing topic at school, and I was totally outnumbered. One girl in particular, Fiona, liked to provoke confrontations with me on an almost daily basis.

If there was a lull in conversation, Fiona would pull out her favorite line, "Let's talk about politics!" The rest of us would groan, knowing where this was going.

"Why don't you want Trump to win?" she would whine at me during our free period. "You're rich. Don't you want to protect your parents' money from higher taxes?"

I was shocked at her brazen reference to my family's economic status but put that to the side.

"You're willing to overlook all these other human rights issues because you don't want your parents to pay more taxes?" I asked. "We've got enough to share. Don't you care about the rights of other human beings?"

She didn't have any other points. It was all about money. I held my tongue and got back to my homework.

"But why *not*?" Fiona barked back.

"I'm not fighting with you, Fiona," I said.

Two of my friends left the room, fleeing at the first sign of conflict. Arielle refused to get involved in politics. Others sat quietly.

I'd always be thankful that the community at CSN embraced me when I came back from St. Paul's and supported me again when I went public as a survivor. But I was frustrated by my friends who couldn't understand that voting for Trump meant turning a blind eye to sexual assault and all the rights I was fighting so hard to safeguard.

I was transported back to St. Paul's, where protecting one's privilege eclipsed everything else, where standing up for your basic rights meant being disloyal. It also angered me that two of my friends who supported Hillary Clinton refused to speak up. Why did I always have to be *the one*?

The election managed to infect everything—even our class T-shirts. Every year, students picked a T-shirt design to wear on the last day of homecoming. They usually featured benign phrases; last year our student council chose "Stay Classy."

During a meeting in early October, some seniors proposed poaching Donald Trump's slogan "Make America Great Again" and designing T-shirts with the words "Make CSN Great Again."

Wisdom prevailed and by the end of the meeting, the seniors settled on a different motto. Everyone seemed to be on board, but later that day, I caught wind that our class representatives had decided to ignore the decision and go with "Make CSN Great Again."

I found my ex-boyfriend Dean in the hallway. He was one of the guys backing the dumb slogan.

"Hey, I thought we agreed on another T-shirt. What happened?" I asked.

"We're not changing it back," Dean said.

He wasn't getting it.

"Dean, I've said this to you guys before, and I know there are other kids in our class that feel the same, but I'm not putting a T-shirt anywhere near my body that has a slogan on it that supports a misogynistic rapist."

"That's not even—" Dean said before I cut him off.

"Whatever, I guess I just won't come to school that day if that's our T-shirt," I said, then pivoted on the balls of my feet.

Another senior class representative tried to "calm me down" in the hallway. I didn't need calming, I needed to be listened to! This was ridiculous. How could they not understand why I would be so upset?

I bolted to the parking lot and slammed the car door shut. I drove straight home and told Mom that I refused to go to homecoming. She was okay with it, but she challenged me: Did you speak up? Then I began drafting an email to my high school principal, Mr. Miles, informing him of the T-shirt debacle:

Dear Mr. Miles,
. . . Donald Trump's ideology goes against everything I've fought for for the last two years, and completely goes

against what I am fighting for now, and I was especially
hurt when my classmates couldn't take that into
consideration. I have decided that since that is the t-shirt
slogan that will be representing my senior class, I will not
be going to school on Friday the 28th, nor will I make a
big deal of it, I just wanted to let you know that this is
how some of us feel in the senior class.
Thank you,
Chessy Prout

A couple of days later Mr. Miles pulled me aside during our morning break and promised that CSN would not allow class T-shirts to feature political messages—for either side.

Later that evening, all anyone could talk about was the *Access Hollywood* tape. Billy Bush's conversation with Donald Trump on the set had leaked out. There he was, the Republican presidential candidate, admitting to sexually assaulting women.

Trump: I just start kissing them. It's like a magnet.
Just kiss. I don't even wait. And when you're a star,
they let you do it. You can do anything.
Bush: Whatever you want.
Trump: Grab 'em by the pussy. You can do anything.

This was who my friends wanted to lead our country. I put my head in my hands as Mom flipped through the news channels, watching wall-to-wall coverage of Trump's vile remarks.

I soon realized that I wasn't the only one triggered by this election. In the wake of Trump's comments, I heard about the author Kelly Oxford asking women to tweet about their experiences of sexual assault. I was astounded by the thousands of women coming together to acknowledge how sexual violence had touched their own lives. For once, the online community was building up survivors, not tearing them down.

On election night, I came home and found Mom hosting a barbecue with my college counselor and her husband, my friend Jackie, Zach and his mom, Aunt Carol, Uncle Pete, Christianna's friend and her mother. Basically all the Democrats in Naples.

I ate a burger by the grill with Mom and her friends while Christianna smuggled empanadas upstairs to her bedroom. Our neighbors who brought champagne talked anxiously about how they'd always remember this night.

We congregated in the family room to watch the news coverage, staring in disbelief as the map turned red, signifying states that Trump had won. The champagne stayed corked.

Everyone was dumbstruck. I kept wondering how people could vote for this man. Did anyone care about survivors of assault and what this election would do to perpetuate rape culture?

Eventually people started to leave around eleven p.m. It was a school night, but we couldn't tear Christianna away from the screen. I fell asleep at one a.m., still holding out hope.

Mom rustled me awake at two forty-five a.m.

"She lost, honey," she whispered, kneeling by my side. "We lost."

I rolled over without responding. I refused to accept that my fellow Americans had elected Donald Trump as president. This was just a nightmare. Reason would rise with the sun in the morning.

I lay in bed the next day in a self-imposed exile.

I had no clue how far off the rails things would get under Trump. But I knew, in those dark days of mourning after the election, that fighting for women's rights was more urgent than ever.

I made my first #IHaveTheRightTo poster for an interview with the *Boston Globe* (left). After the *Today* show interview aired in August 2016, I received messages and gifts from all over the world, including origami cranes made by old friends in Tokyo (bottom right). I was invited that fall to speak at events organized by Together for Girls (below) and Georgetown Day School (previous page).

I appreciated meeting St. Paul's survivor Charlie Pillsbury (above), who invited me to speak at Yale.

TWENTY-THREE

Rocking the Boat

I was supposed to hear back from Barnard College about my early decision application sometime between November and December. By December 13, I was hitting the refresh button on my browser every few minutes.

I tried to temper my expectations—something I'd become an expert in during the last two years. But I really wanted this, more than I'd wanted anything in a long time. My entire future depended on getting into Barnard.

Barnard had everything I valued: female empowerment, great access to the arts, a campus in the middle of a city, and a stellar leadership program where I could take classes in speech writing and gender studies. The campus was plastered with signs and graphics about consent and sexual assault. When I brought my family to visit the school, the posters on the walls spoke to me:

THERE'S NOTHING A BARNARD WOMAN CAN'T DO! This was the place for me.

But my interview back in June was a disaster, possibly enough to ruin my chances. I was flustered, sweating, and almost late because my cabdriver misunderstood the address and took me to 160th Street instead of 116th Street.

I didn't even catch the name of the woman interviewing me as we introduced ourselves. She looked like the famous writer Cheryl Strayed and told me she was a former prosecutor for the city of New York.

I talked about my background growing up in Japan and explained where I had gone to school, gradually building up to my assault, the trial, and my plans moving forward.

"I want to study law to help spread awareness of this terrible crime and fight for other victims and survivors," I said, my voice rising with passion. "I want to be at Barnard, where they value women's strength."

I worried that I sounded too emotional, too outraged, too unstable. I took a couple of breaths to calm down. A few days earlier, a college consultant for a New York City firm had told me that I didn't have to talk about my assault during my interviews if I didn't want to.

"But it seems hard to avoid when I have to explain why I switched schools and my grades slipped," I pointed out to the consultant.

"Just stay positive and focus on the future, not the past," he advised. "And don't sound bitter."

Whoa. I didn't go there to have some man tell me how to act. But his words reverberated in my head. I tried to regain my footing during the last few minutes of the Barnard interview, but I walked out feeling like I blew it. Eventually I tracked down the name of my interviewer and sent a thank-you note.

Back home on the living room couch, my finger was starting to cramp up from hitting the refresh button. I had just put my world history textbook away, giving up on the studying I was supposed to be doing for my exam the next day.

Christianna hung around my neck as I glared at the computer screen.

"Did you get an email from Barnard? Did you get in? Did you get in?" she repeated like a parrot. "Did you? Did you?"

I swatted her away.

Suddenly I noticed my computer screen change. There was now a "View Update" option on the Barnard portal highlighted in yellow. I squeezed my eyes shut and said a little prayer as I clicked on it.

Dear Ms. Prout, Congratulations!

There it was—in black and white—I was in!

Mom rushed over and hugged me as I skipped across the living room.

I exhaled, a huge weight sliding off my shoulders. I kept my history textbook closed and danced around the house with Mom and Christianna for the rest of the night.

Dad was still commuting to his job in New York, and when he came home that weekend, he had a tote bag filled with Barnard swag. It looked as if he had cleared out the school store. Christianna rummaged through the mugs, T-shirts, notebooks, and sweatpants, trying to call dibs on whatever she could.

"Can I have this one?" she asked as she pulled out a gray T-shirt with BARNARD printed across the chest.

"Sure." I giggled. Maybe it would inspire her one day to be a Barnard woman too.

I went on a news diet after the election. Everything sounded the same as Trump alienated the world—friends and foes—before stepping foot in the Oval Office. As word spread of women planning demonstrations across the country, I started paying attention.

Lucy was attending the Women's March in Washington, DC, the perfect send-off before starting her semester abroad studying human rights in New York, Nepal, Jordan, and Chile. The program looked fascinating, with opportunities to learn from activists, feminist leaders, refugees, and grassroots organizers around the world.

Mom wanted to join Lucy in Washington, DC, so the Prouts decided to divide and conquer. Dad would take me and Christianna to the demonstration in downtown Naples while Mom and Lucy marched in the capital.

On January 21, 2017, I woke up and threw my covers off the bed. I put on my white PAVE tank top and pulled my hair back into a ponytail. I had considered buying one of those pink pussy-hats that women were wearing in response to Trump's crude comments, but it seemed too hot for wool in Florida.

Before heading out, we gathered around the dining room table with purple markers and each designed posters. Dad, who could never have enough hashtags, wrote: #IHAVETHERIGHTTO SUPPORT SURVIVORS #SHATTER THE SILENCE

I finished next: #IHAVETHERIGHTTO USE MY VOICE & BE HEARD

Christianna flicked the marker between her pointer and middle fingers as she debated what to put down. I beamed with pride when she settled on: #IHAVETHERIGHTTO GROW UP SAFE AND EQUAL

We stuck the signs in our trunk and picked up Aunt Carol, her eighty-year-old friend, and my college counselor, who'd been at our house on election night. As we drove along Route 41, I worried we'd be the only ones protesting. But when we arrived downtown, hundreds of people were streaming in from all directions under splaying palm trees: there were babies in strollers, people in wheelchairs, and men and women waving American flags.

The sidewalks filled with shades of pink as women and girls thrust signs in the air: WE MARCH AS ONE, WE ARE CREATED EQUAL, WOMEN'S RIGHTS ARE HUMAN RIGHTS.

So many protesters showed up—roughly 2,500 in total—that we took over the streets. March organizers hollered into megaphones, "Women united, we'll never be divided!" and "This is what a feminist looks like!"

We tried FaceTiming Mom and Lucy during the march, but the call dropped as wireless networks in DC caved under the demand of hundreds of thousands of demonstrators there.

I filled up my lungs with dewy air as the sun roasted my shoulders. I loved the sound of my sneakers pounding the pavement, equal rights chants piercing the morning calm. I got goose bumps along my arms as we shouted together: "Whatever we wear, wherever we go, yes means yes and no means no! Hey, hey, ho, ho, sexual violence has got to go!"

I wiped tears from my eyes and grabbed Christianna's hand. I looked around and realized that there really was a community out in the world that was ready to support survivors, no matter where you were. When a jerk stuck up his middle finger as he drove by in a red convertible, top down, I stood taller, held my sign higher, and yelled louder. Because I had the right to.

I took a break from advocacy events for a couple of months to focus on school, but I came back with a vengeance in the new year. Representative Kuster of New Hampshire had invited me, Delaney, and Julia to participate in a panel discussion at the US Capitol about sexual assault at the beginning of February.

I'd met Representative Kuster briefly in the fall when I was in DC for the consent summit at Georgetown Day School. I'd learned that her father and many other family members had attended St. Paul's, and she even served as an assistant clerk for the St. Paul's board of trustees in the 1990s when school leaders were grappling with hazing problems. Representative Kuster suggested that we work together to increase public awareness about sexual violence. I was floored that she wanted to join forces. I felt as if I was starting to live in the light at the end of the tunnel.

It all came together perfectly, with Angela taking on the role of moderator. I wished Lucy could be there to see how far I'd come. She was wrapping up her human rights courses in New York before heading off to Nepal. Before she left, she wrote a sweet note, her most candid thoughts yet on the journey we'd taken.

Dear Chessy,

It is Tuesday afternoon, 2:50 on a snowy day in New York in the fashion district. We had a class session earlier today with the Community Voices Heard organization (ooh you just texted me—telepathy) and I just wanted to bring you there into the folds of the conversation. YOU are bringing the change, Chess. I've had a hard time dealing with this—the personal nature of the work bc of your experience—and grappled w/ the discomfort of the emotional toll. And I've tried/wanted to distance myself from it. This trip is really helping me come to terms with the emotional, personal, exhausting, vulnerable side of s.a. work.

Change does not happen unless you demand it. And no one will demand it until it personally affects them. It is the role of the oppressed to demand humanity—and this is a painful process to liberation. (Freire's

pedagogy of the oppressed—it's awesome)
I am so proud of you for engaging w/the
painful + standing up to share your story.
Your story has and is continuing to change
so much/liberate. You are forcing the world
to confront the human + feel uncomfortable.
Fuck those who are standing in your way—
they are either in the past or will soon be
left behind. Good Luck Wednesday, I know you
will inspire + liberate many.
Love you, XO
Lucy

I walked through the underground tunnels of the Capitol, my heels click-clacking on the marble floor. In the elevator, I recognized Congressman John Lewis; I had seen a clip of the fiery speech he delivered during the Women's March on Washington. I was too intimidated to speak.

Oh. My. God. He marched with Martin Luther King Jr. I locked eyes with Mom.

We eventually arrived in Emancipation Hall for a reception hosted by Representative Kuster. She was announcing the launch of a bipartisan task force to end sexual violence. The group was committed to raising awareness and providing solutions to the challenges posed by sexual assault in the military, on campus, and elsewhere.

At the gathering, a younger redhead quietly introduced himself to me as Congressman Joe Kennedy. He spoke so softly I strained to hear. He mentioned how his old private school struggled to deal with these issues and that he had family who had attended St. Paul's.

Representative Kennedy said he used to work as an assistant

district attorney and knew how difficult these court cases could be. I nodded and recounted a little bit of my own experience at St. Paul's.

After he left, I turned around and exclaimed, "Jeez, that's a Kennedy!"

I was too nervous to eat the cubes of cheese and slices of fruit set out on the reception table. I bear-hugged Delaney this time when she showed up. Some of the representatives shared their own stories of sexual assault and urged me to run for office when I turned twenty-five, the youngest age when you can serve in the House of Representatives. Yikes. I was just focused on getting through senior year of high school.

"We are all Emily Does," Representative Kuster said, kicking off the night's main event in Emancipation Hall.

She told the audience that reading Emily Doe's letter from the Brock Turner case with other members of Congress in June 2016 forced her to confront the secrets she'd been keeping for more than forty years.

Representative Kuster was an eighteen-year-old freshman at Dartmouth College in 1974 when a guy assaulted her at a fraternity party while others cheered him on. She ran home alone, blamed herself, and never told anyone else. She had been assaulted two more times since college—by a famous surgeon who stuck his hand under her skirt at a work lunch and by a stranger as she walked home from Capitol Hill.

She described the lasting effects of the attacks: she's sixty years old and can't be alone. Sometimes she wakes up screaming from nightmares.

She said her silence—and society's collective silence—is part of the reason we haven't made more of a dent in preventing sexual violence. Representative Kuster refused to be complicit any longer: "If I don't speak up, how can I expect young women to?"

When it was my turn to speak, I looked around the room filled with influential lawmakers and young legislative aides. There I was, talking in public about the most uncomfortable moment of my life, and for the first time, I didn't dissolve into tears.

"I feel like my job right now is to make the world a better place for my younger sister, who is growing up in a world that is dangerous and hard to go through as a young woman," I said. "To be here in a place where that seems to be the goal of everyone is pretty inspiring and pretty empowering."

I listened intently to Julia Dixon as she described how survivorship and healing is not linear. It goes up and down like a mountain range. Some days you have the emotional bandwidth to heal and feel positive, she said, and other days you don't.

That really resonated with me. People always talk about moving on. When a member of the board of trustees called Dad after the *Today* show interview, he said, "We'd like to put this behind us."

"I can understand you and the school wanting to move past this," Dad responded, "but unfortunately for Chessy and my family, we're going to have to live with this for the rest of our lives."

You don't just move on from a sexual assault. What happened doesn't just go away with time. As Buzz, my counselor at St. Paul's, liked to say, it moves through you, like grief. It changes shapes and sizes and directions. Some days it's angry devils staging a riot on my rib cage, pricking me with their burning pitchforks. Other times, my assault is cold ice running through my veins, numbing me from head to toe so I can't feel my skin. On better days, like at the US Capitol, my assault is a powerful gust of wind, lifting my heart and my mind to places they've never been.

When the panel discussion returned to me, I talked about the importance of not forgetting us kids. So much attention in recent years has focused on preventing sexual assault on college campuses.

But the only way to do that is to start the conversation earlier—and that's why I was speaking out. Kids of all ages need to learn that it's not acceptable to "show a girl you like her" by poking her with a pencil, grabbing her on the playground, or snapping her bra. High school students and middle schoolers need to talk about consent, entitlement, and healthy relationships. By the time they get to college, it's too late.

Angela ended the evening with a Margaret Mead quote—the same one that Buzz had hung on the wall of her office: "Never doubt that a small group of thoughtful, committed citizens can change the world; indeed, it's the only thing that ever has."

When we met Representative Kuster for coffee in fall 2016, she suggested that we work together and then invited me to participate in a panel in Washington, DC. I spoke with members of Congress at a reception before the event (top). Angela and I also attended the launch of a bipartisan task force to end sexual violence (above left).

It was empowering to join the Women's March in Naples in January 2017 (left) and then speak the next month at the US Capitol with fellow survivors Angela, Julia Dixon, Representative Kuster, and Delaney (below).

TWENTY-FOUR

Reclaiming Concord

had to look at my phone twice before believing what I read. Tabitha texted that she wanted to do a photo shoot for #IHaveTheRightTo at St. Paul's. Tabitha said she was inspired to be stronger and speak up more after attending the Women's March in Concord.

I'd thought a lot about Tabitha over the last few months. She messaged me when the *Today* show interview aired and apologized for not being more supportive.

> Tabitha: The case was already triggering a lot for me, and I was scared that if I reached out to you, I would do more harm than good . . . I was also worried I wouldn't be able to make the memories stop and that my parents' lack of support would become even more obvious, and therefore damaging.

Tabitha was the last person who should be apologizing. I felt terrible that her parents hadn't been there for her when she needed them, something I'd unfortunately heard from many other survivors. I'd hate to think about where I'd be, or whether I'd even still be here, if I didn't have my family by my side every step of the way. I was an anomaly and I wanted that to change.

I had encouraged Tabitha to join #IHaveTheRightTo, but I never imagined she'd want to get others at St. Paul's involved too. I texted her back on Valentine's Day.

> Me: I think that is an incredible idea, to do an I have the right to photo project at school. I really hope this is raising awareness there and making the boys think twice about taking advantage of the removed environment and young girls.
> Tabitha: I'm so glad you're into it; I just wasn't sure and wanted to ask

That text was a cherry on top of a great day. I had recently begun dating Parker, a guy I had known since middle school. He was kind, authentic, and cute. It took me a while to be comfortable with the relationship, but Parker understood. He was patient with me and let me cry on his chest whenever I was overwhelmed.

Our relationship was relatively new so I wasn't sure how, or if, we would celebrate Valentine's Day. In Japan, girls gave boys chocolates and not the other way around. I avoided Parker that morning and talked to a younger classmate about protest opportunities in Naples. Eventually, Parker tracked me down and handed me a small, decorative bag filled with champagne-flavored gummy bears, a pink stuffed pig, and a bar of chocolate. It was definitely the work of his mother, but it was very sweet and I was blushing all morning.

Making myself emotionally vulnerable was really hard, and it was just as tough dealing with the pressures of physical intimacy. But I drew my lines and Parker knew to respect them. I introduced him to Mom, Dad, and Christianna. And I met his family. They seemed so perfect and had that southern hospitality. Mine, not so much. We didn't do small talk anymore, and Mom and Dad were often holed up in the office. Sometimes they'd summon me to catch up on pressing legal matters or to do an interview while Parker was left alone on the couch in the living room. But he acted like he didn't mind and was happy to go with the flow. It was exactly what I needed.

A hearing on Owen's ridiculous request to get a new trial was scheduled for the end of February. It was perfectly timed to spoil my winter break. There was no way in hell I was going—Dad would attend—but I knew I'd have to hear about it somehow.

I was having trouble digesting this latest legal maneuver. Owen was blaming the guilty verdict on the ineffectiveness of his very famous, very expensive lawyer, J. W. Carney Jr. I'd say it was buyer's remorse, but Owen didn't even foot the bill! And Carney was such a monster to me. What more did Owen want Carney to do—go up to the witness stand and murder me?

As the hearing was about to start on February 21, 2017, I saw a text from my old roommate.

> Tabitha: Hey so I mentioned the I have the right to campaign in young women's club, and people were really not into it

I shouldn't have been surprised, but it stung nonetheless. The curt tone of her message made me feel as if I had done something wrong. I immediately went on the defensive, rattled that I thought people at St. Paul's could back the initiative. They were still a disappointment.

Me: Wow, thank you for trying with that though, that was
   really kind/awesome/brave of you to bring it up there.
   That really hurts my heart, because I had this sort of vision
   that doing my project there would show the school that
   the kids really care about making the culture healthier and
   safer, and that it's not about politics or personal injuries
   but about basic human decency. It really hurts me that
   the kids there couldn't see the bigger picture, a picture
   where we can work together and help take away any
   animosity that some kids there have fostered and others
   (like you) have tried so hard to take away. Shit. Thank you
   so much though tabitha. I hope you didn't catch any shit
   because of that.
Tabitha: I completely agree. And dont worry, nobody gave
   me shit at all.

I hoped this wouldn't dissuade Tabitha from fighting for this
cause after she left St. Paul's. We needed as many young warriors as
we could get out there. And Tabitha was a pretty badass one.

Dad settled into his usual spot in Courtroom 1 on the far corner
of the bench behind the prosecutor's table. There was no jury, just
Judge Smukler to listen to this nonsense.

On the first day of the hearing, Owen's new lawyer took aim
at Carney for failing to introduce at trial my full mental health
records, emails from older guys at the school, and photos of me
and Christianna during graduation weekend. Apparently, stitched
together with a thread called lies, these documents would have
revealed that I was a suicidal, slutty alcoholic who had "secret
snuggles" with senior boys and possibly had more than one sexual
encounter on the night of my assault. Oh, and the kicker was that
I clearly could not have been assaulted because I was doing splits

the next day on a trampoline with my little sister.

Dad, in tears, texted Mom.

> Dad: This is worse than the f$&&&&& trial. Cant breathe
> or move . . .

Mom was watching a live video stream from the computer in our home office. Suddenly she flew through my bedroom door, almost out of breath.

"I can't believe they're saying this, but you need to know this stuff is floating out there," she said hotly. "I don't want you to learn about this somewhere else!"

I was thrown off by Mom's outburst. I thought it was pathetic and revolting that Owen could exploit the legal system to abuse me once again. I couldn't deal, so I ran to the beach, where I watched waves pound the sand over and over.

After court that day, Dad drove a few miles down the road to St. Paul's and tried to remember why he loved that school so much. He passed by his old dorm and looked at photos of his 1982 baseball and basketball teams hanging in the athletic center. He checked out the volleyball courts, where Lucy and I used to play, and waved to our former coach. He ran into Tabitha and chatted with her for a few minutes.

Dad crunched dove-white snow under his dress shoes as he walked over to the Upper. Inside, he ran his fingers along the wood panel where his name was carved along with the other graduates from the class of 1982. In the long arched hallway before the senior couches, he found the name of Robert Barrie Slaymaker, Class of '47, and noticed the wood worn down around "Slaymaker," where Owen and the other boys had rubbed it.

Dad had one more stop for the day: a small white shed near the woods known as the Mars Hotel. He had learned about this place from police: it was where Owen and the other guys used to take girls to score. Dad saw keys with a yellow tag in the door and ducked inside. Skis and ski poles were neatly stacked along the unfinished wood walls; gone were the couch and condom wrappers. When he left, he took the keys and half-buried them in the snow near the door so the yellow tag was still sticking out. It was his one tiny act of rebellion.

As Dad drove away, he got a call from our lawyer, Steve. St. Paul's attorney, Mike Delaney, had sent Steve an email and left an urgent voicemail in the last hour.

"Mike knows you're on campus and he's threatening to forcibly remove you," Steve said.

"Tell him I'm in front of the student center and he can come and find me and take me away," Dad hollered, finally losing his cool. "I'm the one who's a St. Paul's graduate. He can't take that away from me."

"Don't shoot the messenger, and keep the faith, Alex," Steve said before hanging up.

I was fuming when Dad told me about the school's latest threats. I knew St. Paul's was being nasty in our civil suit, demanding to see my journal and trying to depose my friends. They didn't seem remotely interested in resolving the case or in addressing the problems they knew too well. They just wanted to make this as painful as possible for me.

But why was Dad the pariah? How could any young person feel comfortable reporting a crime knowing this is how the school treats victims, including their family members and alumni? It's this kind of approach that makes the rape culture and victim shaming at St. Paul's so potent. The school would rather attack me and my family than look inward at their shortcomings, at the lives derailed on their watch.

On the third and final day of Owen's hearing, Carney took the stand. He was a witness for the prosecution, for Catherine. This was beyond bizarre.

The live video stream was spotty, so Dad texted updates to Mom. Carney admitted that he deliberately crafted a trial strategy to keep out damaging information about Owen. This included police interviews with my friends Catie, Ivy, and Faith, who I spoke to immediately after my assault. Carney called these three girls the "most harmful witnesses" because they would have undermined Owen's defense that I fabricated the rape from the beginning.

If Catie had recounted to the jury what I said happened in the mechanical room, "it would be toxic to the defense," Carney conceded.

Catherine showed Carney a photo from the night of my assault when I was demonstrating on Ivy how Owen pinned my arms up against the wall so I couldn't move—something jurors never got to see.

"And do you recall the state's attempt to try to have that admitted at trial?"

"Yes, I do," Carney said.

Catherine then made Carney describe other police reports that never saw the light of day.

"There were a number of references throughout the discovery of other women whom Owen had dated in which he had acted in ways, according to the women, that were very aggressive, that were forceful, that led to Owen having a very bad reputation at the St. Paul's campus among women as someone who would be so aggressive that he would actually go so far as to inflict injury during a sexual act with a woman, such as biting a lip or biting a nipple that would cause injury that was apparent the next day."

These were girls, teenage girls, not women. Whitney, the freshman with braces, told Detective Curtin that Owen brought her to the Mars Hotel, where he was "very aggressive."

"Two things then happened that made her feel like she was being violated," Carney said, summarizing the police report. "Number one, Owen sucked on her lip and gave her a blister, which hurt. Number two, Owen sucked on her breasts, leaving bruises."

Whitney had shown Detective Curtin pictures she took of her swollen lip. She said she hadn't spoken up at the time and told Owen he was hurting her because she felt inferior. I'd never had the strength before to read the police report, but hearing about it now made my heart ache.

Whitney told police that she heard about another girl who felt "very violated by him" and told other people that Owen was "too aggressive" and "close to hurting her."

Then Carney read a police interview with Briana, the senior in my dorm who confided that Owen had done the same thing to her. Catherine asked whether Carney's trial strategy was to prevent Briana's statement from coming out too.

"Absolutely correct," Carney said.

I was so confused as to why Catherine could introduce this evidence now but it had been kept from the jury during trial. Was it *too* damning? I didn't understand our criminal justice system sometimes. All I knew was that it was stacked against survivors every step of the way.

In the afternoon, Carney described a mock trial exercise in which he brought a criminal defense attorney in to cross-examine Owen to prepare him for taking the stand.

"He destroyed him," Carney said. "At one point, Owen was agreeing that 'I guess it's true I am a pedophile who was trolling to have sex with underage girls.'"

I couldn't wrap my head around the fact that all of this information was coming out now, after the trial, after the jurors had gone home, after anyone seemed to care.

The statements these girls made to police didn't surprise me in the least. What did shock me was one paragraph contained in Detective Curtin's report: the vice rector, Mrs. Hebra, *knew* Owen had a problem months before my attack.

Mrs. Hebra acknowledged to Detective Curtin that Briana had told her that Owen was "really rough with girls," "likes to pull girls' hair," and was a "sex addict."

When Mom shared this with me, my mouth dried up. My skin turned white. My legs froze. I thought I might faint. Mrs. Hebra was an adviser in my dorm, the school's vice rector, one of the most powerful women on campus. She'd invited me to her house to write my victim impact statement, sent me a note after I left St. Paul's apologizing for the school's lack of support, dropped groceries at our house during the trial. Was that because she cared? Or because she felt guilty that this all could have been prevented in the first place?

A week after the hearing, I had a panic attack in math class, my first period of the day. My mind went blank, I couldn't focus, and my legs started to shake. I left during a break and hyperventilated in my car before driving home. Mom cooked a feast to try and comfort me: spaghetti and meat sauce, chicken and broccoli, bean sprout salad, mixed greens, and a fresh strawberry pie. I sampled a bit of everything. Later that day, I received a letter from a fellow survivor, a perfect stranger, offering me strength and support.

It was times like these when I was reminded of my faith: "You intended to harm me, but God intended it for good to accomplish what is now being done."

I was still struggling in my relationship with God. I felt alienated from our church since learning that leaders there had pushed out my friend who helped run the Cat Island programs because she was a lesbian. Using religion as a weapon to deny people rights or withhold God's love sickened me.

But it was my faith that helped me arrive at a place of semi-forgiveness, first for myself and then for Owen. I've read the divorce court records where Owen's mother accused his father of sexually abusing Owen once when he was a child, though state authorities apparently couldn't substantiate the claim. In any event, in a college essay Owen gave to police, he elaborated more on his view of his childhood:

> I left for boarding school because I wanted to become
> a better man than my father . . . My father became a
> lustful man and an angry father, and a slew of vices
> earned him virtual expulsion from the world of academia;
> he hasn't held a job in years. At age fifteen, in a moment
> of adolescent self-reflection, I began to fear my father's
> character latent within me. He was not, and is not, the
> man I wanted to become, so I left. In my first few months
> away from home, I found myself still grappling with the
> vices that I, frustratingly, felt as if I had inherited from
> my father. However, presented with the opportunity for
> self-examination and graced with the chance of self-
> reinvention away from home, I was determined.

Owen may have been determined, but he failed miserably. And he was failed miserably by the community that surrounded him—from his father to his friends to the leaders at St. Paul's who did nothing to stop these ritualized games of sexual conquest.

Owen has yet to express an ounce of remorse to me. But hating him takes up too much of my body, too much of my heart. Instead I rely on Grandma Prout's wisdom: "Pity him."

I still hated what he did to me and despised his lack of a con-science. But it was not my job to change him; he had to do that by himself. I had to think about my own future. I was looking forward to Barnard, to advocacy work, to trusting other boys again. Having a new relationship was helping me heal and realize that I really do have the right to respect, patience, and love.

Dad wanted to do an advocacy event with Representative Kuster in St. Paul's backyard in Concord. I hadn't been there since the trial and had serious reservations. But I knew that Concord was a place that was never going away and it wasn't healthy for me to harbor fear and anxiety over it. This was my chance to create new positive associations, to reclaim a city. Returning with Congresswoman Kuster by my side seemed like the perfect way to go back and own it.

It didn't mean I wasn't scared. I asked Delaney, my best bodyguard, if she could come with me. But she was busy taking a well-deserved vacation. Angela promised to attend and bring baby Aryana.

The event was held in mid-April at the University of New Hampshire School of Law, just a few minutes away from St. Paul's, something I didn't know beforehand.

We flew into Boston and hopped into a rental car. On the ride up to New Hampshire, I did a phone interview with a writer from *Seventeen* magazine who was working on a piece about teen activism. I was feeling okay until we turned off the highway and onto Main Street in Concord. Buckets of tears streamed down my cheeks as we drove through downtown and passed all my favorite spots—Siam Orchid, the Works, Live Juice—and then the place I never wanted to see again, the courthouse.

I was stressed and sobbing when we stopped outside the law school. Amanda Grady Sexton, who worked for the New Hampshire Coalition Against Domestic and Sexual Violence and helped organize the event, quickly shuttled us into a small room where we could have some privacy.

I was wailing, Mom was weeping, and by now, Amanda was crying too.

Mom held me tight while Dad yelled at himself for driving past painful sights, for pushing me too hard.

"It's okay, it's okay," Mom soothed, rubbing my back.

"We can send the reporters home. We can send everyone home. We can shut this all down," Amanda said. "None of this has to happen. You don't have to do this."

"No, of course I have to, I'm here," I snapped, with unnecessary attitude.

Then I took a deep breath. I realized what a blessing it was in the first place to be able to speak out, to have a voice, so I shoved to the side my desire to hide in a bunker.

"I want to do this, I need to do this," I said, wiping the tears on the back of my hand. "I'm okay. I'm happy to be back here on my terms."

Amanda looked worried. I knew "happy" was a total stretch. I took ten minutes to compose myself and then did several media interviews. Mom stood guard outside the door.

People began mingling in the lobby for a reception. I didn't feel like talking to strangers, so I huddled behind the PAVE table with Angela, baby Aryana, and Representative Kuster. Mom was close by when she was approached by Lucy Hodder, mother of Andrew Thomson, Owen's roommate, and Haley, one of my former best friends.

Apparently Ms. Hodder wanted to speak to me before the event.

"That won't be necessary," Mom said curtly, the ultimate put-down in her book.

Ms. Hodder choked on her words.

I was proud of Mom for standing up to Ms. Hodder. Her timing was totally off and I was frustrated by her children's behavior. Ms. Hodder, who'd served on St. Paul's board of trustees, had had three years to step up and say something. Her daughter abandoned me when I needed her most, and her son, according to Carney, had faced suspicions of having sex with an underage student at St. Paul's, although no charges were brought. Andrew denied that, but emails suggest he pursued a freshman girl and met up with her at night.

I retreated to the small room to gather my thoughts before the panel. My face lit up when Catherine and Detective Curtin walked through the door. So much had happened since the trial, and I had so much to thank them for. Catherine teared up and Detective Curtin, always stoic and professional, was on the verge of crying.

"We're very proud of you Chessy," Catherine said.

"Yeah, really proud." Detective Curtin nodded.

I felt indebted to these strong women who fought hard to get justice. I knew my case wasn't easy. In fact, I'd only recently learned that the male prosecutor who watched my interview at the Child Advocacy Center days after I was assaulted expressed concerns. He thought the jury wouldn't like that I went with Owen willingly, that I didn't say no when he took off some of my clothes, and that I didn't push back when he kissed me.

But Catherine disagreed. She believed a woman could engage in a certain level of sexual contact but still say no. And as a fifteen-year-old, I wasn't legally able to consent.

These are precisely the kinds of cases that prosecutors need to tackle in order for society to understand that agreeing to kissing is not an invitation to have sex. That victims freeze. That survivors deserve to be believed.

Thankfully, Judge Smukler rejected Owen's request for a new trial and called out the "frivolity" and "absurdity" of some of his claims of ineffective counsel. Owen, of course, couldn't accept that and asked the New Hampshire Supreme Court to review the ruling. The end was nowhere near.

Before the panel discussion started, Catherine said she had a surprise for me. She opened her hand to reveal the knight-in-shining-armor figurine that I'd clutched while I was on the stand during the trial.

"I want you to keep this, even though you don't need it any longer," she said. "You're tough enough."

"Thank you so much," I said, and zipped the figurine safely inside my wallet. "I'll always carry it with me."

We headed upstairs to a classroom on the second floor. Mom and Dad took seats near the front as roughly a hundred people filled the room. I tugged nervously at my gold necklace that featured the symbol for woman and the symbol for man forming an equal sign. I bought the same necklace for Lucy and Mom before the Women's March.

Representative Kuster introduced the other panelists and welcomed me back to Concord.

"We cannot change the culture of sexual violence in this state or across the country unless we all—our entire community—become a part of the conversation," she said.

I glanced around at the strange faces, mostly older adults, wondering if they had any connection to St. Paul's and were there just to keep an eye on me. I needed them to feel a sliver of the pain I lived with every day. And then I wanted to encourage high school students not to accept the status quo.

"I did that for too long at St. Paul's," I said. "I accepted the culture for what it was and thought I couldn't do anything to change it. And there is a lot that needs to be changed."

I looked up again and searched for the faces I knew: Buzz, Detective Curtin, Catherine, Angela, Congresswoman Kuster. This network of female professionals who lifted me up during the most difficult moments of my life was nothing short of magnificent.

"I'm lucky enough to have a supportive family and a supportive community now and people like Congresswoman Kuster who believe in the same things that I believe in as an eighteen-year-old girl," I said. "Some things, I just won't accept them anymore. I believe that it's our time to really stand up and fight for our rights and to fight for our own respect and dignity. I'm tired of being silenced and ashamed."

I returned to Concord, New Hampshire, in April 2017 for an advocacy event with Representative Kuster (below). Angela and baby Aryana came to support me (above). I also reunited with (from left) Detective Julie Curtin, attorney Catherine Ruffle, and Amanda Grady Sexton (on the end next to Mom).

TWENTY-FIVE

May 2017

P arker had burrowed into my heart during these last few months
of senior year. He was my boyfriend, and I was his girlfriend.
I adored his family, especially his three sisters, and I could tell
that the women in his life called the shots. Finally I was enjoying
something normal teenagers did.

I knew our relationship had an expiration date, but I hoped we
could enjoy the rest of the summer together. I tried not to dwell too
much on our inevitable breakup. Dr. Sloane was always reminding
me to be present in the moment, and the moment required something else: a prom dress.

I decided to shop in my favorite place—Lucy's closet. I settled on
the dress she'd worn to her prom, a strapless sky-blue flowy gown
that came to the floor. It was beautiful and ethereal and most importantly, comfortable.

On prom night, Parker showed up all decked out in a black tuxedo, a blue bow tie that I'd bought for his birthday, and a pocket square, carefully selected by his mother so it didn't clash with my dress.

After dinner, I took off my heels and let loose with my girlfriends on the dance floor, twirling around and singing along to the music, just like the way I used to dance with Christianna on the black lacquer table back in Tokyo. At the end of the night, as I was strapping on my heels, the song "Thinking Out Loud" by Ed Sheeran began playing. A couple of seconds in, I felt a hand on my back.

"Forget your shoes, Chessy, come on and dance with me," Parker said, and whisked me onto the floor.

We were one of only three couples on the dance floor. But we didn't care. He held me close, as if no one else was in the room. I knew the year was coming to an end, but I wanted this moment to last forever. I gazed into his eyes and laughed a little; prolonged eye contact always made me uncomfortable. But he just looked back, forehead to forehead, and kissed me. I shut my eyes and rested my head on his shoulder. When the song finished, I fastened the straps on my shoes, and we headed out into the night.

Five days before graduation, I woke up to loud voices bellowing from the office. Dad broke the news: St. Paul's had released a report that morning documenting decades of sexual abuse at the school, but it made no mention of my assault or any assaults that had happened in the last twenty-five years.

I flipped open my laptop and started reading the seventy-three-page report. The investigation initially focused on one former faculty member accused of molesting students at another boarding school. But it was ultimately determined that thirteen former faculty and staff members had engaged in sexual misconduct with St. Paul's students between 1948 and 1988. Investigators hired by the school also looked into another twenty claims and later would identify more predators.

The report faulted past leaders at St. Paul's for ignoring and even concealing abuse. Mom and Dad were familiar with many of the cases from speaking with other survivors and alumni who'd worked on the task force back in 2000. Now the rest of the world would know too.

Transparency and honesty were long overdue. But I was outraged by the school's attempt to frame sexual abuse as a problem of the past. St. Paul's had limited the scope of the investigation solely to examine faculty sexual misconduct. By doing so, Mr. Hirschfeld and other school leaders sealed off any potential criticism of how they had mishandled my case and other student-on-student assaults. This was a slap in the face to many survivors of St. Paul's and they knew it.

When the report was released on May 22, Mr. Hirschfeld and Mr. Cox, the president of the board of trustees, offered apologies for the sins of past leaders and promised "healing and reconciliation" to those wronged by the school.

It was beyond offensive. In no way was I cared for as a survivor of sexual assault. I was a fifteen-year-old rape victim looking for help, longing for support, and instead the school treated me like a publicity problem that needed to be managed.

My heart hung heavy for all the St. Paul's survivors. I wanted accountability for those victims and I wanted it now.

As the summer wore on, the news got worse. The *Concord Monitor* reported that a "relationship map" was found on the underside of a shelf in a basement laundry room. Police were also investigating another sexual assault on campus and a new sexual conquest game that involved a crown.

Roughly eight boys from the same dorm competed to have their names put on a paper crown. The exact rules of the game weren't clear, but the *Concord Monitor* reported that St. Paul's attempted to cover up photos in the yearbook of the boys wearing the crown by placing a large sticker on the page to hide the original images. St. Paul's, of course, tried to deny that there was a competition. But what else was new? This had been going on since before Lucy's time.

One group, the Center for the Study of Boys' and Girls' Lives, sounded the alarms at St. Paul's all the way back in 2002 when it warned in a report: "A culture which describes dating as scoring suggests a cold-hearted, almost predatory, sexuality."

More than a decade later—and just months after my assault—the center bluntly concluded: "For years the relationship culture at St. Paul's has been something of 'an elephant in the room': although many were aware it had problems that needed to be addressed, few students or faculties were willing to openly engage in dialogue about the topic, and it was often only in hindsight that problems were recognized."

It riled me up that an institution in the business of teaching was incapable of learning lessons from its own misdeeds. How many more egregious examples were needed before St. Paul's could admit there was a problem and put the well-being of students ahead of its own reputation? Girls needed to be treated as human beings, not targets.

We got word that New Hampshire attorney general Gordon MacDonald was considering a criminal investigation into St. Paul's and wanted to interview me to garner more information. *Finally.* Someone who could hold the school accountable. Someone who could expose St. Paul's leaders for their horrendous, even criminal, actions.

I was overwhelmed by a sense of responsibility when we met in his office in Concord.

"I'm just so grateful you asked us here," I said, my eyes welling up with tears. Mom broke down too. Everyone in the room jumped up to offer us tissues.

"I think the school needs some kind of oversight. I don't believe kids are safe there," I said. "The school wants to call what happened to me an isolated incident, but these things keep repeating themselves."

Dad was restrained, and Mom sat quiet, until the end.

"This has affected every one of our family members in different ways and changed the course of our lives forever," Mom explained.

"And it will be with our dying breaths that we see this issue through."

"This is what we've dedicated our lives to," said Jane Young, an associate attorney general. "Welcome to the club."

"We will get to the bottom of this," Mr. MacDonald vowed.

All I yearned for was a gentle landing after four tumultuous years of high school. The last time our family had gathered for commencement, I was in shock from my assault. I wanted to reclaim graduation as a day for celebration, not devastation.

Delaney was in the middle of a move and exams, but she still found time to attend the big day. She brought her sweet rescue dog, Ollie, and I raced around with him in our backyard, tumbling on the grass, letting him lick my face. Christianna and I had been begging Mom and Dad for months to buy a puppy and I felt like we were within striking distance. Buzz was a huge advocate of healing through animals and had been pressing Mom and Dad too.

Delaney kept saying how proud of me she was, how there were so many obstacles that could have stopped me, but I was actually graduating. I could hardly believe it either.

"I'm so proud of all that you've overcome, but I'm more proud of the person you still are after everything," Delaney said, squeezing me tight.

"I love you," I said.

"I love you too, girl!"

Ollie got a little too excited at one point and peed all over the floor. Delaney was in the other room, and Mom and Dad were out with Christianna, so I ended up mopping dog urine in my white graduation dress. Never a dull moment in the Prout house!

I put on my four-inch periwinkle heels and drove to the ceremony with the top down. I was anxious about graduation—and not just about tripping onstage to get my diploma. In the last week, Parker had acted distant.

Everything was changing. I was in the beginning stages of writing my book so I was preoccupied, and he was getting ready to go to college. I was afraid to press Parker too much before his family vacation to Ireland in a few days.

Our last names were close in the alphabet, so we sat next to each other, staring stoically ahead. I was very nervous because I had a solo in a song, "If We Hold On Together," that the seniors in my theater class were performing for graduation. I took a few shaky breaths before we began to sing.

When I got back to my seat, Parker tried to grab my hand and say something, but I yanked my hand away and avoided his gaze. It hurt that he had been so aloof. And I didn't want to start blubbering onstage.

It was a mob scene trying to leave graduation. Since the assault, my body had shifted into panic mode whenever I had to navigate crowded spaces. My muscles tensed as I snaked between knots of people in the lobby. I eventually spotted Delaney and introduced her to Parker before we headed out. I was too stressed out by the commotion to have a real conversation, so I halfheartedly told him I'd see him later.

My family had a small celebration outdoors at an Italian restaurant but I felt distant from everyone, and kind of alone, despite the fact that I was surrounded by loved ones. Days earlier, my health teacher from sophomore year handed back the letters that we'd written to our graduating selves. All my friends were so excited to look at them, but I didn't have the same urgency.

It sat unopened on my desk at first. When I finally unfolded the letter, I saw that I'd questioned whether I would even make it to senior year. I thought I would succumb to the darkness that ate away my body and soul. But I hadn't. I had survived. I looked over at Delaney, thankful to have another survivor there who could understand me.

Hours after our family dinner, I reluctantly went to a graduation party, where I leaned on Paige and Arielle for support. Stupidly, I drank a little too much. I regretted it immediately as my head began to spin.

The cops showed up after one of the neighbors complained about the noise and all the cars jamming the street. Everyone cleared out, and I left with Parker even though he was still acting weird. We took an Uber to a local hotel and beach club and went to the top, one of his favorite spots, where you could see the waves crashing on the right and the lights of Naples to the left.

Parker and I stood in silence. I leaned against the railing of the balcony and squinted at the glimmering lights. My vision blurred as tears filled my eyes. Parker tried to get closer, but I pulled away.

Even though I knew we'd have to break up, I thought we still had the summer together.

"It's better to do this now. I leave on Sunday," Parker said.

I didn't want to hear any more, so I left the hotel and started walking home. I told Parker not to follow me, but he did. I took off my shoes so I could move faster.

I eventually put them back on and walked a mile and a half to the five-foot fence behind my house. I climbed up in my platform shoes and hoisted myself over. He didn't follow me. I sat in our driveway, crying and asking myself why. Then I texted Lucy.

Me: Are you awake? Please?

Lucy met me outside by our pool and cradled me on the couch.

"It's going to be okay, Chess," Lucy said, stroking my head.

The next morning I could barely get out of bed. But then I heard the pitter-patter of doggy paws, and the pain in my heart eased a little. Delaney and Ollie were still there, and they both snuggled with me in bed before they left.

During graduation parties that weekend, I mustered fake smiles and small talk, but my insides were pulverized. Parker ignored me and my family, but his mother came up and apologized: "His sisters will not let him forget his timing was terrible. You know how much we all love you."

I bit my lip. It was nice of her to talk to me, but I wasn't sure what to say. It wasn't his mother's place to apologize to me. It wasn't his sisters' job to teach Parker how to be thoughtful, sensitive, and decent. It was his own responsibility.

At home I hid in my room. Christianna tried to joke around and make me laugh, but I wasn't in the mood. Then she crawled on the floor next to me.

"Chessy, if he doesn't know that you're all of this, then he definitely doesn't deserve you," Christianna said, throwing her hands into the air as if she was sprinkling fairy dust. "If he doesn't see that you're this awesome, wonderful, strong girl, then he's definitely not good for you."

I guess this was what it was like to have regular teenager problems. They suck too.

Soon enough my misery had lots of company. The guys were breaking up with their girlfriends one after the other, relationships falling like dominoes. My girlfriends and I tried our best to support one another, gorging on Mexican food and fries, hosting sleepovers and movie nights, and talking about the amazing road ahead.

My friends had college to look forward to. I had decided to take a gap year and write my memoir with Jenn Abelson, an investigative reporter with the *Boston Globe*'s Spotlight Team. I wanted to share my journey so other survivors and those who love them know there is a path forward, however rocky. There is a community ready, willing, and able to support their healing and their pursuit of justice.

While my friends binge-shopped at Bed Bath & Beyond for college supplies during the last few weeks of summer, I helped Mom and Dad pack up our home in Naples and move to Washington, DC.

It was a sobering and excruciating process. The house had been an oasis, but it was scabbed with painful memories. During our last few days together, Mom and Dad had a huge fight. We may have been leaving Florida behind, but the raw emotions from the past several years were coming with us. There were many moments since my assault that threatened our survival as a family. But we always were, and always would be, stronger together.

I cleared out my closet where I used to punch myself during panic attacks and bang my head. Now that it was empty, I could see small dents in the wall. The next person who lived there would probably assume that I aggressively kicked the shoes off my feet, not hit my head with hangers.

It reminded me how our deepest wounds are usually invisible, how easy it is to misjudge each other's pain, how the most important thing we can do is to treat one another with kindness and respect. Everyone has a story.

Once in a while, my thoughts returned to Parker, to the picture I kept in my mind of us holding each other on the dance floor at prom. My heart has healed, and I am able to look back on our relationship with gratitude and fondness. He helped me reclaim many things: intimacy, my sexuality, and emotional vulnerability.

I wasn't going to let my past, however painful, get in the way of my future. Not then, not now, not ever. I have big dreams and want to help lots of people. I knew Uncle Ron was out there somewhere, smiling down on us.

Mom and Dad were focused on launching a nonprofit to help survivors and make schools safe. They had assembled an all-star group to get it off the ground: Steve Kelly, Angela Rose, Laura Dunn, and Eric Singleton, who helped defang the Internet trolls posting hate sites.

Our lawsuit against St. Paul's was expected to go to trial in 2018, but Dad held out hope that the school would come to its senses and settle, and be the first to work with our organization.

I'm on the board of directors, but I told Mom and Dad that my priority right now is joining Barnard's class of '22 and taking care of JJ, our new family puppy.

After unpacking boxes all day at our home in Washington, DC, I needed to get some fresh air. I laced up my black Nike sneakers and jogged by Georgetown Waterfront Park, near the hotel where I'd first met Steve and Laura. I blasted a remix of "Stand by Me"—Dad's favorite song—as I headed toward the National Mall, past the US Capitol, where I had shattered the silence months earlier with my friends Angela, Delaney, and Representative Kuster.

I stopped for a few minutes to catch my breath. I sipped in the humid August air and felt possibility open up around me: the Supreme Court and the Capitol to my right and the White House straight ahead. Maybe I'll be a lawyer. Maybe I'll be a politician, a producer, a writer. Maybe I'll be an activist. I still have time to figure it all out. But I know one thing: I have the right to live my life fearlessly.

I never could have made it to graduation in May 2017 without the support of my family (left). And I was grateful to have my new friend Delaney by my side (below). During our celebratory dinner, we all got silly with my graduation cake.

AUTHOR'S NOTE

My story is my truth: a retelling of as much as I can remember with the aid of recollections from some people included in the book, police reports, court transcripts, court exhibits, photos, emails, text messages, letters, and other records. I understand that my story is not unique, as sexual assault and rape culture is so deeply ingrained in society today.

As I send the last draft of this book to my publisher, the world is changing around me. The #MeToo movement, started by Tarana Burke, is becoming a widespread mission.

I see people being held accountable for their actions for the first time. I'm disappointed by the legions of respected men who abused their power. I'm frustrated by people who care more about their downfall than about the victims or who question whether their idols could be capable of such behavior.

At the same time, I hear hourly conversations—thoughtful ones—about where we go from here and how to treat one another with respect. As this book goes out into the world, I am hopeful.

In this memoir, I am not attempting to speak for all victims/ survivors of sexual assault. Despite my Japanese heritage, I am a white, straight, blond-haired girl from an upper-class family. I grew up privileged, and my parents had the ability to fly back and forth between our home in Florida and the court hearings in New Hampshire to make sure the judge didn't forget about the human behind the word "victim." Too many victims are forgotten or afraid to report because of the intersectionality of racism and sexism.

It's also important to recognize that justice comes in many ways, shapes, and forms. That's why advocacy is so important—whether it be in the public arena or in private. It allows victims and survivors to find peace and justice in their own way, at their own pace.

Consent and sexual assault/rape education also need to be taught in schools from as early as kindergarten all the way through high school. Conversations about consensual touching—"Can I hug you?"—are appropriate for children as soon as they can start communicating. Waiting until college is just blatantly too late.

I have included a resources section below to help survivors, their loved ones, and others in the community. I've listed crisis hotline numbers and assistance for the criminal justice system, along with educational documentaries and activism opportunities.

Too many sexual assault victims are bullied into silence, which is why I want to remind you that you have the right AND responsibility to stand up for the survivors in your community, to make sure none are left behind.

RESOURCES

HOTLINE SUPPORT FOR SURVIVORS

National Sexual Assault Hotline: 1-800-656-HOPE (4673) / rainn.org
National Child Abuse Hotline: 1-800-422-4453 / childhelp.org
National Suicide Prevention Lifeline: 1-800-273-8255 /
  suicidepreventionlifeline.org

LOVED ONES OF SURVIVORS

Paving the Way for Parents: pavingthewayforparents.org

TEEN-DATING VIOLENCE

Love Is Respect: 1-866-331-9474 / Text "loveis" to 22522 /
  loveisrespect.org
Break the Cycle: breakthecycle.org
Join One Love: joinonelove.org

LESBIAN, GAY, BISEXUAL

The Anti-Violence Project: 212-714-1124 / avp.org

LGBT National Help Center: Hotline 1-800-246-PRIDE (7743) /
glbthotline.org/chat.html

Gay Men's Domestic Violence Project: 1-800-832-1901

The Network La Red: 800-832-1901 / tnlr.org

TRANSGENDER SURVIVORS AND LOVED ONES

Forge: 414-559-2123 / forge-forward.org

MALE SURVIVORS

1in6: Online chat support and peer support group / 1in6.org

Male Survivor: malesurvivor.org

MILITARY SEXUAL ASSAULT

Safe Helpline: 877-995-5247 / safehelpline.org

Protect Our Defenders: protectourdefenders.com

DOMESTIC VIOLENCE

National Domestic Violence Hotline: 1-800-799-7233 / ndvh.org

National Coalition Against Domestic Violence State Coalitions:
ncadv.org/stay-connected/state-coalitions

CRIMINAL JUSTICE

SurvJustice: 202-869-0699 / survjustice.org

National Crime Victim Law Institute: 503-768-6819 /
law.lclark.edu/centers/national_crime_victim_law_institute

It Happened to Alexa Foundation: ithappenedtoalexa.org

Office of Victim Services: www.jud.ct.gov/Publications/vs030.pdf

GLOBAL RESOURCES

Mukwege Foundation: mukwegefoundation.org

Rape Crisis Network of Europe: +44 (0) 1413314180 /
  rcne.com/links/sources-of-help-for-survivors

International Rape Crisis Hotline Directories:
  ibiblio.org/rcip/internl.html

Overseas Citizen Services for Americans Living Abroad:
  1-888-407-4747 from the US or Canada;
  1-202-501-4444 from overseas

ACTIVISM

Promoting Awareness/Victim Empowerment: shatteringthesilence.org

It's On Us: itsonus.org

EROC: endrapeoncampus.org

No More: nomore.org

Survivor Love Letters: survivorloveletter.tumblr.com

Joyful Heart Foundation: joyfulheartfoundation.org

Know Your IX: knowyourix.org

ENGAGING BOYS AND MEN TO END SEXUAL ASSAULT

ReThink: we-rethink.org

Men Can Stop Rape: mencanstoprape.org

Consent Is Campaign: consentis.org

POLICY

National Alliance to End Sexual Violence: endsexualviolence.org

Bipartisan Task Force to End Sexual Violence: bipartisantaskforce.com

Erin's Law: erinslaw.org

Together for Girls: togetherforgirls.org

RESOURCES

CHILDHOOD SEXUAL ABUSE

National Children's Advocacy Center: nationalcac.org
Darkness to Light: d2l.org

DOCUMENTARIES

The Hunting Ground: thehuntinggroundfilm.com
  Exposé of rape culture on college campuses.
Audrie and Daisy: audrieanddaisy.com
  Examines cases of high school sexual assault.
Breaking the Silence: https://itunes.apple.com/us/tv-season/breaking
  -the-silence/id1031325588
  Shines light on child sexual abuse and where people can turn for
  help.

STUDIES

The "Justice Gap" for Sexual Assault Cases; Kimberly A. Lonsway,
  Joanne Archambault
*The Lifetime Prevalence of Child Sexual Abuse and Sexual Assault
  Assessed in Late Adolescence*; David Finkelhor, et al.

LETTER FROM SUSAN AND
ALEX PROUT

There is no road map for victims and families surviving sexual assault. Perpetrators and institutions, however, have a well-established playbook. Isolate. Shame. Blame. Silence.

That's why we have supported Chessy in writing about her experience—so that the price she has paid, and that we have paid as a family, the lessons we have learned and the pain we have felt, might be mitigated for someone else. We hope others will think twice about how they treat a victim of sexual assault and perhaps join us in shattering the silence.

This is Chessy's account of how she made it through the aftermath of the sexual assault and the institutional and community backlash she faced, almost as painful and damaging as the crime itself. We went into this process knowing nothing about sexual assault and the path to justice. We ended up learning far more than any parent ever hopes.

In the weeks since Chessy finished this memoir, we have been astounded by a shift in social conscience regarding sexual harassment and sexual assault. As the #MeToo movement dominated headlines, St. Paul's identified another fifteen victims of faculty sexual misconduct but failed to mention recent cases of student-on-student sexual assaults, including Chessy's. Many of these survivors remain voiceless and unsupported.

While the rest of the world awakens to the realities of the scourge of sexual assault and its life-changing effects in places like Hollywood, Wall Street, Congress, and Silicon Valley, we question why St. Paul's school called Chessy's assault "an isolated incident" and continues to deny present-day problems in its school culture, like the Senior Salute and other "games" that have led to sexual harassment and sexual assault. Until we address these issues in our educational institutions, we have little hope of eradicating the conditions and attitudes that allow rape and rape culture to flourish.

There is no *one way*, of course, to prepare for a traumatic life event or sexual assault, just as there is no way to prepare for the effects of a devastating earthquake or a life-threatening illness. From the beginning, we agreed as a family that we would make every decision with these three things in mind:

1. Chessy's recovery and well-being is always our top priority
2. That Owen Labrie be held accountable for his crime
3. That her perpetrator be prevented from sexually assaulting another victim

We made some good decisions with careful thought, and other actions we took were made by chance—like not questioning Chessy when she called late that night about why she went with Owen Labrie, or demanding to know why she didn't tell us sooner. We told her we loved her and we would get through this together, one step at a time. Of course, her older sister, Lucy, had said the most important words of all, right from the start: *It's not your fault.* That her sister knew to respond that way was a blessing, pure and simple.

It was a painful decision to let Chessy go back to St. Paul's School. As parents, our immediate reaction was that there was <u>no way</u> we could entrust her to that kind of environment again. Chessy, however, wanted wholeheartedly to return to the St. Paul's community, to continue her studies, sports, her friendships. We were told by her counselor, whom we trusted and looked to for guidance, that Chessy needed to feel some control over her life, when she had been robbed of the most intimate form of control. We channeled our deep hurt and anger and went where we normally go in tough times—to our knees. And then to our feet.

One of us traveled to St. Paul's School in Concord every week to work with school leaders to handle the latest bullying incident, assess Chessy's well-being, and offer her the support she was not receiving from her school community. We assumed that administrators, trustees, parents, alums, and students would be a source of compassion and support to Chessy upon her return to school. She had done "the right thing" by reporting and cooperating with the authorities, hadn't she? Instead, she faced isolation, hostility, and bullying. St. Paul's School and the community failed our child and our family. They have been failing students under their care for decades. It is a betrayal that we will never get over.

FINDING A SUPPORT NETWORK

Sexual assault is a hugely uncomfortable topic. If you knew a friend's child had been robbed and beaten, you would offer support. Not so with sexual assault. We lost nearly all the community we'd once had at St. Paul's School—fellow parents, alumni—with the exception of a small group of people. Other friends from our wider circle and colleagues simply dropped us, without conversation, for reasons we cannot really fathom.

Know that silence and isolation might try to envelop you and those who care about you. Friends may abandon you, or remain silent and ignore what you're going through, tell you to get over it, and move on without you.

In the aftermath of trauma, it is critical to find people who will listen, love, and support you. Sometimes we were slow to figure out what that meant. It took us two years to find and speak to another survivor's parent and learn about the commonalities all survivors and their families face. What a comfort that was, to know we were not alone as parents! The shame many survivors face is isolating, and can extend to the family of survivors, affecting every aspect of your lives, from where you live, work, and send your children to school, as you are trying to seek justice and healing.

We tightened and reworked our network of support. We will always be indebted to our family, old friends, some friends of Alex from the class of '82, several teachers, and other sexual assault survivors who became our new friends and perhaps most inspiring community. We relied heavily on members of our children's school community in Naples and were grateful for their support.

CRIMINAL JUSTICE SYSTEM

We were also given good advice by Chessy's counselor in Naples not to rely on the criminal justice system for healing, because that was beyond our control. Chessy and our family, perhaps naively, had faith in the justice system when we decided to cooperate with authorities.

Luckily, we were in good hands, although we realize not everyone is as fortunate. Laws differ state by state in terms of how crimes are defined and what victims' rights are. So much depends on the attitudes of the police and district attorney in handling sexual assault cases. The Concord authorities cared about what happened to Chessy, about sexual assault crimes, and about high school students in their city, as did the district attorney involved. But we didn't know what they would make of it, and let them do their jobs. While there were disappointments along the way about how the process works and the way the justice system is tilted to protect perpetrators, we still feel it was the right decision.

We remained very engaged in the process, calling, emailing, and asking questions.

Lucy challenged us to think of Chessy first and foremost—and what justice would look like to her, and not us, her parents. We immersed ourselves in New Hampshire laws surrounding sexual assault and the court process we would potentially face. It took us a very long time to find the knowledge, help, and advice we needed.

WHAT WE WISHED WE KNEW

We love our daughters and were interested in everything they did, before they went away to school and while they were there. We had good relationships with each of them, with typical parent-child struggles, but nothing that warranted "I think you would be better off out of the household and *away*." It was hard to be apart from our kids, and for our family, it was a sacrifice on many levels to let them go away to boarding school. We had thought the gains would outweigh the sacrifices. We were wrong.

While we knew a lot of information about St. Paul's academics, sports, and ideals of serving the world, in hindsight, we didn't really know *anything* of the daily culture, even after having a child attend for three years.

Looking back, we are painfully reminded of the questions we didn't ask when we sent our daughters to St. Paul's School, and the assumptions we made:

- That our daughters' bodies would be respected and that they had complete control over their sexual interactions and environment.

- That the school recognized it was important to teach its students how to treat one another, and enforced ethical policies when these standards were violated.
- That female students are as important to the community as male students.

Those assumptions and unasked questions have had a huge impact on all our lives. We learned the answers in the hardest way possible. We discovered St. Paul's had turned a blind eye to sexual assault for decades. We realized that in a fully residential boarding community like St. Paul's, there appears to be little oxygen to keep the cultural corners clean, bright, and safe—functioning as parents would expect.

We encourage parents and guardians to take the time to learn what lies beneath the veneer of any institution—whether it's a boarding school, college, or summer program. Ask the questions we wish we had asked: What traditions does the school culture hold near and dear? How many sexual assaults are reported? What training is provided to administrators, teachers, and coaches? What support is available to victims?

TALKING TO YOUR CHILDREN

Reading Chessy's book, we were sad to learn what a burden she felt she was on the family. It reminds us how critical it is for parents to let their children know how important they are to them, how important they are, period. What courage is, and what courage it takes to grow up well, and honestly. That when your child enters high school, you never lose sight of making sure your kid is the kid they have been and are meant to be.

As much as parents are uncomfortable discussing sex with children, tweens, and teens, our culture has taken the wheel from us and is charting the course, if not steering the ship. As parents of three daughters with a ten-year age gap, we have witnessed this quickening pace of widespread sexually charged culture.

Sex is a part of the school curriculum, whether it's official or not: jokes, teasing, social media, and real pressures—along with devastatingly criminal games of sexual conquest and predation.

Parents must have conversations with boys and girls from a young age about what consent and healthy relationships mean. It's not enough to wait for schools to take the lead.

The conversation has to be shifted away from blaming the victim: Why did you drink too much? Why did you go with him? What were you wearing? Instead, we need to talk about changing the behaviors of the perpetrators. In particular, mothers and fathers need to talk to their sons about respect, entitlement, and consent.

Sexual assault is a physical violation of your body, but it also damages your self-esteem and self-worth. It can have a devastating effect when transitioning from child to minor teen to young adult. It can stunt your education or growth as a person. Sexual assault made Chessy question her basic rights as a deserving member of the community we call humanity.

We have grappled throughout this journey with how to explain sexual assault in age-appropriate ways to Chessy's younger sister, Christianna. She was just seven when her sister was assaulted, and we had never discussed sex or sexual assault at that point. It has been very important to us as parents to convey what Chessy experienced and how her sister has struggled and fought to regain a sense of control over her life.

We started with "a young man at school hurt your sister, and the authorities are asking him to take responsibility." But suffice it to say, we were so encouraged by her role in coming up with the #IHaveTheRightTo initiative and her simple statement: "Sounds like it's time for a girls' bill of rights!" It's a good step in the right direction.

We will never forget when we picked Christianna up from two weeks at sleepaway camp at age ten and an adult counselor told us that we should be proud of her for standing up for herself to some mean-girl activity. It will be a process, we recognize, to develop her understanding of what her sister has experienced. The conversation is ongoing.

OUR FAMILY TOLL

Our family has leaned heavily on each other and tried to avoid the paralyzing abyss of sadness and anger when challenges arose. We struggled with daily anxiety over our reputation and our long-term finances. There were many times we wanted to lash out in anger and defiance. When one of us felt overwhelmed or despaired, the other parent rallied and refocused our lens on healing and justice.

Despite our hopes and best intentions, our family suffered at the expense of the time spent on this process. This was a sad by-product, especially for our youngest daughter. We hope someday she will forgive us, and understand that the toll exacted on her childhood, the hours behind closed doors, were not for lack of love for her.

We also want to acknowledge Lucy's strength and wisdom to say the right words to her sister and have the wherewithal to hold Owen accountable by punching him in the face. She has lost her SPS peer community. She has changed the course of her studies to justice and peace and is trying to impact the world in a positive manner.

We humbly recognize that our ability to find strength was God-given and continues to be a blessing and a matter of grace.

SUPPORTING SURVIVORS

Some days, it has been easy to figure out what to do to support Chessy. We tried to show her in words and action that her family's love for her is stronger than the hateful crime against her, against her body.

We bound ourselves together with the things that make Chessy tick and make her an integral part of our family dynamic of three daughters: her incredible love of all kinds of music and food; her sense of humor and distinctive laughter; her encyclopedic knowledge of funny YouTube videos and pop culture; her love of sports, all things Japanese, babies and children, and puppies; her ever-growing and inquisitive faith. And, more recently, we've had much discourse on the political landscape with our children, to engage them in their futures and what kind of world they want to live in.

We made sure family was around Chessy whenever she would permit herself to be surrounded. We are so grateful we had that support from our families. We are trying to do whatever we can to make sure that Chessy lives the life she was meant to live. Chessy will decide how much she wants to make advocacy a part of her life. But we as parents are committed to this fight until our last breath.

Other days, it was and is still difficult to know what to do to help ease her pain, except be with her. Or nearby. We are not perfect and are certainly not experts in any way—just parents who love their children. The journey after sexual assault to survivorship is jagged, not linear. At this stage of our lives, we depend on love and faith to guide us and hold us together. And we continue to educate ourselves on how rape culture thrives and ways to combat it.

We entered into the nightmare tunnel of sexual assault together— and will keep trying to find the light at the end, together. We are committed to seeing that we each arrive safely to the other side, however long it takes!

YOU ARE NOT ALONE

We have come to understand that sexual assault happens far more often than people have been willing to admit, and that sometimes it takes many years to name an experience. One in four girls has been the victim of sexual assault or sexual abuse by the age of seventeen.

No one wants to believe it can happen to them, to their child, sister, mother, aunt, friend. We understand that, and also had that mind-set. But the fact is quite different. It has happened to someone close to you. But they have remained silent, like so many other victims.

To teens and survivors, we parents are often not perfect—but we can be a good place to start. Communicating with a trusted teacher, an adult in your church or religious community, a mature friend, or an older sibling can make all the difference. You are not alone, nor should you be. You deserve love, compassion, and support.

You deserve information on what your options are to move forward. Gather more information, not less. Call your local rape crisis center. Find out about the statute of limitations. In many places, you can get a rape kit test done now and decide later whether you want to pursue the case in criminal court.

All victims and circumstances are unique. Every family's experience is unique. Everyone has a story, and they are all a little different—but this is what motivates us to shine a light, to recognize you are not alone in searching for your right to justice and healing.

When Chessy went public on the *Today* show, we heard from people all over the world, and it gave us hope that justice can prevail and survivors can regain their voice. By speaking out, our family has formed a new community, a real community, with survivors, advocates, and supporters. This community is out there for you.

A NOTE FROM COWRITER
JENN ABELSON

My mission as a reporter for the *Boston Globe* is to hold powerful people and institutions accountable.

As a member of the paper's Spotlight Team—which gained international attention because of the Oscar-winning film about its work (*Spotlight*)—I've exposed top surgeons secretly operating on two patients at once and slumlords cramming college students into dangerous apartments.

My most complicated work began in 2016, when I joined a team of reporters who turned their attention to sexual misconduct in private schools. I journeyed into a world of privilege and elitism, where high school teenagers lived on their own like adults and were left to make up their own rules.

In our investigation of these institutions, we discovered a pattern of horrific abuse of boys, reminiscent of the Catholic Church abuse scandal uncovered by the Spotlight Team in 2002. We also saw evidence of pervasive sexism and entitlement that enabled male teachers and students to prey upon girls. School leaders turned a blind eye; fellow students shamed those who spoke out against this culture; and administrators, trustees, and alumni tried to silence victims. It was epidemic.

During our prep-school investigation, I talked with more than one hundred survivors and learned the devastating toll that silence takes on victims. I heard about struggles with substance abuse, suicide attempts, and failed relationships. Most of these abuse survivors had little hope for systematic change—or closure.

One institution that refused to participate in our investigation altogether was St. Paul's School in New Hampshire. I was shocked when they accidentally forwarded an internal email that said, "We want to be polite but don't want to add anything new to the conversation."

St. Paul's had come under intense national scrutiny in recent years after a popular senior, Owen Labrie, was arrested and put on trial for sexually assaulting a fifteen-year-old in a ritualized game of sexual conquest.

Chessy Prout, unlike many victims, reported her attacker to police, testified against him in court, and won a conviction. When St. Paul's refused to take steps to address the toxic sexual culture, Chessy and her family filed a civil lawsuit. And when St. Paul's tried to bully the teenager by threatening to reveal her identity, Chessy fought back and appeared on the *Today* show, speaking publicly for the first time in 2016.

I'd long been inspired by Chessy's willingness to stand up to her perpetrator and to one of the country's most prestigious schools. Once we met, though, I knew I wanted to help her tell her story. I felt a responsibility to shatter the silence that surrounds victims of sexual assault. It was time for a young survivor to have her voice heard. And it was time for leaders at St. Paul's and the entire school community of students, parents, faculty, and alumni to be held accountable.

As a reporter, I was deeply impressed by Chessy's attention to facts and details. She'd kept journals, text messages, Facebook exchanges, emails, photos, and other records that helped tell her story. She even documented mistakes she made—like the time when she posted a comment on the *Concord Monitor*'s website and thought it was anonymous. She took a photo before removing the comment. We spent hours together every day, week after week, exploring the most intimate, uncomfortable moments of her life. Nothing was off-limits.

I'm sure it was difficult for her to let me into this private part of her world, but she trusted me, and I am grateful.

I'll disclose that the bond I felt with Chessy was also deeply personal. More than two decades ago, I had a crush on a public high school English teacher that veered into uncharted waters when he began sending me William Butler Yeats's poetry and calling me his muse. I remember his hand lingering on my back moments longer than it should have while I stood in the private office he had as chairman of the department. After a fleeting sense of excitement, I felt dread. I stopped going to his class. I panicked every time I saw him. I felt partly responsible. My mother found emails from the teacher on our new AOL account and confronted me. I pleaded with her to wait until I graduated to say anything to the superintendent.

The next year, when I discovered that the teacher had behaved similarly with another friend, I knew I had to speak up. I didn't want anyone else to feel the same guilt and shame. During a visit home on a break from college, I stormed into his office with a tape recorder in my purse. I closed the door behind me and told the teacher I knew how he was treating girls and it was wrong. He needed to stop. I'd be watching him.

Years later, as I saw Chessy tell her story with such courage, I started thinking about how frightening my experience could have been if I had attended boarding school, where I didn't see my parents every day. What would I have done if there had been no boundaries between school and home?

Chessy's trauma is far worse, and she is confronting it in a different, more public world where people can find her online and harass her on social media. From the moment she told her story, even to close friends, she's been called names. Shamed. Punished.

I was—and continue to be—in awe of her strength. It was a great honor to work with Chessy on this book, named for her incredible campaign. She risked everything to do what's right, even when it involved taking the most difficult path.

I hope this book will encourage others to speak up for what's right in the face of injustice. I hope it empowers survivors and makes them feel less alone. I also hope her story inspires real change. Chessy has the right to demand that. The rest of us should too.

ACKNOWLEDGMENTS

CHESSY PROUT

Thank you to Catherine Ruffle for taking my case and fighting for justice, and to the victim advocates Barbara Jacobs and Sarah Heath, who made sure to educate me and my family on the criminal justice process and for calling me a "rock star" on some of my lowest days. Thank you to Grandma Prout for showing me what graceful strength and determination looks like, and Uncle Tom for helping me find my path in faith, reminding me that every day is a blessing, and to keep fighting no matter what. Thank you, Uncle John and Aunt Judy, for your help and support in Concord. I'm grateful for the constant support of my aunts Frannie and Cathy, and cousin Katie, throughout my entire life. Thank you to Uncle Bernie and Aunt Blair—who in the midst of it all had their own obstacles to deal with—for their unconditional patience, care, and support. Thank you to AC and UP for taking care of us always in Naples, and to Aunt Carol, Aunt Linda, Aunt Deb, and Uncle Jon for their support, compassion, and strength, which I admire so much. Thank you to my cousins Peter and Tony and Cameron and Christian for showing support and sympathy at the courthouse, and for your ongoing support and interest in the issue of sexual assault prevention.

Thank you to Detective Curtin and Detective DeAngelis for believing me and for seeing my case through, something few survivors experience. Without Detective Curtin, I never would have met Laura Dunn. Laura's tenacity, strength, patience, and fierce compassion helped keep me in line when anger got the best of me, and kept me going when sadness overwhelmed me. Thank you for speaking out for my family during the trial, and for introducing us to the Steves. I am grateful for Steve Grygiel, who taught me that if a loaded question from a defense attorney cannot be answered with a yes or no, I have the right to explain myself, because I am only speaking up to tell the whole truth and nothing but the truth. Steve Kelly's patience with my father will always impress me, but his passionate pursuit of justice will always inspire me most. Amanda Grady Sexton, director of public affairs at the New Hampshire Coalition Against Domestic and Sexual Violence and city councillor in Concord, New Hampshire, as well as the entire team at NHCADSV, are the fiercest advocates in the truest sense of the word. During the trial, letters, emails, phone calls, and notes from other survivors and strangers made me feel less alone and showed me that there really is a community of people in the world who care about survivors.

So many survivors of sexual assault are met with doubt and blame, but Deputy County Attorney Catherine Ruffle and Assistant County Attorney Joe Cherniske met me with compassion, respect, and determination to fight for the truth. They also gave me and my family a safe space to retreat to during the trial, and helped preserve our privacy as much as they could. The many family friends who have been by my family's side and have stayed there through the tumult will always hold a place in my heart.

Too many people turn a blind eye to sexual assault, but thank you to the professionals for helping me reclaim my story. To Cinny Murray and Eric Singleton, thank you for helping us fight back on the Internet. Dan Hill, thank you for showing us how to communicate effectively with the media, and for standing up for this issue so strongly.

This book would not have been possible without the expertise and energy of our family friend and my book agent Carla Glasser, and the dedicated, kind team at Simon & Schuster and Margaret K. McElderry Books. Ruta Rimas, our editor, and the entire team of professionals who gathered for our first meeting with S&S: thank you for believing in me. Thank you for giving me an amazing outlet to tell my story.

My counselor Buzz at St. Paul's did the right thing and called the police after my mom disclosed to her that I had had an "unwanted sexual experience" and called it what it was: rape. I owe a lot to Tabitha, my freshman-year roommate, for keeping me grounded when the St. Paul's culture would consume me, for continuing to fight on campus for change, and for inspiring me to continue to fight for survivors because too many survivors don't have the family to do so. Catie also was a grounding force, someone who always knew how to cheer me up and stood by me even when it meant social ostracism.

Naples, Florida, was the perfect place to land after two traumatic events, and I have a close community of friends and family to thank for that. My teachers at the Community School of Naples (CSN) helped me make it to graduation, a day I couldn't really see in my future after the assault. Arielle, Scott, Zach, and the rest of my friends at CSN, the love and support you've shown me keeps me hopeful. Also, the Cat Island Mission team with Youth 4 Orphans replenished my soul after a traumatic event and reminded me that all pain is relative, and that I have a lot to be thankful for. Thank you also to my Sacred Heart Sisters and friends in Japan.

I thoroughly believe in the power of therapy and will always be grateful for my sessions with Dr. Sloane, who helped me navigate my feelings toward the earthquake in Japan and my ongoing experience with depression, and helped me unpack and come to terms with being sexually assaulted. She helped teach me that things don't "get better with time," they just change, and sometimes it's happy change, and other times it's tough change. Nothing is ever fully good, and nothing is ever fully bad.

And I would not be who I am today if not for the incredible support and work of PAVE and the PAVE family: founder Angela, Delaney, Julia, Jill, Jean, Sierra, Dom, Ilana, and Ally. Angela Rose is a strong survivor who lives a beautiful, genuine life advocating for others, and she gives me hope for my own future. Delaney Henderson's selflessness and deep love for others inspires me every day.

Thank you to Mr. Pillsbury for acknowledging my story publicly, and then for sharing your own, helping to shatter the silence around sexual assault. I'd like to thank Together for Girls, Quinnipiac and Yale Law, Georgetown Day School, and Representative Annie Kuster for giving me the opportunities to tell my story and speak out. I'd also like to thank Chief Justice Barajas, executive director of NOVA, for giving me the privilege to speak at the 43rd Annual NOVA Training Conference among superheroes Tina Frundt and Ana Morales on the Victim Tribute panel.

Finally, familial support is so important to helping survivors heal. My mom, dad, sisters Christianna and Lucy, and I have gone through a lot together, but constantly go back to one thing: love.

Last but not least, thank you, thank you, thank you, Jenn. Thank you for listening to me ramble, for helping me make sense of my life, for feeding me yummy goodies because I'm always hungry, and for letting me take puppy breaks intermittently throughout the day. This book would not have been possible without you helping to make this process as painless as it could be even as I reached back into the most painful crevices of my memory. Thank you for your patience and compassion. I am so lucky to be able to call you my cowriter, and my friend.

JENN ABELSON

I am grateful to *Boston Globe* editor Brian McGrory and my current and former colleagues on the Spotlight Team for their commitment to investigating sexual abuse and holding powerful institutions accountable. Jon Saltzman, Bella English, Todd Wallack, Scott Allen, Mark Morrow, Amanda Katz, Sacha Pfeiffer, Mike Rezendes, Matt Carroll, and Marty Baron: Your work has changed lives—and the world—for the better. Thank you to my guardian angels at the *Globe*: Walter Robinson, Ellen Clegg, and Tom Farragher.

I'm indebted to the victims, advocates, and lawyers who helped me understand what it means to be a survivor of sexual assault. This crime has been shrouded in shame and silence for far too long.

I'm forever grateful to Meredith Goldstein for her friendship, advice, and confidence in me. When I questioned whether I had what it takes to help Chessy write a book, Meredith told me not only could I do it—I had to do it.

Thank you to my literary agent, Katherine Flynn, and book agent, Carla Glasser, for getting *I Have the Right To* into the hands of the fantastic team at Simon & Schuster. Ruta Rimas at Margaret K. McElderry Books is an editing wizard.

I am lucky to have amazing friends who took on multiple roles as readers, editors, fact-checkers, and cheerleaders to make sure I did justice to Chessy's story: Matt Lebovic, Eric Hudson, Gina Favata, Kevin Blinkoff, Jon Gorey, Jenna Russell, Scott Helman, Sarah Grafman, and Scott Leibowitz.

I am so appreciative of Kathleen and Michael Fina for their

incredible hospitality in Naples and Joan Fina for her chilly condo in Washington, DC, and her impeccable grammar skills.

Thank you to Ralphie and Paul Faircloth for being the best second set of parents I could ever ask for. Emily Faircloth Barker, Peter Barker, and Kate Faircloth have brought love, humor, and a passion for competitive board games to my life in Boston.

I am honored to be surrounded by strong females in my professional and personal life, including my nieces and their mothers.

Thank you to my sister, Jodie Abelson, for always being a light in my life, and to Alex Sommer for helping her burn brighter.

I am grateful to my mom and dad, Sue and Joe Abelson, for supporting my goals, my choices, my path. I inherited my investigative chops from my mom and listening skills from my dad. I would not have my dream job and a fearless ability to challenge authority without them.

Thank you to my love, Paul Faircloth, for lifting me up at every step of the way.

I feel blessed to have become part of the Prout family. Lucy and Christianna Prout warmly let me into their lives and reminded me of the power of sisterhood.

Thank you to Susan and Alex Prout for providing a sanctuary of truth, bravery, and grace. Thank you for making your home my home and for raising three incredible daughters who are helping to change the world.

Above all, thank you to Chessy Prout, my friend, my cowriter, my rock star. Your kindness and honesty, your humility and courage, and above all, your towering integrity, will inspire me always. You are a fierce warrior who gives me hope for girls everywhere. You are the reason why I do what I do. You are a force of nature and I am so honored to have shared this journey with you.

Cowriters hard at work!

Friends for life.

I Have the Right To

A High School Survivor's Story of Sexual Assault,
Justice, and Hope

A memoir by Chessy Prout
with Jenn Abelson

About the Book

The numbers are staggering: nearly one in five girls ages fourteen to seventeen has been the victim of a sexual assault or
attempted sexual assault. In 2014, Chessy Prout was a freshman at St. Paul's School, a prestigious boarding school in New
Hampshire, when a senior boy sexually assaulted her as part of a
ritualized game of conquest. Chessy bravely reported her assault
to the police and testified against her attacker in court. Then,
in the face of unexpected backlash from her once-trusted school
community, she shed her anonymity to help other survivors find
their voice.

This gut-wrenching memoir is more than an account of a
horrific event. It takes a magnifying glass to the institutions that
turn a blind eye to such behavior and a society that blames victims rather than perpetrators. Chessy's story offers real, powerful
solutions to upend rape culture as we know it today.

Prepare to be inspired by this remarkable young woman and
her story of survival, advocacy, and hope in the face of unspeak-
able trauma.

Discussion Questions/Writing Prompts

These questions can be used as targeted questions for discussion and reflection or, alternatively, they can be used as writing prompts.

1. In the introduction by U.S. Congress member Ann McLane Kuster, Kuster suggests we are at a cultural tipping point in regard to sexual violence against women and the often unstated expectation that survivors remain silent. She goes on to ask the critical question: "What are we going to do about it?" How does Kuster's admission of her own personal experience as a survivor of sexual assault frame Chessy's story? What can readers gain from this knowledge in better understanding the scope of sexual assault?

2. Kuster encourages Chessy and all survivors to "rock the boat." What do you believe she hopes they will do? Why is this action so important? In your opinion, in what ways does Chessy accomplish this?

3. In the prologue, Chessy provides readers with an overview of her experiences on the night she was sexually assaulted, and closes with the advice given to her by Dr. G., who tells her, "Call your mother. How you handle this will inform the rest of your life." How does Chessy's choice to reach out to her family ultimately change the course of her life?

4. From your initial introduction to Chessy as the book opens, what are some of your impressions about her as a young teen? In what ways is her life similar to your own? How is it different?

5. Early in the book, Chessy shares her memories of growing up

in Japan, including the earthquake and its aftermath that eventually causes her family's move back to the United States. How does her life there seem different from what she experiences in Florida and eventually at St. Paul's?

6. *I Have the Right To* is a memoir told in first person. Do you think if anyone besides Chessy were telling her story, the reader would have the same type of experience? In what ways does reading a memoir impact you as a person? Does knowing that Chessy's story is real make the experience more poignant?

7. How do the experiences that Chessy's father had at St. Paul's initially frame Chessy's opinions about the school? Why does learning that a stark contrast exists between expectations and the reality of the climate and culture at St. Paul's prove to be difficult and painful to both Chessy and her family?

8. Chessy states, "Tabitha said she refused to be used by anyone ever again. She tried to make sure I didn't either by calling me on my bullshit. . . ." Do you believe Tabitha's attitude and willingness to share her struggles with self-harm, anxiety, and overcoming sexual assault ultimately help Chessy? If so, in what ways?

9. After hearing details of the events with Owen, Buzz tells her mother, "'Susan . . . that sounds like rape.'" Why does hearing this declaration impact Chessy so strongly? In what ways does Buzz help her understand what has actually happened? Do you believe Buzz proves herself to be an important supporter for Chessy during this time?

10. In what ways is Chessy's relationship with Lucy typical for two sisters? Though Lucy struggles to deal with Chessy's assault,

what are some of the ways she ultimately shows she is an advocate for Chessy and other survivors?

11. Discuss St. Paul's tradition of the Senior Salute and "slaying." What about it did you find most disturbing? How does this impact your understanding of the idea of tradition? In your opinion, what are the best ways to defend against these types of misogynistic behaviors?

12. Other female students suggest that Chessy is attention-seeking when speaking about what happened to her. Why do you think this kind of attitude toward those who bring awareness to being victims of rape and sexual assault is often prevalent?

13. Though some girls admitted to knowing Owen was a predator, why did so many girls choose not to believe Chessy after she came forward about being sexually assaulted?

14. Chessy states, "Dad was my hero. He had literally dropped everything and risked his career to make sure I was supported and protected each and every day." Why is having the support of her father and the rest of her family so critical to Chessy? Why can this battle be so difficult for survivors without family support systems? What advice would you offer to those who are suffering?

15. In *I Have the Right To*, fear both incapacitates and motivates Chessy and her family. Consider how each one deals with these emotions. In what ways do they acknowledge them? How are they able to turn to others for help? What are the consequences of their reactions?

16. How does learning that the parents of other St. Paul's students

raised money for Owen's defense impact Chessy? What was your reaction to this knowledge?

17. Do you think Chessy's experience is a unique one? Why might it take someone time to understand what's happened to them? Why does Chessy refuse to be seen as a powerless victim?

18. Examine and discuss the significance of St. Paul's faculty and leadership in perpetuating a toxic culture at their school. In your opinion, why would adults supposedly committed to the education and well-being of children choose to behave this way?

19. Given what you've learned in *I Have the Right To*, what elements about the criminal trial against Owen and the aftermath surprised you the most?

20. Regarding her mother, Chessy states, "She assumed that her daughters would be treated equally at St. Paul's, that our bodies and voices would be respected. She'd never imagined the most dangerous thing she could ever do was send us to boarding school." How does Chessy's mother ultimately deal with the gravity of what has happened to her daughter and her family? In what ways does her effort to help her girls state their rights impact each of them?

21. Discuss Chessy and her #IHaveTheRightTo movement. How does this hashtag become a catalyst for change within the framework of schools and communities, as well as with the survivors themselves? Do you think participants are better off for having joined forces instead of choosing silence, advocating for themselves as part of the team of survivors who speak up and out?

22. How does Chessy's work with PAVE help her continue to find her voice and use it as an instrument of empowerment and good for all those battling to survive sexual assault?

23. Thinking about what you've learned from Chessy and her family's experiences in *I Have the Right To*, what advice would you give to young women and men facing similar situations?

24. Explain the significance of the title, *I Have the Right To*. In what ways does it accurately describe the events and relationships portrayed in this memoir?

25. Using the phrase "This is a story about . . ." supply five words to describe *I Have the Right To*. Explain your choices.